Cory Marsh investigates the contr
identity. What I love about this bo
on doctrine, focusing on theolog)
reminds us that evangelicalism is ab
that evangelicalism relies on the Bible as God's authoritative and
infallible word. He also captures the missionary spirit and ecclesial
focus that characterizes those who are faithful to the scriptures.
Even if one might dissent here and there from what Marsh says,
we can be grateful for this important contribution to evangelical
identity.

Thomas R. Schreiner
Professor of New Testament Interpretation, Southern Baptist
Theological Seminary Louisville, Kentucky

Another book on evangelicalism today? If that is your response to
Cory Marsh's latest title, hear me out. Marsh is not just a critic of
what is going on today by the adjective "evangelical," he understands
the sickness thoroughly and clearly prescribes "the cure for what
ails us!" This book is current (he cites contemporary literature); it is
critical (he thoroughly analyzes the real nature of evangelicalism's
sickness); and it is curative (he knows what can bring permanent
healing to these great maladies). Marsh's description of his
prescription is sometimes long and his recommended treatment is
not a quick fix but will offer a long-lasting cure!

William Varner
Professor of Biblical Studies
The Master's University, Santa Clarita, California

Every year when I teach on eighteenth-century evangelicalism,
I find myself captivated by those early believers. Their unshakeable
love for Scripture, their theology that kept the cross and Christ at
the center of everything, and their burning passion to make Jesus
known to the ends of the earth is infectious. Two centuries later,
Cory Marsh tackles the messy question of what evangelicalism has
become and what we should do about it. He doesn't pull punches
about what needs to go, but he also carefully preserves what's worth
keeping. For anyone wrestling with what it means to be evangelical

today, this book offers both honest critique and hopeful direction for reclaiming our roots.

Ryan L. Rippee
President, The Cornerstone Bible College and Seminary; Pastor, Trinity Church of Benicia, Benicia, California

Cory Marsh has offered a thoughtfully conceived, clarifying, and convictional understanding of evangelical identity. Frustrated by the sociological interpretations that seek to frame evangelical identity primarily in terms of politics and other trends, leaving a vacuous perception of evangelicalism, Marsh calls for a "vintage faith" that is theologically anchored and historically informed, grounded in the commitments of a fully inspired Scripture and Christ-centered gospel. Moreover, he connects evangelicalism with the priority of evangelism, church involvement, and theological education. Critiquing the obsession with brand, platforms, and celebrity, Marsh urges his readers to connect belief with behavior, exhorting followers of Christ to lives of discipleship and biblical faithfulness. While not everyone will be persuaded by all aspects of Marsh's presentation, I joyfully applaud the sincere efforts to invite a new generation of evangelicals to reprioritize the place of Scripture, theology, and the gospel of our Lord Jesus Christ.

David S. Dockery
President and Distinguished Professor of Theology, Southwestern Baptist Theological Seminary

Over time, words that once carried clear meaning can become confused and contested. In today's climate, "evangelical" and "evangelicalism" have become such words, leaving many Christians wondering whether to abandon these terms altogether. Dr. Marsh demonstrates why this would be a mistake and calls us back to a "vintage" understanding of what it means to be evangelical. This book is grounded in theological depth and clarity. Essential reading for both scholars and everyday believers.

Joel Muddamalle
Director of Theology and Research, Proverbs 31 Ministries
Author, *The Hidden Peace*

CORY M.
MARSH

*Recovering
a Vintage
Faith*

Five
Fundamentals
of Evangelical
Identity

MENTOR

Copyright © Cory M. Marsh 2026

paperback ISBN 978-1-5271-1348-0
ebook ISBN 978-1-5271-1408-1

10 9 8 7 6 5 4 3 2 1

Published in 2026
in the Mentor imprint by
Christian Focus Publications Ltd,
Geanies House, Fearn, Ross-shire,
IV20 1TW, Scotland.

www.christianfocus.com

Cover design by Rubner Durais

Printed and bound by Bell & Bain, Glasgow

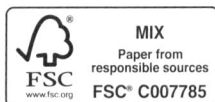

FSC
www.fsc.org
MIX
Paper from responsible sources
FSC® C007785

To Ryan Day

Pastor, friend, and stalwart defender of the vintage faith

"A man of too many friends comes to ruin,
But there is a friend who sticks closer than a brother" *(Prov. 18:24)*

Contents

Part 3
A Few Rants and Things

Acknowledgments

This book began as an idea centered on the word "vintage." I always liked that term but couldn't say why. It's probably because it recalls flashes of nostalgia in ways better than "old" or even "old fashioned" does. I managed to insert the word once in a previous book where I argued that churches need to get "vintage" and train their people in basic Bible study.

That word must have had the same effect on my friend Jeff Campa (serving in Alaska in the US Army's only Airborne arctic division) who texted me in December 2022 with: "'Vintage Faith' as your next book title has a nice ring to it!" While I dismissed the notion as forever tainted by a controversial mega-pastor who had the word "vintage" in a book title years ago, I couldn't entirely shake the idea. Like most Gen-X'ers, the older I get, the less embarrassed I am about what Millennials and Gen-Z'ers think is old and dorky, but we know is cool or fun to remember. Growing up in a world pre-social media, pre-cell phones, and pre-ChatGPT meant having friends who were real, and living a life more adventurous and genuine. Ultimately, I sided with Jeff, reaffirmed my love for the word, and used "vintage faith" as a way to express the fundamentals of classic, genuine evangelicalism. Thank you, brother; without your text message that day, this book would not exist.

Expressions of gratitude are due to several others as well. I am especially grateful for the institution where I teach full time, Southern California Seminary (SCS), for granting me the space during a hectic school schedule to work on the manuscript for this book. My dean and co-laborer in all things theology, Dr. James Fazio, graciously offered to step in for many (most!) of my classes which proved immensely helpful in allowing me to work on this and another book project simultaneously. He also read early drafts of the manuscript and gave points to consider, virtually all of which I implemented and reflect his helpful impressions. SCS colleagues Drs. Jeremiah Mutie, John Yeo, and Ward Crocker also bore with what probably sounded like drivel during ad hoc conversations that ultimately sharpened my thinking on various matters in this book. To them I offer my thanks and express my joy in counting them as friends and colleagues.

I'd also like to acknowledge Pastor Jesse Randolph of Indian Hills Community Church in Lincoln, Nebraska for reading drafts of early portions of the manuscript and offering helpful feedback and encouragement. Likewise, Pastor Ryan Day of Revolve Bible Church (my own pastor to whom this book is dedicated) offered encouragement along the way as he read sections of the book. Both Jesse and Ryan gave close pastoral examinations to various areas where I tend to be theoretical and academic. These men serve on the front lines of local church ministry with remarkable diligence, which has enriched my own heart for the local church. With that I also offer my gratitude to the elders, deacons, and saints at Revolve Bible Church in San Juan Capistrano, California where I serve with joy as their Scholar-in-Residence.

Working with my editor Colin Fast and the team at Christian Focus (CF) has been a wonderful experience. Colin's attention to detail and clear expression turned my efforts into a book worth reading. I also want to thank CF's director of publishing, Willie Mackenzie, who, at a chance meeting at ETS in San Antonio in 2023, reassured me that my proposal was not dead in the water. That brief conversation breathed the life needed to complete this project! Finally, I am at a loss for words (quite uncommon) for how to express proper thankfulness to my wife of sixteen years, Shannan Marsh. She has heard countless versions of the chapters in this book during our hikes, drives, and us sitting somewhere doing nothing. Next to my thankfulness to Jesus my Savior—whose grace made this work possible—my gratitude for her help, critique, and encouragement goes beyond what words can relay.

.

PART 1

An Evan-Jello-Cal Identity Crisis

Introduction

I believe the word of God,
the teaching of the Holy Ghost in the divine word,
and not the Evangelicals[1]

— J. N. Darby.

E vangelicalism is like Jell-O. It's hard to define and just as jiggly. Is Jell-O a food or drink? I believe I was in high school when I first thought of that question. Up until I wrote this line, I still didn't know the answer. I heard Jell-O had something to do with feet.[2] You don't chew it, so it must be a liquid. But you can't use a straw, so it's not really a drink. Some people, me included, do *something* with their jaws while rolling the bouncy substance around in their mouth while slurping it. So that sort of makes it

---

1. J. N. Darby, "A letter on the righteousness of God," in *Collected Writings of J. N. Darby*, ed., William Kelley, 34 vols. (London: Morrish, 1862), 7:498.

2. I actually looked this up. Turns out Jell-O is not made of cow or horse hooves. It's a powder mix that's considered a food product or premade desert made primarily of the protein gelatin (a derivative of animal collagen).

1

a food, I suppose. In the end, a case can be made for Jell-O being either a food or a liquid—or a hybrid! Evangelicalism is similar.

What is evangelicalism? The current landscape is all over the map. In the US especially, there is no consensus as to what evangelicalism actually is. It's a Protestant tradition, on that much we can all agree. Or is it? There are groups of "evangelical Catholics" and "evangelical Hindus."[3] Who is authorized to define evangelicalism? Many appeal to the National Association of Evangelicals (NAE) as the flagship organization for answers, while others view the NAE as passé, political, or largely irrelevant. The amount of "evangelical" groups staking their claim is overwhelming. They include: Evangelicals for Social Action, Evangelicals for Peace, Evangelicals for Biblical Immigration, Evangelicals for Middle East Understanding, Evangelicals for Life, The Evangelical and Ecumenical Women's Caucus, and so on. Each of them offers a different definition of what makes someone "evangelical." In the end, the word "evan-jello-cal" may be the best descriptor.

On an academic scale, the consensus becomes a bit narrower; but struggles of identity remain. At the time of writing this book, I not only teach full time at a historically evangelical seminary, but I also serve as president of a region of the Evangelical Theological Society (ETS) that covers seven states, from Colorado to Hawaii. Surely, the assumption would go, I know precisely what makes someone "evangelical," since it is only those-types who are allowed membership in the largest evangelical academic society in North America. But if I am writing with pure honesty, there are some members of ETS whose bona fides I question. There are only two convictional requirements for joining ETS and publishing in their journal: a belief that the Bible is God's Word and inerrant

---

3. For variations of these labels, see George Weigel, *Evangelical Catholicism: Deep Reform in the Twenty-First Century* Church (New York City: Basic Books, 2014); The Evangelical Catholic, evangelicalcatholic. org; Merwin-Marie Snell, "Evangelical Hinduism," *The Journal of Religion* 6, no. 4 (Oct 1895): 270–7.

in the autographs, and that God is triune in essence.[4] That these are evangelical doctrinal stances is without question. The question is if these are the *only* doctrinal stances that comprise evangelicalism. Can evangelicalism really be reduced to just two theological positions? If so, then it is not surprising to find Roman Catholics and members of the Orthodoxy tradition identifying as "evangelical," as they too believe in the Bible as God's inerrant Word (however nuanced) and in the Trinity.

Even so, the amount of *Protestant* academics willing to sign off on this doctrinal basis without the consistency of personal belief is alarming. One leading evangelical uses the term "theoretical inerrantists" for those who affirm the doctrine of inerrancy, for example, in order to maintain a ministry job or teaching position while lacking submission to its divine authority. These less-than-genuine evangelicals have the "satisfaction of verbal affirmations and signatures on documents rather than by lives lived in humble submission and conformity to Scripture."[5] Cases like this are all too common as the pressure for professors to gain (or retain!) tenure in evangelical universities and seminaries can be unreal. To compromise one's beliefs for job security does happen, even among self-identifying evangelical scholars.

Not only am I an officer of ETS, but I participate in other scholarly evangelical groups as well. I am an active member of the Evangelical Philosophical Society, Institute for Biblical Research, and the Evangelical Foundation for Biblical Research.[6] Each of these venues provides excellent publishing platforms as well as camaraderie for the more academically-minded who care

---

4. Evangelical Theological Society, https://etsjets.org/. These two doctrinal bases are listed on their membership application form requiring signatory agreement. They are also printed on the inside cover of every issue of JETS (*Journal of the Evangelical Theological Society*).

5. Tom Ascol, "Theoretical Inerrantists," Founders Ministries, n.d., https://founders.org/articles/theoretical-inerrantists/.

6. Evangelical Philosophical Society, https://www.epsociety.org/about/; Institute for Biblical Research, https://www.ibr-bbr.org/; and the Evangelical Foundation for Biblical Research, https://efbr.net/.

about advancing Christian scholarship in service of the church and the academy.[7] They are dedicated to advancing knowledge and scholarship from a Christian worldview and formed around certain doctrinal stances, such as the authority of Scripture and the gospel of Jesus Christ. But again, having just one or two broadly "evangelical" positions inevitably opens the door for just about anyone to participate who identifies as "Christian."

I do not list my scholarly associations here in a subtle attempt to advance my *curriculum vitae* (not really). Rather, it is simply to point out that I engage and interact with self-identifying evangelicals at the highest academic levels and have come to realize that the term "evangelicalism" is anything but identifiable. It's as jiggly as Jell-O and just as unstable. And like evasive substances, it seems the only way to identify what is truly "evangelical" is by no other means than personal intuition. Perhaps, that is where we've gone awry. In the free-spirited vein of Western individualism, self-identifying evangelicals have *personalized* evangelicalism to such an extent that it has become anyone's right to define.

Critical theorists, political pundits, and social media influencers all join the sea of opinion of what makes someone "evangelical." For many, the word evangelical is a synonym for republican, or worse, *white-male-racist-conservative-republican-facist-misogynist*.[8] If such is accepted, it is not long before a reference to Donald Trump gets thrown into the mix, eventually morphing "evangelical" into "Trumper" as a shorthand for the longer moniker. Thomas Kidd highlights the problem when self-identifying evangelicals who lack historic evangelical convictions intuitively understand "evangelical" as an ethnic and political designation, rather than a theological or devotional one. "Some critics of evangelicals might say they're right: to such observers,

---

7. "Promoting scholarship in service of the church" is the stated vision of Bible Faculty Summit (www.biblefacultysummit.org), another annual academic group of conservative Bible teachers and seminary professors on whose steering committee I proudly serve.

8. Several books mentioned throughout either define or strongly suggest "evangelical" as this very thing.

'evangelical' carries as much racial and political freight as theological significance. That freight, critics would say, bolsters Trumpism."[9] From there, the downhill slide is inevitable. At best "evangelical" gets cataloged as a particular voting bloc and, at worst, is discarded as a label for anything resembling white supremacy or oppressive patriarchy.[10]

Taking as virtually useless the modern descriptor "evangelical," this book argues a few things. First, it is possible that defining evangelicalism simply by those who *self-identify* as "evangelical" has resulted in vain attempts to define the movement. (Is it even a movement?[11]) In other words, the "-ism" signifying the noun *evangelicalism* is not the same as the "-al" when used as an adjective identifying an *evangelical*. If accurate, then it is quite possible—even expected—to have so many self-identifying "evangelicals" who do *not* fit at all within "evangelicalism." In such cases, I believe there is no warrant for designating evangelicalism as their theological tradition.

Thus, contrary to most treatments on the subject, some of which are very helpful,[12] this book does not argue for *who evangelicals are* but rather *what makes up* (or should make up) *evangelicalism*. In doing so, it raises questions of retaining "evangelical" as a moniker as the best step forward for those who hold to traditionally conservative theological beliefs. As

9. Thomas S. Kidd, *Who Is an Evangelical? The History of a Movement in Crisis* (New Haven: Yale University Press, 2019), 151.

10. Such are the relentless premises behind Anthea Butler, *White Evangelical Racism: The Politics of Morality in America* (Chapel Hill: University of North Carolina Press, 2021), and her *Women in the Church of God in Christ: Making a Sanctified World* (Chapel Hill: University of North Carolina Press, 2012).

11. David Wells, *No Place for Truth: Or, Whatever Happened to Evangelical Theology?* (Grand Rapids: Eerdmans, 1993), 8, offers several criteria that suggest evangelicalism may not qualify as a "movement" at all.

12. One example is Mark A. Noll, David W. Bebbington, and George M. Marsden, eds., *Evangelicals: Who They Have Been, Are Now, and Could Be* (Grand Rapids: Eerdmans, 2019).

I contend, it is not about belonging, but belief. That is to say, evangelicalism is not about social-identity or self-identification. Instead, it *is* about belief and the behavior that results from belief. There are certain doctrinal positions, what I call "vintage," that historically set evangelicalism apart from other faith traditions. And these beliefs become tangible as they work themselves out in Christian conduct. Identifying evangelicalism as a vintage expression of biblical Christianity, rather than by gender, race, genetics, or political preferences, has the advantage of staying clear of virtually every (misleading) poll that documents an "evangelical" constituency.[13]

Of course, this book is not the first to argue for a set pattern of beliefs as the benchmark for what makes someone "evangelical" in a meaningful sense. The best-known example is historian David Bebbington's noteworthy "quadrilateral" of evangelicalism.[14] Bebbington classified evangelicalism in the UK under four main convictions, what he termed *conversionism* (the need to be "born again"), and *activism* (expressing gospel-belief through effort), *biblicism* (a high regard for the Protestant Scriptures), and *crucicentrism* (a strong emphasis on the atoning work of Christ on the cross). Bebbington's laudable metric offers a helpful guide in defining evangelicalism. However, I believe there are fundamental elements missing in it that this book includes.

Another relevant and more recent example is a 2016 article by Leith Anderson and Ed Stetzer entitled, "A New Way to Define

---

13. Most mainline polls (e.g., Pew, Gallup, and Barna) usually categorize "evangelicals" by how they *self-identify* regardless of whether they actually believe a constellation of core biblical positions, such as the infallibility and inerrancy of Scripture, the deity of Christ, the triune nature of God, the conscious reality of heaven and hell, the need for personal repentance and trust in the exclusivity of Jesus Christ for salvation, or the need for consistent church fellowship.

14. David W. Bebbington, *Evangelicalism in Modern Britain: A History from the 1730s to the 1980s* (New York: Routledge, 1989), 2–3. An updated and expanded version of collected essays is David W. Bebbington, *The Evangelical Quadrilateral: Characterizing the British Gospel Movement* (Waco: Baylor University Press, 2021).

Evangelicals" published by *Christianity Today*.[15] In it, Anderson and Stetzer offered a fresh way to identity who is genuinely "evangelical" via several traditional *beliefs* rather than by simply asking who *identifies* as one. Instead of the typical political, geographical, ethnic, or other self-identifying measures used by contemporary critics, they offered a belief-based metric that kept at bay denominational affiliations and social statuses.

Avoiding the rubrics "white," "suburban," "American," "southern," and "Republican" that customarily comprise such research, Anderson and Stetzer pointed out: "The desire to survey white evangelicals to determine their political interests inadvertently ends up conveying two ideas that are not true: that 'evangelical' means 'white' and that evangelicals are primarily defined by their politics."[16] Their point finds agreement here. In the end, the article, which was based on a two-year study, demonstrated that, despite large number of *self-identifying* evangelicals, many of them did not actually hold to traditional evangelical beliefs (which in their study numbered four that related to: the Bible's authority, personal evangelism, the exclusive and sufficient atonement of Christ for sins, and exclusive belief in Christ as Savior for eternal salvation). The approach was valuable in shedding light on the overemphasis many place on evangelicals *belonging* (as in a social construct) to the exclusion of *beliefs* and *behavior* which are more definitive expressions. While acknowledging a debt of gratitude toward theirs and Bebbington's model, the current work will differ in some noticeable ways.

What to Expect

It goes without saying that I am not the only person to offer criticism or to try and "recover" a true evangelical identity. I also don't pretend to have the last word on the matter. You should not expect

---

15. I'm having fun imagining several of my fundamentalist friends' faces as I appeal to something they call *Christianity Astray*.

16. Leith Anderson and Ed Stetzer, "A New Way to Define Evangelicals," *Christianity Today* (April 2016), 54.

a fully exhaustive accounting of everything that needs tightening in evan-jello-calism. This book is only a modest appraisal that seeks to elevate certain core beliefs which historically find a home within the particular Protestant expression of Christianity called evangelicalism. That some will likely disagree or feel the book is left wanting, I have no doubts. I merely offer my experience and qualifications as an active "evangelical scholar" to bear on a conversation which is ongoing and may never end. My take is merely one step on a staircase.

But I do have something to contribute. Firstly, this book is not only about the elasticity of the term "evangelical" that has occurred over the past several decades, but also how its vintage form needs to be recovered according to a set of core fundamental beliefs. Though the beliefs that I think should be "recovered" build upon numerous works that are helpful (and appear throughout this volume), I've included a few that are often overlooked. In the end, I am convinced that evangelicalism, in any meaningful sense of the term, cannot exist without the ones mentioned below and that unfold in the pages that follow.

My main argument is that evangelicalism should *not* be categorized according to political blocs, Christian celebrities, race, or "other evangelicals" adopting the nomenclature (progressives, feminists, transgenders, gay Christians, etc.) as is often the case today. Rather, it *should* be classified by its vintage doctrinal expression that results in behavior befitting of genuine evangelical identity. As this book contends, the constellation of fundamental positions around which true evangelicalism orbits can broadly be classified according to five major components: (1) a high view of Scripture; (2) the exclusivity of Jesus for salvation; (3) a zeal for evangelism; (4) the importance of theological education; and (5) the necessity of consistent local church fellowship. These will each receive detailed explanation as the book progresses. Ultimately, I aim to offer a helpful counterbalance to the current and explosive conversation dominated by critical and progressive thinkers publishing (sometimes correct) critiques of "white," "republican," and "American" evangelicalism, though driven by a leftist culture advocating for an evangelicalism inclusive of beliefs and lifestyles antithetical to the tradition's original identity.

My Audience(s)

The primary audiences I have in mind as I write are pastors and churched lay people. I'm thinking of faithful shepherds and informed congregants who usually aren't compelled to pour over lengthy footnotes with the obsession of an academic.

For those who are jaded or confused over the industry that evangelicalism has become but who also regularly engage in preaching, counseling, baptizing, marrying, burying, and budgeting in evangelical churches, this book is for you. Such ministers who love Christ and his church yet simply don't have the time to read a scholarly monograph will hopefully find this volume valuable to their ministries. Secondly, I envision entry-level Bible college or seminary students benefiting from this book, perhaps those taking introductory courses in contemporary religious movements. Though it's far from a "scholarly" work, it does incorporate many scholarly voices to help strike a balance between the church and the academy.

Exorcising the Jello out of Evan-Jello-Calism

It turns out that Jell-O has an actual core that identifies it as a food product. Perhaps there is hope for identifying evangelicalism the same way—getting to the core of what it's made of. Though squishy, there must be an identifiable center that makes up a tradition that continues to have a seismic impact for the glory of God.

Then again, maybe the squishiness is signaling that it's time for a name change. As Darby implied in the quote at the outset, even in his nineteenth-century context, evangelicalism was less than stable.[17] Apparently, the dilemma is not new. The inevitable

---

17. Darby went so far as to declare the church in "ruins" due to its fragmented, denominational and political nature. Given the clerical abuses he witnessed not only in Roman Catholicism but in high-

question raised is if "evangelical" is a useful label anymore. Should we put up with the label, entirely discard it, or attempt to redeem it with some nuance? Maybe there's just too much Jell-O in the middle of "evangelicalism" for it to be a useful descriptor of a specific Christian tradition. In addressing the perennial issue, this book offers answers on how to recover a *vintage*—that is, a genuine and fundamental—evangelical identity.

---

church Protestantism, he may have had a point. See James I. Fazio, *Darby, Dispensationalism, and the Ruin of the Church* (Edinburgh: T&T Clark, forthcoming).

CHAPTER 1

The Elasticity of Evangelicalism

Evangelicalism has become an elastic enterprise. It seems that everything under the sun attaches the label "evangelical." Whether historic convictions are kept no longer matters. In his introduction to a book that strives to identify various brands of evangelicalism, Colin Hansen diagnoses the frustrating problem of evangelical identity with several statements that deserve to be quoted at length. After centering the *evangel* (gospel) as the core component supposedly agreed upon by all self-identifying evangelicals, he goes on to observe:

> Yet all is not so clear within the evangelical camp either. Simply labeling ourselves evangelical no longer suffices. We are conservative, progressive, postconservative, and preprogressive evangelicals. We are traditional, credal, biblical, pietistic, anticreedal, ecumenical, and fundamentalist. We are "followers of Christ" and "red letter Christians." We are everything, we are nothing. If the descriptor *evangelical* cannot stand on its own, then it has little use. There is no coherent movement, only an endless collection or self-styled labels created by Christians for their Facebook profiles.[1]

---

1. Colin Hansen, "Introduction," in *Four Views on the Spectrum of Evangelicalism*, eds. Andrew David Naselli and Colin Hansen (Grand Rapids: Zondervan, 2011), 9.

Hansen's assessment may be more poetic than precise. Still, it carries an alarming pulse that deserves pause—there's an obvious problem in evangelicalism. One can imagine a huge blender with every possible, even contradictory, marker for someone thrown in and then hit start. The result is anything but helpful. It's a total mess. Such is the inevitable result of defining evangelicals according to culture, self-identification, or by socio-historical analysis. It seems every possible candidate is entitled to the label "evangelical"—despite whether or not they maintain traditionally held biblical doctrines. Therefore, it is not surprising that one sociologist of religion reduced evangelical identity to someone who merely "practices a distinct style of religious devotion popular in the US."[2] Another prominent sociologist thought it best to understand evangelicalism as a "religiocultural phenomenon unique to North America."[3] But are these descriptions accurate? When do *beliefs* come into play? There are certainly cultural implications of evangelicalism, no one would deny that. But implications are just that: implications. This book contends that at its core, evangelicalism is (or should be) entirely biblical-theological. The sequential order of what should affect what is this: Bible—theology—evangelicalism—culture. Reversing the order wreaks havoc and results in the evan-jello-calism of today.

According to James Hunter, "an Evangelical is a Protestant who attests to the inerrancy of Scripture and the divinity of Christ and either (1) believes that Jesus Christ is the only hope for salvation or (2) has had a religious experience—that is, a particularly powerful religious insight or awakening that is still important in his everyday life that involved a conversion to Jesus Christ as his personal Savior or (3) both (1) and (2)."[4] That these

---

2. Alan Wolfe, *The Transformation of American Religion: How We Actually Live our Faith* (Chicago: University of Chicago Press, 2003), 36.

3. James Davison Hunter, *American Evangelicalism: Conservative Religion and the Quandary of Modernity* (New Brunswick: Rutgers University Press, 1983), 7. Hunter does offer several core doctrines that he sees as comprising evangelicalism, three of which are touched upon in chapter two of this book.

4. Ibid., Appendix 1.

are solid evangelical beliefs and implied behaviors is not doubted. The question is, as touched upon in this book's introduction, are these two or three criteria helpful enough to encapsulate a genuine evangelical identity in today's world? Hunter's grid allows for "religious experience" to stand on its own to qualify someone as an evangelical. But religious experience is a slope that is notoriously slippery. Many quasi-Christian cultists claim something similar regarding an experience in relation to Jesus, as do others outside of Protestantism altogether. Personal religious experiences that venerate Jesus's saviorhood can occur at divine liturgies in the Eastern Orthodox tradition or at masses in Roman Catholicism. It's not surprising, therefore, for sociologists to conclude there is "a sense in which we are all evangelicals now."[5]

If anyone who feels like adopting the label "evangelical" does so, how useful is it as an identity marker? The question is not particularly new. Almost three decades ago, Richard Mouw raised a salient point: "I must say something about the 'evangelical' label itself. Labels can outlive their usefulness, and it's important to keep monitoring the identification tags we wear to see whether they still make sense. A good label will inform. If a term we use to describe ourselves ceases to live up to the standards of truth-in-advertising than we should drop it."[6] If Mouw's reflection was relevant then, how much more now? Today's highly politicized, celebrity-driven, and culturally saturated "evangelicalism" should raise doubts as to the value of the label itself.

Terms of derision like "Big Eva" and "Big Tent Evangelicalism" have become catch-alls for what has eroded into an industrial complex over the past several decades shaping American evangelicalism. Coined by Carl Trueman, "Big Eva" (short for "big evangelicalism") refers to a populist conglomerate of neo-Reformed elite evangelical powerbrokers who have created a

---

5. Alan Wolfe, *The Transformation of American Religion*, 36.
6. Richard J. Mouw, *The Smell of Sawdust: What Evangelicals Can Learn from Their Fundamentalist Heritage* (Grand Rapids: Zondervan, 2000), 20.

conservative celebrity culture with minimal accountability.[7] Big conferences with big personalities are the driving mechanism. They entail lots of memes, merchandise, and mega-pastors with the word "gospel" thrown in. Of course, popular conferences, speakers, and books are not problematic in themselves, nor is every evangelical conference plagued by disingenuous motives. In fairness, many of their organizers and speakers are fine Bible expositors who really want to bless the wider church with their gifting. "What is problematic," observes Trueman, "is that some of these conferences and their concomitant celebrities have an intentional significance beyond offering a time for some fellowship and some good teaching."[8] Lines are drawn forming who's in and who's out of the movement without accomplishing any real ecclesiastical substance. The local church is routinely overshadowed by the stream of these big evangelical events. With little surprise a new group of "exvangelicals," has since emerged; former evangelical millennials jaded by the Big Tent scene who have walked away from evangelicalism (or Christianity) entirely.[9]

Complicating the matter, it is now trendy—even expected—for scholars to place the adjective "white" in front of "evangelicalism." Doing so helps gain a reading by the academic elite or perhaps a spot on a bestseller list. Some go so far as to paint American evangelicalism as a sort of racist and powerful old boys club: "conservative white men who have always been in charge of

7. Carl Trueman, "Revoice, Evangelical Culture, and the Return of an Old Friend," *Reformation* 21, July 31, 2018, https://www.reformation2.org/mos/postcards-from-palookaville/revoice-evangelical-culture-and-the-return-of-an-old-friend.

8. Ibid.

9. T. M. Luhrmann, "God Can You Hear Me?" *The American Scholar*, Jan 25, 2021, https://theamericanscholar.org/god-can-you-hear-me/. See also Jim Davis and Michael Graham with Ryan P. Burge, *The Great Dechurching: Who's Leaving, Why Are They Going, and What Will It Take to Bring Them Back?* (Grand Rapids: Zondervan, 2023), 65–78; Alisa Childers and Tim Barnett, The *Deconstruction of Christianity: What It Is, Why It's Destructive, and How to Respond* (Carol Streams: Tyndale Elevate, 2024), 29–42.

the twentieth-century US America version of the movement."[10] Others offer technical rubrics that conflate white evangelicalism with right-wing populism and driven by an obsession for Trump and racist foreign policies.[11] Doing so overlooks the hard fact that, globally speaking, "Evangelicalism is a predominantly non-White movement within Christianity, and becoming increasingly more so, with 77 per cent of all Evangelicals living in the Global South in 2020," according the co-editor of *World Christian Encyclopedia*, who also reports that as of 2020, nine out of ten countries with most evangelicals are in the global south.[12] Additionally, a 2020 Ligonier survey demonstrated that up to 93 per cent of Christians affiliated with historic Black Protestant churches agreed with the core beliefs that identify someone as an evangelical as compared to the 90 per cent of Christians affiliated with mainstream evangelical denominations. Commentating on the figures, Robert Bowman and J. Ed Komoszewski observed that according to these standards, "Black Protestant churches are just as 'evangelical' as the 'evangelical' church groups, if not more so."[13]

Clearly evangelicalism should not be defined by race or nationality. There may be more "white evangelicals" in the US than in other parts of the world, but why should that matter? It seems that scholars who critique "white evangelicalism" are ironically blinded by the very ethnocentrism for which they blast others. Evangelicalism for them is a purely American white phenomenon because *they* are American (and often white).

---

10. Isaac B. Sharp, *The Other Evangelicals: A Story of Liberal, Black, Progressive, Feminist, and Gay Christians—and the Movement that Pushed Them Out* (Grand Rapids: Eerdmans, 2023), xvii.

11. Marcia Pally, *White Evangelicals and Right-Wing Politics: How Did We Get Here?* (New York: Routledge, 2022), 1–10.

12. Todd M. Johnson, "Evangelicals Worldwide," *The Inquiry,* Gordon-Conwell Theological Seminary, March 25, 2020, https://www.gordonconwell.edu/blog/evangelicals-worldwide/.

13. Robert M. Bowman Jr., and J. Ed Komoszewski, *The Incarnate Christ and His Critics: A Biblical Defense* (Grand Rapids: Kregel Academic, 2024), 28.

Defining evangelicalism in terms of "whiteness" or American is parochial and ignores the overwhelming evidence that American and/or white evangelicalism is a global minority by far. This being the case, why the constant barrage of published volumes critical of "white evangelicals"?

To omit the racially embedded "white" adjective from modifying "evangelicalism" would result in no small number of progressive authors having virtually nothing to write about. Race peddling sells books; it always has. And ironically, a majority of such works are written by *white* evangelicals (or exvangelicals) who conveniently overlook their own "whiteness" in their critiques. There is no question that today's scholarly venues are obsessed with anything critical of "white" and "evangelical." Indeed, maybe it is time we once and for all drop the "evangelical" tag altogether.

What Others Are Saying

This book offers both a complement and contrast to several new releases that are critical of the evangelical version portrayed above, particularly Western influenced and American evangelicalism. Some are largely correct in their criticisms. Others go too far and exacerbate the problem, painting evangelicalism as a target deserving of only relentless assaults. As primary conversation partners, the first two books are more complementary, and the last two are more contrastive to my project.

The first is Katelyn Beaty's *Celebrities for Jesus*, which delivers an accessible and noteworthy critique of evangelicalism's intoxication with Christian celebrity.[14] Beaty helpfully defines celebrity as "social power without proximity" and with it, offers a sobering diagnosis of today's evangelicalism. "Celebrity is social power without proximity," she explains, "the chance to influence without knowing or being known by those you

---

14. Katelyn Beaty, *Celebrities for Jesus: How Personas, Platforms, and Profits are Hurting the Church* (Grand Rapids: Brazos, 2023).

are influencing."[15] Allowing pastors and Christian leaders to acquire broad-scale influence without genuine accountability inevitably leads to abuses of power, fixation of profits, and cults of personality—a constant nuisance within evangelicalism. "And the absence of true knowledge, and true accountability" argues Beaty, "leaves abundant opportunity for their social power to be misused and abused. To have immense social power and little proximity is a spiritually dangerous place for any of us to be."[16] Beaty is right to blast a somber warning to evangelicals being led by the nose by leaders with an insatiable appetite for fame. It seems American evangelicalism has failed to challenge celebrity culture; instead, it mimics it.[17] Headlines of evangelical mega-pastors with moral failures, evangelical consumerism, and a stream of evangelical social media "influencers" who deceivingly inflate their influence with "purchased fake followers" are all indicators of a toxic Christian celebrityism.[18]

A clear danger presents itself when committing one's devotion to a popular human. "If one's faith could be sealed by a particular celebrity, it makes sense that it can also be capsized by one too."[19] How many Christians have become jaded, discouraged, or even apostatized entirely when they came to grips with the fact that their favorite evangelical celebrity is anything but virtuous! Also worth pointing out is that Christian celebrityism is not restricted to heterodox "evangelical" prosperity teachers alone but can easily run rampant among orthodox mega Bible expositors as well. Apparently, this is an ancient problem, going back to the factions formed in Corinth. True evangelical faith is in the man Jesus Christ; no competing mediator will take that spot (see 1 Tim. 2:5). All famous men will inevitably disappoint, whereas the God-man never will. These ideas will be fleshed out more later.

---

15. Beaty, *Celebrities for Jesus*, 100.
16. Ibid., 19.
17. Ibid.
18. Ibid., 110–11.
19. Ibid., 158.

Suffice to say here, I largely agree with Beaty's assessment of American evangelical culture that has, in a sense, redefined itself by chasing platforms and abandoning "ordinary" or a vintage faithfulness in the gospel of Jesus. But there is a cure, which this book offers. A re-routing is needed that turns us back home. Though some fields get better when they progress, evangelicalism isn't one of them (thus "progressive evangelicalism" is a misnomer). We need to return to *fundamental* beliefs that make up a genuine evangelical identity. With this, we need to kill Christian celebrityism. Doing so will help situate our allegiances back to God in Christ as revealed in the infallible Scriptures—not to whoever is building the biggest ministries, hosting the biggest conferences, or accruing the most likes on social media. We need to get vintage.

The second complementary work is Constantine Campbell's *Jesus v. Evangelicals.*[20] Like Beaty, Campbell offers an accessible critique of American evangelicalism, but from the perspective of a non-American (who resided and taught in the US for years). Campbell's view of American evangelicalism is one of a cultural and political movement largely defined by power-mongering, divisiveness, greed, and hypocrisy. "The term *evangelical* no longer means what it once did, posing a significant problem for evangelicals," argues Campbell.[21] He accuses American evangelicalism of several lapses, including distorting its spiritual nature with an emphasis on politics; having an "us v. them" mentality; and creating divisive tribal boundaries over cultural and finer theological issues.[22] Though it may hurt Americans to be criticized to such an extent by an "outsider" (Campbell is Australian), all it takes is a perusal of Facebook, X, Instagram, and other socials belonging to American evangelicals to see how valid his assessment is.

---

20. Constantine R. Campbell, *Jesus v. Evangelicals: A Biblical Critique of a Wayward Movement* (Zondervan Reflective, 2023).
21. Constantine R. Campbell, *Jesus v. Evangelicals*, 11.
22. See Ibid., 10–11.

The biggest help Campbell brings to the table is his taxonomy for "evangelical."[23] The first category he calls "Theological evangelicals," composed of Christians who identify as evangelical by conviction over certain theological doctrines. These include belief that the Bible is God's authoritative Word, and belief in Christ's deity and atonement for eternal life. The second he terms "Cultural evangelicals": those who identity as evangelical not by conviction over beliefs, but for merely belonging to a crowd that has been influenced by theological evangelicalism. Campbell's third category, "Political evangelicals," are not evangelical by conviction or even culture but identify as evangelical out of shared political commitments that get conflated with an evangelical constituency. It is possible that a self-identifying evangelical can fit into more than one of the three groups simultaneously. However, and here's the point: "The blurriness of these three groups partly accounts for the confusion around the term *evangelical*."[24]

If we are to adopt these categories it would be the first one—theological evangelicals—that finds most agreement with the current book. "This kind of evangelical," contends Campbell, "has the best historical claim to the term, since these theological convictions have been part of evangelicalism since the Protestant Reformation in the sixteenth century."[25] As the book plays out, Campbell spends far more attention criticizing the second and third group and does so *without* the helpful monikers he coined at the outset. The result is an imbalanced impression that evangelicals are *only* cultural and political. Theological evangelicals are either irrelevant, *in absentia,* or dead. Still, there is value in Campbell's three-tiered metric as the distinctions he makes are helpful in categorizing much, or all, of American evangelicalism.

The value of his book notwithstanding, Campbell's assessment focuses too much on *who* evangelicals *are* rather than on *what* evangelicalism *is.* As a complement, my central focus is on

---

23. Campbell, *Jesus v. Evangelicals*, 4–6.
24. Ibid., 5.
25. Campbell, *Jesus v. Evangelicals*, 5.

the latter which by necessity strips away any right to claim the evangelical label for the latter two groups in Campbell's metric. As I argue, evangelicalism should be defined solely by a constellation of biblical-theological beliefs that results in living lives that reflects those beliefs. Otherwise, the label is useless. That said, there is a sense in which Campbell is right that no one truly "owns" language, and as such, none of the three groups can claim exclusive rights to the label.[26] Whether we like it or not, self-identifying evangelicals are always going to identify as such, regardless of whether they meet certain criteria. But this just highlights the problem along with the question raised earlier of whether we should throw out the label since it's been trampled beyond recognition.

Admittedly, I take exception to his claim of "white nationalism" being the current *de facto* criteria for American evangelicalism.[27] Such charges of racism are customary of left-leaning views of American political culture that tend to overlook evangelicalism's actual and historic stance on Scripture. Yet, in the end, my project agrees with Campbell's assessment of the rampant tribalism in American evangelicalism over secondary interpretive matters dividing Christians into warring camps, which *includes* (but is not defined by) the recent explosion of Christian nationalism. Campbell's assessment, even when only based on personal experience, highlights the messy confusion over evangelical identity as raised and recovered in this book.[28]

If the previous two works find general agreement with this book, the next two are quite the opposite. These projects argue

---

26. Ibid., 6.
27. Constantine R. Campbell, *Jesus v. Evangelicals*, 14–19.
28. Campbell's more personal and anecdotal complaints, such as evangelicals treating divorced people unfairly or his own views on gun control (along with a few other personal laments) should not detract from the book's larger argument that evangelicals are looked upon, at least from outside the US, as far removed from Jesus's commands of genuine love and unity as well as Bebbington's quadrilateral. Such argument deserves reflection.

for everything antithetical to classic, vintage evangelicalism. As they see it, evangelicalism is *not* held together by a pattern of historic beliefs centered on the inerrant Scriptures. Rather, it is dominated by white-supremist, misogynist homophobes who oppress every progressive voice feeling entitled to the label "evangelical." Yet there is value in these works. For one, they underscore the need for the current book. Through bombastic rhetoric and sensationalized titles, they serve as important indicators that evangelicalism, particularly in America, may have morphed into something unrecognizable from its vintage expression. Another point worth retaining from this crowd is the obvious danger of what happens when evangelicalism abandons its identity according to fundamental theological beliefs. A rotten evan-jello-calism emerges to take its place.

A recently explosive, slightly academic, work that offers a sharp contrast to my book, is Kristin Kobes Du Mez's *Jesus and John Wayne*.[29] A professor of history and gender studies at Calvin University, Du Mez presents a revisionist history of American evangelicalism corrupted by white politically conservative, ultra-masculine males. For Kobes Du Mez, American evangelicalism is a movement spearheaded by patriarchy, authoritarian rule, aggressive foreign policy, and Islamophobia—all of which was brought to a climax with American Trumpism. Instead, evangelicalism should be redefined in such a manner that embraces modern cultural movements #MeToo, Black Lives Matter, and the LGBTQ community. "Despite evangelicals' frequent claims that the Bible is the source of their social and political commitments," argues Kobes Du Mez, "evangelicalism *must* be seen as a cultural and political movement rather than a community chiefly defined by its theology."[30]

29. Kristin Kobes Du Mez, *Jesus and John Wayne: How White Evangelicals Corrupted a Faith and Fractured a Nation* (New York: Liveright, 2021).
30. Ibid., 297–98, emphasis added.

It is unclear if by "must" Kobes Du Mez is thinking in terms of description or prescription. Maybe it's a little of both. If she's merely *describing* what she sees in American evangelicalism, then there is some truth to her assessment. This book agrees that cultural and political "evangelicalism," which is no true evangelicalism at all, has corrupted and dominated a vintage faith that should be centered on the exclusivity of Jesus Christ as revealed in the inerrant Scriptures. Politicians on both the right *and* left are guilty of leveraging prooftexts from the Bible to support their cause or candidacy.

How often has some community leader or politician—across the spectrum—exploited biblical concepts like "hope," "unity," "healing," "justice," and so forth for their own campaigns? Though, like virtually all progressive scholars, Kobes Du Mez aims her guns (pardon the pun) at white republican macho gun owners to the exclusion of leftist politicians and social activists who equally exploit the Bible. If, however, she is levelling a prescript, an imperative *demanding* that we identify evangelicalism as purely cultural and political, this book takes serious exception. Instead, I believe we must identify evangelicalism according to fundamental beliefs and behaviors *regardless* of the surrounding politics and culture. But if we cannot do so because of wide-scale corruption, then, unfortunately, Kobes Du Mez has a point.

Throughout her book, Kobes Du Mez never defines what she means by "white evangelicalism," despite the alarming subtitle that this group has corrupted a faith and fractured a nation. Viewing everything through the lenses of critical race theory, she simply conflates evangelicalism with its "white" constituency, more specifically, its white-male-conservative-gun toting-Trump supporting constituency. Doing so effectively—and ironically— silences all ethnic minority evangelicals who she (presumably) hopes to elevate. Though the book is pervasive with examples, the conflation can clearly be seen in the following quotes that are listed in the same sequence in which they appear at the start of her concluding chapter. Without any demarcation or explanation, *white evangelicalism* simply becomes interchangeable with *evangelicalism.* Maintaining the same sequence from her book, I've italicized the blending of the two phrases below which subtly begins to occur by the third quote:

- A 2017 survey revealed that 41 per cent of *white evangelicals* owns guns, a number higher than any faith group and significantly higher than 30 per cent of Americans overall who own firearms.[31]

- For conservative *white evangelicals*, guns carry a symbolic weight that can only be understood within this larger culture of militancy.[32]

- Or consider *evangelical* views on immigration and border security. More than any other religious demographic, *white evangelicals* see immigrants in a negative light.[33]

- Yet *evangelicals* who claim to uphold the authority of the Scriptures are quite clear that they do not necessarily look to the Bible to inform their views on immigration; a 2015 poll revealed that only 12 per cent of *evangelicals* cited the Bible as their primary influence when it came to thinking about immigration.[34]

- It's no surprise, then, that the majority of *evangelicals* would agree that "building walls is not non-Christian," that there is "nothing anti-gospel about protecting our nation from those who would do our nation harm," and that those perceived as threats are members of *nonwhite* populations.[35]

It appears that for Kobes Du Mez, "white evangelicalism" *is* "evangelicalism." They are one and the same. This unspoken obsession to amalgamate whiteness, evangelicalism—and even

---

31. Kristin Kobes Du Mez, *Jesus and John Wayne,* 296.

32. Ibid.

33. Ibid., 297.

34. Ibid.

35. Ibid. Kobes also references her article, "Understanding White Evangelical Views on Immigration," *Harvard Divinity Bulletin* 46, nos. 1 and 2 (Spring/Summer, 2018), see 342, n.5.

Christianity as a whole—results in demeaning statements like, "Hobby Lobby is beloved by crafters and *white women* alike,"[36] to more aggressive ones such as: "Hobby Lobby masculinity . . . is a mix of gun-toting bravado, nostalgic imperial conquest, and flag waving (white) Christian nationalism."[37] What is the purpose in restricting Hobby Lobby shoppers to *white* women? Are there not women (and men) of *all colors* who enjoy crafts or American nostalgia—even if it annoys some on the left? Statements like hers are less than helpful.

Pardon my own anecdote for a moment. I'm not an avid Hobby Lobby shopper by any stretch, but my wife drags me out on occasion (we live several minutes away from *two* of them in southern California). Each time we've been inside either store, we've encountered women and men—both employees and customers—who are white, black, Hispanic, Asian, etc. But as I said earlier, race peddling sells books, and Kobes Du Mez is as guilty as her publisher for doing so.

There is a caution here about mixing Christianity with politics, nationalism, and merchandise. But where "white" makes the difference is anyone's guess. In contrast to Kobes Du Mez, my argument pushes back on a method of looking to culture as the starting point for identifying evangelicalism. Instead, as this book contends, a true historic (vintage) expression of evangelicalism should be defined by *fundamental orthodox beliefs* about Scripture, Jesus, evangelism, theological education, and local church involvement. Grounding evangelicalism in *doctrine* which leads to *behavior*—not culture or race—provides surer footing for those questioning their identity as professing Christians.

The final major contrastive voice to my project is Union Theological Seminary visiting professor Isaac B. Sharp's *The Other Evangelicals*.[38] A more scholarly assessment than Kobes Du Mez, Sharp offers an unbending critical revisionist history of

---

36. Kristin Kobes Du Mez, *Jesus and John Wayne*, 300, emphasis added.
37. Ibid., 301.
38. Isaac B. Sharp, *The Other Evangelicals*. Full citation earlier.

"canonical" (standard) evangelicalism. He argues that twentieth-century American evangelicalism has become an exclusionary conservative movement that has abandoned its minority voices represented by progressive, gay, feminist, and other theologically and politically liberal "evangelicals." According to Sharp, "Evangelical identity in the context of the contemporary United States has become a propriety trademark reserved almost exclusively for its most fundamentalistic, theologically and politically conservative, white, straight, and male-headship affirming claimants."[39]

The impression one gets from Sharp's project is that twentieth-century evangelicalism is exclusively controlled by a homogenous group of white, militant, American fundamentalists who view themselves as superintendents of orthodoxy, men belligerently pushing out all minorities who deserve a place in their big tent. "In so doing," contends Sharp, "a succession of powerful evangelical gatekeepers thereby defined themselves and their followers— who, not coincidently, thought, believed, voted, and looked like them—as *the* evangelicals, claiming the evangelical label as their proprietary trademark in the process."[40] Maybe this critic is on to something. There are doubtless influential evangelical leaders of the past who, though perhaps originally driven by their evangelical convictions, erected monuments and funded causes that certainly went further than evangelicalism's vintage expression. That conservative evangelicals can lobby for causes drifting from their original core identity hardly needs proof.[41]

Still, is it fair to characterize *all* of evangelicalism as a homophobic, misogynistic power struggle championed by bigoted white men? Moreover, who are these victimized groups that deserve to be included as "evangelicals," but are unfairly kept at

---

39. Isaac B. Sharp, *The Other Evangelicals*, 32.

40. Ibid., xviii.

41. Previous conservative political influencers that come to mind are Jerry Falwell, Tim La Haye, and Pat Robertson as do current evangelicals Rick Warren, Robert Jeffress, and Franklin Graham.

bay by the guardians of evangelicalism? The answer according to Sharp helps bring into focus exactly what he is proposing. According to him, these "other evangelicals" include theological liberals, progressives, feminists, noninerrantists, Barthinan, and even "gay evangelicals"—none of whom, I would argue, have any right to appropriate the term "evangelical" for themselves to begin with.[42] Sharp's thesis, like Kobes Du Mez's, is entirely culturally driven. Historic evangelical convictions matter little in his assessment other than to suggest they are passé. Yet, like the others, his work serves an important role leading to this book. Unwittingly, he underscores my thesis—abandonment of a fundamental core set of doctrine leaves the door open for every voice screaming for a place at a table that was never meant to be theirs.

As I see it, genuine evangelical *beliefs* will inevitably determine evangelical *behavior* resulting in evangelical *identity*. All three— belief, behavior, identity—form the *sine qua non* of evangelicalism. Of course, this assumes a benchmark, a set pattern of doctrines, by which to measure authentic evangelicalism, and, conversely, disqualify dissenters who contradict the benchmark. Because of various accretions that have muddied evangelical identity, it's not hard to sympathize with Sharp pointing out how nebulous defining "evangelicalism" really is. Without an agreed upon constellation of beliefs as its benchmark—the very elements that make evangelicalism a *vintage faith*—there really is no reason to discard the options he's included as what to call it: a tradition, a subculture, a style, an aesthetic, a worldview, a faith, a tradition, a cult, a social group, a belief structure, a spirit, a coalition, a movement.[43] Clearly, all of these fit the bill of an evangelicalism missing a set pattern of beliefs by which to define it.

Furthermore, like other attempts, if we define evangelical identity by *who* instead of *what*, then Sharp has as good a case as any to contend that the most acceptable version of evangelical identity

---

42. Isaac B. Sharp, *The Other Evangelicals*, 270–71.
43. Ibid., 254.

is someone defined by what they are *against* rather than what they are for. And, when left to most historians and social commentators, such a method inevitably ends in defining an evangelical primarily as anyone who takes exception to leftist ideology who then gets stamped with the quarrelsome labels "fundamentalistic," "militant," or the perennially-selling "white" (these terms shrewdly become synonymous). Someone who believes like an *anti*modernist *anti*liberal *anti*inerrantist, thinks like an *anti*feminist *anti*gay complementarian, and votes like a white Republican is what becomes the accepted criteria for evangelical identity, according to such cultural critics.[44] Unfortunately, the narrative continues to be advanced by current trends in academic publishing.

My project is markedly different. By situating evangelicalism according to a vintage constellation of *beliefs* and *behaviors* reflecting those beliefs, instead of people who *claim* to be evangelical, I am avoiding Sharp's and Kobes Du Mez's charges of racism, sexism, and personal discrimination as characteristic of evangelicalism. Simply put, positions such as the inerrancy of Scripture, the exclusivity of Jesus for salvation, a zealous passion for evangelism, for theological education, and for local church fellowship have no racist undertones. Moreover, my argument provides a positive platform for minority voices, such as the historic black fundamentalists, who have been unfairly muted by the dominance of critical scholars defining evangelicalism in cultural terms of race, politics, and celebrity.[45] These valiant Christians were convicted and motivated by classic evangelical *beliefs*, which I argue, makes them *evangelical* in a true and meaningful sense. But their existence simply does not fit within the progressive "white" narrative, so they remain largely forgotten in American evangelical history.

What I Am Saying

This book contends that the constellation of fundamental positions around which true evangelicalism orbits can broadly be classified

---

44. Cf. Ibid., 271.
45. This is taken up further in chapter nine with examples.

according to five major components: (1) a high view of Scripture; (2) the exclusivity of Jesus for salvation; (3) a zeal for evangelism; (4) participation in theological education and learning; and (5) the necessity of consistent local church fellowship—all of which are governed by position one. If a self-professing "evangelical" rejects any of these five convictions, either in belief or behavior, they have no right to the label "evangelical."

I anticipate that some will question why I chose these five positions as encapsulating a *vintage* or genuine form of evangelicalism. Admittedly, there is some subjectivity to the model, though it is based on years of study, experience, and reflection.[46] Though the first two or three beliefs are generally recognized across the board as "fundamentals" of evangelicalism (they comprise three-fourths of Bebbington's quadrilateral), the latter two—education and church fellowship—usually end up on the periphery (if considered at all). But something I question is that if everyone agrees that the classic fundamentals of evangelicalism include the first two or three of my metric, along with believing doctrines such as the virgin birth, the reality of miracles, the still-future physical second coming of Christ, and so on, then why is there such confusion over evangelical identity today? One would think these staple orthodox positions would be the impenetrable gatekeepers for authentic evangelical identity. However, today's evan-jello-calism is proof that something more than these beliefs is necessary for a genuine evangelicalism.

I contend that it is precisely because of the neglect of supposed "peripheral" or secondary positions that the erosion of evangelicalism has occurred to the extent it has. In the list above these are positions four and five which, in my model, are elevated (so to speak) to "fundamentals"—growing in theological education (see 2 Pet. 3:18) and thriving in consistent local church fellowship (see Heb. 10:25).[47] Why are these two often overlooked

---

46. I may not be an expert on evangelicalism, but I hope my evangelical "bona fides" in the previous chapter are worth *something*.

47. I am not alone in arguing for church fellowship being a "fundamental" of evangelicalism as Allister McGrath included it in his list of six fundamental convictions along with the standard set.

in modern evangelical identity? I believe it is because it is these two in particular that speak of *behavior*, which demonstrates actual *belief* in the first three convictions (a high view of Scripture, the exclusivity of Jesus for salvation, and zeal for evangelism). Thus, they have an embedded accountability. I would even classify these two behaviors as the *application* of believing the Scriptures are truly authoritative (relating to all three positions). Without living out an evangelical belief in Scripture, there is no true evangelicalism. As Ken Casillas rightly maintains, "Application is the only way the Bible can exercise its authority over our lives. Similarly, application is the only way the Bible can be sufficient for our lives."[48]

It is not unusual, therefore, that matters considered "secondary" in reality have enormous value and get overshadowed by what are historically considered more "essential" doctrines. The reason for the primary / secondary taxonomy is probably because the historic fundamentals of the faith virtually all revolve around one main thing: soteriology—*what a Christian must believe to be saved*. Of course, salvation is important; that goes without saying. But I believe that focusing on salvation while neglecting other important elements is too narrow to comprise a vintage or true evangelical identity; that identity *must* include behavior.

How this plays out is that the more one grows in their faith (education), the more one realizes that Christianity is far more than a binary category of who's in and who's out. Furthermore, the more one commits to a group of fellow-believers under faithful Bible teaching (church fellowship) the more seasoned and mature they become to serve others. God is then glorified in Christ through evangelical behavior that reflects evangelical belief. A genuine evangelical identity results, forming the *sine qua non* of evangelicalism (belief, behavior, identity). I believe that Paul had this very thing in mind when he envisioned the church

---

See Allister McGrath, *Evangelicalism and the Future of Christianity* (Downers Grove: InterVarsity, 1995), 55–56.

48. Ken Casillas, *Beyond Chapter and Verse: The Theology and Practice of Biblical Application* (Eugene: Wipf & Stock, 2018), 152.

building itself up in love by anchoring our identity in Christ: "For you have died, and *your life is hidden with Christ* in God. When *Christ who is your life* appears, then you also will appear with him in glory" (Col. 3:3–4; cf. 5–17). An evangelical identity sourced in anything other than Christ and his Word is no evangelical identity at all.

Though secondary doctrinal beliefs and behavioral ethics may not warrant the high ranking as fundamentals for salvation, that's not my argument. I am contending for a genuine *evangelical identity*, which *includes* primary salvation doctrines (e.g., belief in the Trinity, justification by faith alone, etc.), but also extends to behavior or how an already-saved evangelical thrives as an evangelical. For the latter to occur, I believe that growing in one's theological education (formally or informally in the biblical languages, theological disciplines, church history, and so on) as well as maintaining an active church life of serving others and being served under the faithful exposition of the Bible are necessary. These "secondary" ideas are part of what makes my model different from other, even conservative, metrics offered for evangelical identity.

A recent example is by Lifeway Research via Ligonier Ministries which identities an evangelical according to four beliefs, two of which focus squarely on what one must believe to be saved.[49] While the other two include a correct stance on the Bible, and "encouraging" non-Christians to trust in Jesus, a zealous practice of evangelism and missions work, participating in theological education, and the need for consistent local church fellowship did not make the cut. But I contend that my two positions on theological education and church fellowship along with the three other beliefs about the Bible, Jesus, and evangelism are not secondary or tertiary in any sense for evangelicalism to be genuinely evangelical. Rather, they are *fundamental* for true

---

49. Joe Carter, "The State of Theology: What Evangelicals Believe in 2022," The Gospel Coalition, September 22, 2022, https://www.thegospelcoalition.org/article/state-theology-2022/.

evangelical identity. And, as it turns out, this has been the case for quite some time.

Evangelicals and Evangelicalism

Before moving on, we must come to grips with what exactly is *evangelical*, *evangelicalism*, and the *vintage* form of it that I am proposing. Should evangelicalism be defined by power brokers controlling the political side of the movement since the mid-twentieth century? The obvious answer is no, but some say that is precisely what has happened. According to D. G. Hart, the *-ism* fixed to *evangelical* is historically nothing more than the addition of an incoherent abstraction by post-World War II neoevangelical leaders who vied for academic respect and cultural relevancy. It was formed by conservative Protestants looking to influence American religion, culture, and politics in the wake of the modernist-fundamentalist wars.[50]

Going a step further than Mouw, who earlier questioned the label *evangelical[-ism]*, Hart questions—even argues—that *evangelicalism* has become such a popular category, that it has definitely ceased to be useful.[51] Hart's goal of "deconstructing" evangelicalism is alarming and his assessment more aggressive than Mouw's. He says, "The one response that few have considered is perhaps the most radical. . . . Instead of trying to fix evangelicalism, born-again Protestants would be better off if they abandoned the category all together."[52] His explanation may be jarring but it's worthy of pause: "The reason is not that evangelicalism is wrong in its theology, ineffective in reaching the lost, or undiscerning in its reflections on society and culture," clarifies Hart. Rather, "Evangelicalism needs to be relinquished as a religious identity because it does not exist."[53] According to

---

50. D. G. Hart, *Deconstructing Evangelicalism: Conservative Protestantism in the Age of Billy Graham* (Grand Rapids: Baker Academic, 2004), 23–32.

51. D. G. Hart, *Deconstructing Evangelicalism*, 18.

52. Ibid., 16.

53. Ibid.

Hart, it was really pollsters, journalists, and scholars who are responsible for "evangelicalism" being a thing since the word serves only as a trendy analysis tool.[54] Though its theological convictions are not the problem, everything else about it is.

It is not difficult to sympathize with this view. In fact, historian Thomas Kidd points out, "The term *evangelical* has, since 1980, become associated with a particular kind of politics, namely white Christian support for the Republican Party. Yet we should not let today's political use of the term confuse its origins. At the outset, the word *evangelical* primarily related to spiritual reform and awakening."[55] Still, maybe Hart goes too far. Is it really true that "evangelicalism" is nothing but a wax nose, a modern invention of conservative mid-century elites without any discernable features? That is a hard sell given a history that predates twentieth-century America along with the uncalculated impact evangelicalism has had all over the world. In any case, if we're stuck with a label for theological identity that is not going away (despite Hart's insistence or my suggestion in chapter nine) then we need to recover its historic form. To do so, it is helpful to begin by tracing the history of its key terms and how their historic usage argues for what I call a "vintage faith."

Historical Definitions Matter

The word "evangelical" has a long history though not one plotted along a straight line. Several Indo-European languages are part of its evolution, including Greek, Latin, German, and English. The Latin adjective *evangelicus* and noun *evangelium* is where the English counterparts "evangelical" and "evangelicalism" are derived, both finding their origin in the koine Greek term *euangelion*—meaning "good message." This word appears seventy-six times in the Greek New Testament (eighty-four times if counting book titles as in the Tyndale House Greek New Testament) to depict the good

---

54. Ibid., 29.
55. Thomas S. Kidd, *America's Religious History: Faith, Politics, and the Shaping of a Nation* (Grand Rapids: Zondervan Academic, 2019), 35.

news or "gospel" of God and of Jesus Christ or of their kingdom (e.g. Matt. 24:14; Mark 8:35; Rom. 1:16; 1 Peter 4:17).[56]

The German word *evangelisch* originally described the Lutheran wing of the Reformation as essentially "gospel-confessing" before turning into a synonym for any group that is denominationally Protestant. One major theologian who predates the Protestant Reformation and adopted the evangelical label was the morning star of the Reformation—John Wycliffe (c.1330–84)—who was known as the "Evangelical Doctor." According to historian Nick Needham, Wycliffe earned his evangelical title "based on his commitment to popular preaching, grounded in holy Scripture as the Word of God and the Church's only infallible source of truth, as the primary and essential task of ministry."[57] From early on, an evangelical was someone who held to the unalterable truth and authority of the Bible and believed and preached the saving message of Christ.

The term evangelical later gained prominence as a way to describe Christian churches experiencing movements of the Holy Spirit during the Great Awakening periods in England and America. Assemblies that would include non-believers met together regularly and were visibly converted by the preaching of the gospel and the power of the Spirit, heightening the need for church fellowship. According to Kidd, the outpouring of the Spirit was believed to reflect the early church revivals in Acts, and the adjective "evangelical" became a way to describe accompanying traits such as "evangelical preaching" or an "evangelical book."[58]

---

56. The modern English word "gospel" evolved from the old English term "god-spell," which pictured a memorizing story or good tale. See Patrick Schreiner, "The Meaning of Εὐαγγέλιον: Lexical and Tradition-Historical Explorations," in *Paul's Letter to the Romans: Theological Essays*, eds., Douglas J. Moo, Eckhard J. Schnabel, Thomas R. Schreiner, and Frank Thielman (Peabody: Hendrickson Academic, 2023), 86–99.

57. Nick Needham, *2000 Years of Christ's Power* (Ross-shire, UK: Christian Focus, 2023), 5:89.

58. Thomas S. Kidd, *America's Religious History*, 35.

It was not until nineteenth-century revivalism with its emphasis on evangelism, that the English noun *evangelicalism* became a household term, especially in the United States. Particularly impactful was the American Bible Conference Movement which placed a high premium on biblical literacy and education and furthered the Reformation principle *sola Scriptura*, all of which was centered on the Bible's authority. "[These evangelical leaders] made it clear that they believed in all the fundamentals of the faith," explains Larry Pettegrew. "Some of the Bible conference teachers were voluminous writers, turning out volume after volume and publishing numerous articles for the religious journals and periodicals defending orthodox theology."[59] The eventual result was the formation of Bible teaching institutions and Christian colleges.[60] Evangelism, the Bible, and education are clear markers of this era that carried over into twentieth and twenty-first century evangelicalism.

To sum up, at its core, the *evangel* or gospel message of the kingdom and of salvation originally formed the very heart of the words "evangelical" and "evangelicalism." Evangelicalism was about spreading the gospel to everyone concerning repentance in Christ's name for the forgiveness of sins (Luke 24:47). This quickly expanded to include the highest view of Scripture, fellowshipping with saints under the exposition of the Scriptures, and growing in Christian theology resulting in fruitful Christian living—all for God's glory. These are the five components that I argue make up a *vintage* (evangelical) *faith.*

---

59. Larry D. Pettegrew, "Translation Across the Atlantic: American Bible Conference Movement (1875–1910)" in *Discovering Dispensationalism: Tracing the Development of Dispensational Thought from the First to the Twenty-First Century*, eds. Cory M. Marsh and James I. Fazio (El Cajon: SCS Press, 2023), 276.

60. Ibid., 251.

PART 2

The Five Fundamentals of a Vintage Identity

CHAPTER 2

The Supremacy of Scripture

Authority Matters

Evangelicals often disagree among themselves over the exact number and order of positions that make up evangelicalism. But there is virtually no disagreement that its major theological positions about the triune Godhead, salvation, eternity, and so on, are derived from what *Scripture* teaches about these great doctrines. In other words, evangelical identity, however it be defined, should be the result of a distinguishable pattern of beliefs that are sourced in Scripture. Everything "evangelical" begins with the Bible, making the authority of Scripture the first leading principle that determines all other beliefs. The premium evangelicalism places on Scripture immediately sets this vintage faith apart from other Christian traditions.

According to the nineteenth-century Bishop of Liverpool, J. C. Ryle, "The first leading principle of Evangelical religion is 'the absolute supremacy it assigns to Holy Scripture, the only rule of faith and practice, the only test of truth, the only judge of controversy.'"[1] There is irony in Ryle's claim since it's couched

---

1. J. C. Ryle, *Knots Untied: Being Plain Statements on Disputed Points in Religion from the Standpoint of an Evangelical Churchman*

in a book that defends evangelicalism not only from the Bible, but also from the Thirty-Nine Articles and Prayer Book of Anglicanism. This made sense for the Anglican bishop who was seeking to distinguish the "Evangelical" school of thought from two parties in the Church of England at the time he called "High Church" and "Broad Church," both of which neglected Scripture as their primary governing identity. As Ryle demonstrates, there are often competing authorities for the Christian which can include denominations and different traditions. Still, Ryle's "first principle" is entirety accurate. The Holy Scriptures hold *absolute supremacy* for the evangelical.

The Quadrilateral of Authorities

Everyone has an authority by which they live and make decisions. Throughout church history, a quadrilateral of authorities emerged as an intuitive model that Christians employ when appealing to *why* they personally hold to a belief.[2] All Christians, including evangelicals, instinctively use the model when they appeal to their own reason, tradition, personal experience, or Scripture (the "quadrilateral") to validate a position.

However, only one authority of the four is ultimate because it is consistent, trustworthy, and of divine origin, which is Scripture alone.[3] According to evangelical scholar Ben Witherington III, there is a relationship between the quadrilateral of authorities. An

(London: National Protestant Church Union, 1898), 4. Ryle's following evangelical principles were: human sinfulness and corruption, the work and office of Christ as Lord, the inward work of the Holy Spirit, and the outward expression of the Spirit's work in the Christian life. He understood these other positions to have their anchor in a high view of Scripture.

2. Though others have used the phrase, I borrow the term "quadrilateral of authorities" from Ben Witherington III, *Sola Scriptura: Scripture's Final Authority in the Modern World* (Waco: Baylor University Press, 2023).

3. It is outside of this book's scope to exhaust the different canons throughout Church history, but for clarity's sake, appeals to "Scripture" throughout the book are referring solely to the Protestant canon.

evangelical's reason, tradition, and experience may help *illustrate* or *communicate* the Bible, but they should never be presented as having the *same authority* of the Bible (and certainly not higher!). He explains:

> We can say that reason, tradition, and experience can all be seen as windows into the Scripture or avenues out of the Scripture by which we may express the truth of Scripture, but in no case and on no occasion should reason, tradition, or experience be seen as a higher authority than Scripture by which Scripture could be trumped *on some issue that Scripture directly addresses* and about which it makes claims on God's people.[4]

When Scripture addresses a clear theological matter, such as the exclusivity of Christ, (John 14:6), or simple ethical injunctions like honest work and trade (Eph. 4:28), or presents historical reporting such as the rise and fall of Israel's kings (1and 2 Samuel) the evangelical believes it to be infallibly true as God's Word—and submits to its truth as an act of faith in the authority of Scripture. As Fred Zaspel argues, "In all of Scripture's affirmations and declarations—whether in matters of history, faith, or practice—we hear God speaking and are obligated therefore to embrace it as true and receive it in submission, trust, and obedience."[5]

In some contexts, the term *prima Scriptura* is used of the same idea in that Scripture is not normed by theological tradition or human reason, but neither should these lesser authorities be jettisoned for an isolationist view of Scripture. Experience, reason, and tradition are helpful guides, but they can err. In contrast, only the Bible is infallible, divinely authoritative, and thus *primary*.[6]

---

4. Ben Witherington III, *Is there a Doctor in the House: An Insider's Story and Advice on Becoming a Bible Scholar* (Grand Rapids: Zondervan Academic, 2011), 103, emphasis in original.

5. Fred G. Zaspel, "Inerrancy, Adam & Eve, and B. B. Warfield (1851–1921)," *Detroit Baptist Seminary Journal* 29 (2024), 54.

6. Some traditions understand *prima Scriptura* as Scripture being the foremost authority over other supposedly "divine" sources such as angelic visits, creeds and confessions, mystical insight, or charismatic

A person's logical reasoning, experience, or theological tradition can help guide in such matters, but for vintage faith, these other authorities *must* submit to Scripture's supreme authority; it is this principle that connects the relationship between the quadrilateral of authorities. Genuine evangelicalism is to be governed ultimately by Scripture's authority, or it is no true evangelicalism. For the vintage or genuine evangelical, no higher measure on earth exists than the finality of the Bible.

The meaning of this first principle—and traditional governing identity marker of evangelicalism—is that there is no source in the world that is co-equal with the Bible. Scripture holds the ultimate and supreme place for testing truth claims both within and outside of itself. This claim has proven controversial as the belief in the supremacy of Scripture is the historical culprit that became the dividing line between "conservative" evangelicals on the one side, and "liberal" or "progressive" evangelicals on the other side.[7] Regardless, those who wish to identify as evangelicals must stand up for this first fundamental belief of vintage evangelicalism. Nothing true will ever contradict Scripture which is entirely true and the final arbiter of all truth. While truth exists outside of Scripture, *everything* Scripture reports is true and authoritative. This means the Bible holds dominance over all other common authorities that often compete with Scripture, such as human reason, tradition, or personal feelings and experience.

Unfortunately, most modern evangelicals take their sense of direction from the culture rather than the biblical witness. The reason for this shifting of authority-priority is the inevitable result of failing to hold to the high view of Scripture that has historically identified evangelicals since the days of John Wycliffe. The elasticity of modern evangelicalism from the previous chapter

---

views on the Spirit apart from the Bible. My definition above rejects such a view and uses the term in its most conservative manner.

7. As David W. Bebbington noted, "The importance attributed by Evangelicals to the Bible eventually led to something approaching schism in their ranks." *Evangelicalism in Modern Britian: A History from the 1730s to the 1980s* (London: Routledge, 2005), 14,

demonstrates this to be the case: when Scripture is not placed first, culture or self takes the place of evangelical identity. The result is the "jello" discussed earlier. Thus, the first component of what makes up a truly evangelical faith—in my words, a *vintage faith*—is a high view of Scripture. Scripture *alone* has ultimate authority.

Sola Not Solo Scriptura

The evangelical principle *sola Scriptura* should not be confused with "solo" or *nuda Scriptura*. The latter is the idea that the Bible is the only rule of faith to the *exclusion* of all other sources. This is not the case since God has revealed himself not only in Scripture (typically called "special revelation") but in nature as well ("general revelation").[8]

Moreover, the unalterable, fundamental laws of logic are true (though one's application of them is not always so). We also learn truths from other places outside the Bible such as theologians of the past and present, ancient writings of the Church Fathers, pastors, commentaries, journal articles, Bible dictionaries, etc. Indeed, God has blessed the church with a wealth of authoritative resources that help us learn about him and humanity's place in the world.

Still, only the Bible is divinely inspired and infallible and thus carries *ultimate authority* over all these other sources. As Gavin Ortlund explains, "*Sola Scriptura* is simply the position, that, as the Bible is unique in nature, so it is correspondingly unique in authority."[9] This first principle is what guided the Reformers in their disputes against Roman Catholicism. "At an early stage in his controversy with Eck," relays historian Norman Sykes, "Luther had taken up the position that the Bible alone was authoritative, so that *sola scriptura* took its place side by side with *sola fide*.

8. Yet, we ultimately know this is true *because* it is revealed in Scripture! (See Ps. 19 and Rom. 1).

9. Gavin Ortlund, *What It Means to Be Protestant: The Case for an Always-Reforming Church* (Grand Rapids, Zondervan Reflective, 2024), 78.

Calvin was even more emphatic in his iterated assertion of the same principle."[10] Authorities outside the Bible are helpful in that they play a ministerial role in the Christian life. Nevertheless, they are subordinate to Scripture. All others must be "normed" by Scripture. Only Scripture is magisterial. That means that if a book or teacher says something that contradicts clear teaching of Scripture, it is *Scripture that is correct*; the others must change. Same goes for when a person's reason or experience is challenged by Scripture. Only *Scripture* is normative and authoritative as God's Word, so the others must form to it. This is the idea behind the Reformation principle *sola Scriptura*. It is not that Scripture is the *only* authority, it is that Scripture is the *ultimate* authority by which we know and follow the true God (Deut. 6:4; John 17:3).

Of course, appeals to Scripture's authority are based on interpretations of Scripture. And interpretations of Scripture are themselves based on the *a priori* belief that that Bible has objective meaning that is authoritative. In his perennially relevant text *Exegetical Fallacies*, D. A. Carson pushed back against what he called a "new hermeneutic" that rejects objective meaning for Scripture and argues for multiple meanings equally true for any given text, despite the contradictions that result.[11] Such a method directly compromises biblical authority since it relativizes all meaning of biblical texts and shifts their authority away from the biblical authors to the minds of readers instead.[12] Carson observed just how high the stakes are: "I do not know what biblical authority means, nor even what submission to the lordship of Jesus Christ means, if we are unprepared to bend our opinions, values, and mental

---

10. Norman Sykes, "The Religion of the Protestants," in *The Cambridge History of the Bible*, ed., S. L. Greenslade (Cambridge: Cambridge University Press, 1963), 3:175–76.

11. D. A. Carson, *Exegetical Fallacies* (Grand Rapids: Baker, 1993), 128–31.

12. I deal with this matter more in my article, "Synchronic with Caveats: A Fourth Wave of Interpretation of the Fourth Gospel," *The Journal of the Evangelical Theological Society* 65.1 (2022), 93–109.

structures to what the Bible says, to what Jesus teaches."[13] The Bible has objective meaning and has objective authority. The reader, therefore, forms to Scripture, *not* Scripture to the reader (see Rom. 12:2; cf. Heb. 5:14).

The hermeneutical method used to support *sola Scriptura* was a reformational approach that sought to recover the intended meaning of the Bible's original writers. This approach turned the focus to studying Scripture's original languages of Hebrew and Greek, as it was these languages (along with portions in Aramaic) in which the Bible was originally written. It was a "recovery" because the dominating interpretive method up to that time was medieval scholasticism using Jerome's Latin text of the Bible (called the Latin Vulgate) along with centuries of Roman Catholic interpretations by various popes, councils, and theologians such as Thomas Aquinas and others.[14]

But with the return to studying the Bible's original languages, a recovery likely begun in the preceding Renaissance era, a corollary doctrine to *sola Scriptura* emerged that became known as the "perspicuity of Scripture." From the Latin *perspicuitās* meaning clear, transparent, even self-evident, Scripture was understood to be clear in matters of most importance. This idea of Scripture's perspicuity quickly became the primary bone of contention between Luther and the Roman Catholic Church. Rick Holland argues, "It is no overstatement to suggest that the causality for the 'protest' in the Protestant Reformation was rooted in a fundamental disagreement over the clarity of Scripture."[15] Authority is inseparable from clarity. To say that the Bible is authoritative is to say it is *clearly* authoritative.

---

13. D. A. Carson, *Exegetical Fallacies*, 130.

14. See the excellent chapters by Kallistos Ware and David Knowles in Hubert Cunliffe-Jones, ed. *A History of Christian Doctrine* (Philadelphia: Fortress, 1980), 181–286.

15. Rick Holland, "The Perspicuity of Scripture and Expository Clarity," in *To Seek, To Do, and To Teach: Essays in Honor of Larry D. Pettegrew,* eds. Douglas D. Bookman, Tim M. Sigler, and Michael J. Vlach (Cary: Shepherds Press, 2022), 223.

The bedrock of *sola Scriptura* established the Protestant Reformation, which necessitated the Bible's clarity and was supported by an interpretive approach that sought the literal intended meaning of the biblical authors. A magisterial interpreter such as the pope was seen in direct conflict with Peter's clear insistence of the priesthood of all believers.[16] The Scripture was authoritative on its own and clear in its most essential affirmations. With this recovery, the Bible broke through centuries of accretions simply by seeking the literally intended meaning of the original authors in their original languages.[17] The fundamental shift from submission to conflicting Roman Catholic dogma to submission to Scripture's clarity exalted the Bible's supremacy over the Christian life and, with it, became the first concrete marker for evangelical identity.

A Vintage (High) View of Scripture

When scholars explain what makes up historic evangelicalism, almost without exception the first element identified is a high view of the Bible and its authority. Historian George Marsden began his list of "essential evangelical beliefs" with "the Reformation doctrine of the final authority of the Bible."[18] Theologian Albert Mohler included "the authority of Scripture" in his theological triage of first-level evangelical doctrines.[19] Indeed, as historian

---

16. See Martin Luther's tract, "An Open Letter to the Christian Nobility of the German Nation Concerning the Reform of the Chistian Estate," in Martin Luther, *Three Treatises*, trans. Charles M. Jacobs, rev. by James Atkison (Philadelphia: Fortress, 1970), 1–112.

17. Jeremiah Mutie argues that the concept of a literal grammatical-historical method of biblical interpretation was "clearly embedded" into the Reformation doctrine of perspicuity of Scripture. See Jeremiah Mutie, "Neither Woodenly Literal nor Allegorical: The Dispensationalist Legacy of the Reformers' Doctrine of Sola Scriptura," in *Forged from Reformation: How Dispensational Thought Advances the Reformed Legacy*, eds. Christopher Cone and James I. Fazio (El Cajon: SCS Press), 362.

18. George M. Marsden, *Understanding Fundamentalism and Evangelicalism* (Grand Rapids: Eerdmans, 1991), 4.

19. R. Albert Mohler Jr., "Confessional Evangelicalism," in *Four Views on the Spectrum of Evangelicalism*, eds. Andrew David Naselli

David Bebbington declared without hesitation: "Evangelicalism has been nothing if not biblicist."[20]

In his final book, the evangelical philosopher, cultural critic, and theologian Francis Schaeffer identified what he called a "full view" of Scripture as the "watershed of the evangelical world." Giving up that ground meant giving up evangelicalism. "The first direction in which we must face," argued Schaeffer, "is to say most lovingly but clearly: evangelicalism is not consistently evangelical unless there is a line drawn between those who take a full view of Scripture and those who do not."[21]

The Bible is divine revelation—"God-breathed" (*theopneustos*, 2 Tim. 3:16)—and is therefore inerrant and infallible in all that it states. Each verse is entirely authoritative and sufficient "so that the man of God may be complete, equipped for every good work" (2 Tim. 3:17). Everything else in historic evangelicalism must flow from Scripture's view of its own ontology and function. Because evangelical beliefs about the Trinity, redemption, the afterlife, ethics, and so on are sourced in the Bible, a genuine evangelical identity necessarily begins with the highest view of Scripture's authority. "The truthfulness and authority of the Holy Scriptures must... rank as a first-order doctrine," observed Mohler, "for without affirming the Bible as the very Word of God, we are left without any adequate authority for distinguishing truth from error."[22]

The stakes are huge. If the Bible is not the authority for evangelicals, something deficient *will* take its place. Daniel Hyde rightly points out, "If Scripture is not breathed out as 2 Tim 3 says, then preachers become something other than proclaimers and heralds of the words of God. Preachers become entertainers,

and Colin Hansen (Grand Rapids: Zondervan, 2011), 78.

20. David W. Bebbington, *The Evangelical Quadrilateral: Characterizing the British Gospel Movement* (Waco: Baylor University Press, 2021), 36. See chapter nine's discussion on the term "biblicist."

21. Francis A. Schaeffer, *The Great Evangelical Disaster* (Westchester: Crossway, 1984), 51.

22. R. Albert Mohler Jr., "Confessional Evangelicalism," 79.

stand-up comics, or therapists."[23] The idea of entertainment and therapeutic preaching models becoming part and parcel of modern evangelicalism will be revisited later in the book. The point here is the absolute need for the primacy of Scripture if we are to recover a true or *vintage* evangelical identity. This is because the Scriptures' divine authority governs all that evangelicals should believe and how they should behave as evangelicals.

Is the Bible *actually* revelation from God and inscribed by a group of diverse men with diverse styles that carries God's ultimate authority? The answer for historic evangelicalism is yes.[24] Through the miracle of inspiration, God's very words were breathed through chosen men who, through their own distinct styles and personalities, wrote precisely as the Spirit "carried them along" (*pheromenoi*) to write (2 Pet. 1:21). In fact, any deviance from the highest view of Scripture inevitably unravels evangelicalism into the confusion of evangelical identity today. "It is to be expected that evangelical Christianity should often be under attack," began Fuller Seminary charter faculty member Wilbur M. Smith in his mid-century apologetics text.[25] Smith viewed secular philosophy's rejection of divine revelation as undermining the very core of evangelicalism. He argued, "Christian religion and its documents, claiming to be the inspired product of a divine communication, insists that the truth therein set forth comes with unquestionable authoritativeness, and, proceeding from God, must be eternally true."[26] Of first importance is that the supremacy of Scripture is what has governed—and what *should* govern—evangelicalism.

---

23. Daniel R. Hyde, *This is the Word of the Lord: Becoming Confident in the Scriptures* (Fearn, Ross-shire: Christian Focus, 2022), 50.

24. The best treatment defending the authority and inspiration of Scripture remains Benjamin B. Warfield, *The Inspiration and Authority of the Bible* (Phillipsburg: P&R, 1948).

25. Wilbur M. Smith, *Therefore Stand: A Plea for a Vigorous Apologetic in this Critical Hour of the Christian Faith* (Boston: W. A. Wilde Co., 1950), 1.

26. Ibid., 7.

Vulnerable Appeals to Authority

Taking a fundamental stance on Scripture's divine authority does place genuine evangelicalism in a vulnerable position. Attacks made on evangelicalism can usually be traced in some form or another to its views about the Bible.

Critics recognize that evangelicals have historically been identified with a high view of Scripture, which offers them a convenient dogma to exploit. With not-so-subtle disdain, Kristin Kobes Du Mez complains, "Yet evangelicals who claim to uphold the authority of the Scriptures are quite clear that they do not necessarily look to the Bible to inform their views on immigration."[27] In her mind, evangelicalism is heartless because many American Republicans believe in national border security. Overlooking any real distinction between American conservatism and historic evangelicalism, Kobes Du Mez is puzzled by evangelicals *claiming* to hold to the authority of the Bible while not acting accordingly regarding policies on immigration (naturally, her beliefs about immigration are biblical). The confusion is compounded with, ironically, an appeal to Scripture *as authoritative*: "Given that the Bible is filled with commands to welcome the stranger and care for the foreigner."[28]

Setting aside the biblical fact that God's covenant to Abraham included land borders (Gen. 15:18–21), Moses and the prophets divided up land according to Jewish tribal borders (Num. 34:1–15; Ezek. 47:13–21), and Paul preached that God determined earthly borders for all nations (Acts 17:26), Kobes Du Mez and others who appeal to the Bible for their immigration policies fail to make the critical biblical distinction between the nationality of Israel and the spirituality of the church. Commands given to welcome strangers and foreigners comprised the Mosaic law code which regulated Israel's witness as a theocratic, covenanted nation

---

27. Kristin Kobes Du Mez, *Jesus and John Wayne: How White Evangelicals Corrupted a Faith and Fractured a Nation* (New York: Liveright, 2021), 297.

28. Ibid., 297.

(Deut. 14:21; 1 Kings 8:41–43; Zech. 7:9–10). To apply them to America's border polices or to bind them to the church as law is to violate their contextual usage.

Not only is the United States *not* a theocratic nation governed by way of divine covenant (it is a secular republic governed by way of human democracy), which places America in an entirely different context than biblical Israel, but the church is a spiritual entity governed not by law but by God's grace (Eph. 3:2–8; cf. Gal. 5:1). Unlike a nation, there are no land borders that fence in the church. Unlike a nation, there is no earthly king, president, or prime minister ruling the church.[29] Therefore, when the New Testament speaks of caring for the "stranger" (*xenos*) the context is never a legal policy legislating the church.

Now, it should go without saying that Christians caring for all people, including non-Christians, is part and parcel of what it means to be Christian. History has demonstrated this to be the case from Christians refusing to flee disease-ridden Europe and choosing to help those dying of plague, to historically Christian humanitarian agencies and churches always first to respond to victims of natural disasters. After all, the apostle was clear that Jesus-followers are to do good, not just to fellow Christians, but to *everyone* (Gal. 6:10; 1 Thess. 5:15). Christians are to pray for *all people* (1 Tim. 2:1). They are to show hospitality to people they don't even know (Heb. 13:2). That's what Christians do as baptized members of the spiritual body of Christ that shows love to neighbors. But these New Testament injunctions are a far stretch from the legal requirements demanded in the Mosaic covenant that governed the nation of Israel in the Old Testament. Distinct from the church, Israel was governed by covenantal law, which the Gospels report Jesus fulfilled (Matt. 5:17; cf. Rom. 10:4).[30]

---

29. Protestantism, which subsumes evangelicalism, does not believe the pope or any other human candidate has divinely inherited authority over the universal church. See Gavin Ortlund, *What It Means to Be Protestant,* 103–31.

30. For more on how Christ relates to each of the divine-human biblical covenants, see my article, "A Dynamic Relationship: Christ, the

When it comes to caring for the "stranger" (*xenos*), in the New Testament the context is either eschatological (end times) when Christ returns in judgment and rewards believers who displayed acts of love to fellow believers (Matt. 25:31–40), or when commending Christians for welcoming other Christians who are literally strangers (*xenous*)—those from another region who have gone out for the sake of "the Name" (3 John 5).[31] Though passages like these are commonly appealed to by critics judging evangelicalism's supposed lack of sympathy for non-citizens, contextually, they have absolutely nothing to do with the ethics of national immigration policies.[32]

Biblical Inerrancy

A logical corollary to the Bible being "breathed out" by God is that it is inerrant. It has to be. If God himself is inerrant, then whatever he breathed out is inerrant. The Bible contains no authorial errors because it is breathed out by God who makes no mistakes.

In fact, the evangelical goes a step further and argues that not only does the Bible *not* err—it *can't* err. In other words, Scripture is inerrant and infallible. In the words of Jesus, "the Scripture *cannot be broken*" (John 10:35). God's Word will never fail because it *cannot fail* since it originates from an unfailing God (see Isa. 55:11). Thus, Scripture's "inerrancy" (*does not* contain errors) and "infallibility" (*impossible* to contain errors) are inextricably linked.[33] Such a

---

Covenants, and Israel," *The Master's Seminary Journal* 30, no .2 (Fall 2019) 257–75.

31. See Chris Miller, *Matthew*, NTEC (Elgin: Regular Baptist Press), 289–99; David B. Capes, *Matthew Through Old Testament Eyes*, BAC (Grand Rapids: Kregel Academic, 2024), 381 n.8; Andreas J. Köstenberger, *A Theology of John's Gospel and Letters*, BTNT (Grand Rapids: Zondervan Academic, 2009), 272.

32. It is worth noting the reference to "strangers" in Hebrews 13:2 is supplied by translators. The context is fitting, but the word is absent in the Greek New Testament.

33. There are "errors" that the Bible contains in the sense of factual reports of intentional lies, deceit, or unintended mistakes committed by various characters throughout narratives in Scripture (e.g., 2 Sam. 6:7;

position is either true or it is not. For vintage evangelicalism this must be true, since God inspired the biblical text; there are no other options.[34] The Prince of Preachers, C. H. Spurgeon, was resolute: "We care little to any theory of inspiration: In fact, we have none. To us, the plenary verbal inspiration of the Holy Scripture is a fact and not a hypothesis."[35]

It should make sense that if a Christian believes that Jesus is truly divine and that his life, death, and resurrection are factually necessary for the salvation of lost sinners, then the Bible is not wrong or contradictory. The reason is because such unfathomable mysteries are revealed in *errorless Scripture*, not in gurus, councils, dreams, or any other competing source that can err. In other words, we only know what the purpose of Jesus's ministry is *because* it is sourced in an inerrant Bible and is therefore authoritative and trustworthy (Luke 19:10; John 20:31). If the Bible contains authorial errors, then it loses its trustworthiness in areas as important as eternal life. If it's untrue in less significant matters (e.g., historical or scientific accounts), then what confidence do we have that it's true in the areas that matter most?

Holding to the inerrancy of Scripture is a hill that evangelicals must defend and should never be a cause for retreat or embarrassment. Contrary to opinions that suggest the doctrine of inerrancy is arrogant and unwilling to accept the historical reconstructions or form-theories of critical scholars, biblical inerrancy produces *humility*. Biblical inerrancy teaches readers of Scripture that God's ways are higher than theirs, and when a

---

Job 19:4; Eccles. 10:5; Ezek. 45:20; Rom. 1:27; Jude 11). Such instances are truthful and inerrant reports of errors performed, *not* cases of authorial errors, the latter of which concerns the doctrine of inerrancy.

34. I am aware of modern evangelical scholars who argue against aspects of the classic doctrines of inerrancy and infallibility. Though some nuances to the doctrines are helpful, any proposed revisions that call for anything less than the Bible being entirely free from error in the autographs must be rejected if one is to identify as a genuine evangelical.

35. Charles H. Spurgeon, *The Greatest Fight in the World* (London: Paternoster, 1896), 27.

tension arises in the text in an especially challenging way, it is the *reader* whose understanding is limited or needs correcting—not the Bible. Why is that? The reason is because only Scripture is inerrant and infallible. As evangelical scholar Hans Madueme contends, "Far from being a demerit of the person, holding the inerrancy of Scripture dogmatically is a function of *humility*. It is faith seeking understanding and holding as true all that God has revealed to us in Scripture....Pride and hubris are antithetical to the real meaning of dogmatic inerrancy."[36]

Biblical inerrancy has defined evangelical identity implicitly since the pre-Reformation era and explicitly ever since.[37] According to Hunter, evangelicalism can boil down to a three-pronged doctrinal core all of which *begins* with the inerrancy of Scripture: (1) the belief that the Bible is the inerrant Word of God, (2) the belief in the divinity of Christ, and (3) the belief in the efficacy of Christ's life, death, and resurrection for the salvation of the human soul.[38] This model overlooks other fundamentals argued in this book, such as evangelism, education, and church fellowship. Nevertheless, Hunter's list identifying evangelicalism as *beginning* with belief in the inerrancy of Scripture is certainly correct since that truth governs what the Bible says about Christ and his saving work—as well as every other evangelical belief.

Biblical inerrancy is the defining marker for vintage evangelicalism. In the late 1970s, multiple conservative evangelical leaders formed an alliance called the International Council on Biblical Inerrancy (ICBI). Convinced that both the authority and accuracy of the Bible are the foundations of the Christian faith, this group of scholars, pastors, and theologians thought they were

---

36. Hans Madueme, *Defending Sin: A Response to the Challenge of Evolution and the Natural Sciences* (Grand Rapids: Baker Academic, 2024), 54. Emphasis original.

37. Harold Lindsell, *The Battle for the Bible: The Book that Rocked the Evangelical* World (Grand Rapids: Zondervan, 1976), 17–27.

38. James Davison Hunter, *American Evangelicalism: Conservative Religion and the Quandary of Modernity* (New Brunswick: Rutgers University Press, 1983), 7.

witnessing the erosion of such values. As they saw it, halting the downhill trajectory must begin with defending the inerrancy of Scripture.

The ICBI was trans-denominational and global in its constituency as the conviction over biblical inerrancy was purely *evangelical* (not ethnocentric or denominationally controlled). Over three days in October 1978, what became the largest and broadest group of conservative evangelical leaders ever to assemble up to that point, came together for the shared cause of defending biblical inerrancy. They produced what they termed "The Chicago Statement on Biblical Inerrancy" (CSBI), a landmark document for evangelical belief on the inspiration and authority of Scripture. Viewing inspiration, authority, and inerrancy as necessarily intertwined, the statement (consisting of nineteen affirmations and denials) explained biblical inerrancy in multiple, sophisticated ways.[39]

For example, Article Six of the CSBI reads, "We affirm that the whole of Scripture and all its parts, down to the very words of the original, were given by divine inspiration. We deny that the inspiration of Scripture can rightly be affirmed of the whole without the parts, or of some parts but not the whole." This speaks to plenary verbal inspiration—every part of Scripture is God-breathed and inerrant, even down to the very words. According to Article Eleven, "We affirm that Scripture, having been given by divine inspiration, is infallible, so that, far from misleading us, it is true and reliable in all the matters it addresses. We deny that it is possible for the Bible to be at the same time infallible and errant in its assertions. Infallibility and inerrancy may be distinguished but not separated." Thus, the Bible is both inerrant and infallible since it not only contains no errors it is also impossible for errors to be in the Bible in *all* matters that it addresses, not merely religious matters of faith and practice. Article Twelve is most definitive:

---

39. The original CSBI documents are housed in the archives at Dallas Theological Seminary. The following quotes are from The International Council on Biblical Inerrancy, "The Chicago Statement on Biblical Inerrancy," *The Journal of the Evangelical Theological Society* 21.4 (December 1978): 289–96.

We affirm that Scripture in its entirety is inerrant, being free from all falsehood, fraud, or deceit. We deny that biblical infallibility and inerrancy are limited to spiritual, religious, or redemptive themes, exclusive of assertions in the fields of history and science. We further deny that scientific hypotheses about earth history may properly be used to overturn the teaching of Scripture on creation and the flood.

Such an affirmation and denial pushes against theories that try to minimize non-salvific propositions in Scripture as being less than inspired and inerrant, such as the creation narratives. It also draws a clear line between authentic authorship and pseudepigraphy, the latter being a writing *pretending* to be from a genuine biblical author (what the Article calls "fraud" and "deceit").[40] For the framers of the CSBI, all of Scripture—down to the very words in whatever literary genre they appear—is authentic and free from error and deceit. This included not merely the redemptive facts of the gospel (1 Cor. 15:3–4), but also the biblical creation accounts (Gen. 1–2; Ps. 104; Job 38–42), the global flood account (Gen. 6–8), and biblical genealogies (Gen. 5; Matt. 1; Luke 3), along with everything else it says.

Taking all this into account, Paul Feinberg offers a helpful explanation of biblical inerrancy: "Inerrancy means that when all facts are known, the Scriptures in their original autographs and properly interpreted will be shown to be wholly true in everything that they affirm, whether that has to do with doctrine or morality or with the social, physical, or life sciences."[41] While the doctrine of inerrancy pertains, strictly speaking, only to the original writings (often termed "autographs"), evangelicals can be confident that God's Word is preserved in the various manuscripts and mainline

---

40. For an argument demonstrating how pseudepigraphy necessarily (and negatively) affects biblical authority see my chapter, "Forgery and the Fourth Gospel: Implications of Pseudepigraphy and Authority in the Johannine Corpus," in *Does It Matter Who Wrote the Bible? The Pastoral Implications of Pseudonymity and Anonymity in the New Testament*, ed. David B. Capes (Eugene: Pickwick, 2025), 75–97.

41. Paul D. Feinberg, "The Meaning of Inerrancy," in *Inerrancy*, ed. Norman L. Geisler (Grand Rapids: Zondervan, 1980), 294.

translations over the years despite any variants between them.[42] As the Psalmist says, "Forever, O LORD, your word is firmly fixed in the heavens" (Ps. 119:89). A vintage faith trusts that the Word of God is fixed, preserved, and errorless.

The Relation between Biblical Inerrancy, Biblical Literacy, and Biblical Hermeneutics

It should be obvious by now that the evangelical doctrine of biblical inerrancy is not a standalone position. It flows directly from the doctrines of Scripture's inspiration, authority, and perspicuity. It also necessarily intertwines with the idea of biblical literacy and the need for proper biblical interpretation. However, Christians do not always hold these positions consistently.

For example, a recent Gallup poll entitled, "Fewer in U.S. Now See Bible as Literal Word of God" reports: "The majority of Christians (58 per cent) say the Bible is the inspired word of God but not everything in it is to be taken literally, while 25 per cent say it should be interpreted literally and 16 per cent say it is an ancient book of fables."[43] Questions over polling aside, these statistics suggest that to believe that the Bible is inerrant is not always consistent with a hermeneutical method that justifies the claim. How can the majority of believers hold to the Scriptures being entirely free from error, fraud, and deceit, and yet a good chunk of that number view Scripture as a non-literal book of ancient fables? The answer is that the majority of Christians (at least those polled) are biblically *illiterate*. This raises the question, What is biblical literacy?

---

42. A helpful discussion is Wayne Grudem, C. John Collins, and Thomas R. Schreiner, eds. *Understanding Scripture: An Overview of the Bible's Origin, Reliability, and Meaning* (Wheaton: Crossway, 2012), 101–20.

43. Frank Newport, "Fewer in U.S. Now See Bible as Literal Word of God," *Gallup*, July 6, 2022, https://news.gallup.com/poll/394262/fewer-bible-literal-word-god.aspx#:~:text=The percent20majority percent20of percent20Christians percent20(58,an percent20ancient percent20book percent20of percent20fables.

As I have explained elsewhere, biblical literacy does not mean mastery over all of Scripture's contents.[44] The concept is more modest, centering on two key ideas: awareness and proficiency. I define biblical literacy as a continual process whereby the believer progressively develops in their *awareness* of God by reading through the Scriptures, while gaining *proficiency* in their understanding of Scripture's meaning. This definition makes clear that biblical literacy is tied directly to hermeneutics. This must be the case since biblical literacy develops with recognition of the various historical contexts and literary genres in Scripture that God used to reveal himself, and from there, grows in discerning the Scripture's meaning expressed through those contexts.

Repeated themes of creation, sin, grace, justice, covenant, Christ, eternal life, and others in Scripture become apparent, forming an arc in the biblical storyline—all of which point to God's glory. Evangelical scholar Ched Spellman encourages believers to develop an "intentional canon consciousness" when reading Scripture—viewing the Bible as a "whole mental construct" in order to maintain the overall unity of the Scriptures.[45] Increased awareness and proficiency are the twin goals of biblical literacy which provide the necessary guide rails for responsible application. For vintage evangelicalism, such an interpretive process is superfluous if divorced from believing that the Bible is inerrant, infallible, and sufficient.

More will be said later about the legacy of Christian reading and writing, but for now it's important to understand the relevance that biblical literacy and biblical interpretation have on a high view of Scripture—the latter of which has historically defined evangelicalism above everything else. If Scripture is the ultimate authority by which we know and obey God, then understanding

---

44. Cory M. Marsh, *A Primer on Biblical Literacy* (El Cajon: SCS Press, 2022), 26–28.

45. Ched Spellman, "The Canon After Google: Implications of a Digitized and Destabilized Codex," *Princeton Theological Review* 17, no. 2 (Fall 2010): 42.

Scripture correctly is our most crucial endeavor. Yet doing so requires the basic belief that God *really has* revealed himself in Scripture, and that he *really does* want us to understand what he has revealed. "[God] communicates with the assumption of being understood," contends Holland. "The premise of the continued intelligibility of Scripture is the most basic presumption of its nature."[46]

A principle I often relay to my students in class is that a Christian's relationship with God is directly proportionate to their relationship with God's Word. When believers dedicate themselves to a consistent engagement with the Scriptures, they grow in grace and in their knowledge of God in accordance with 2 Peter 3:18. What a wonderful adventure that awaits those who cherish the supremacy of Scripture! As Old Testament scholar Michael Shepherd states, "The intricacies of the Bible and the Bible's rich history of interpretation are more than enough to keep believers occupied for a lifetime, and there is no better way to live a life of faith than to be busy with the details of God's Word."[47]

The connection between a high view of Scripture (authority, inerrancy, etc.) and literal hermeneutics go hand in glove for historic evangelicalism. Scholars recognize the relationship between the two is essential for the vintage faith. Gordon Fee argued: "It has long been my conviction that the battle for inerrancy must be settled in the area of hermeneutics."[48] As David Bebbington observed, "A body of Evangelical opinion…began to insist from the 1820s onwards on inerrancy, verbal inspiration and the need for literal interpretation of the Bible."[49] Summing up his poll quoted earlier, Frank Newport concluded: "The most prominent of these positions is the belief that the Bible is inerrant and must be viewed as literally true, a position adopted as part of

---

46. Rick Holland, "The Perspicuity of Scripture and Expository Clarity," 221.

47. Michael B. Shepherd, *An Introduction to the Making and Meaning of the Bible* (Grand Rapids: Eerdmans, 2024), 169.

48. Gordon D. Fee, *Gospel and Spirit* (Peabody: Hendrickson, 1991), xv.

49. Bebbington, *Evangelicalism in Modern Britian*, 13–14.

the evangelical movement in this country over the past centuries and by a number of Protestant denominations."[50]

If evangelicalism is historically traced to the highest view of Scripture, then its dependence on biblical inerrancy and literal hermeneutics cannot be ignored for its identity. Every essential evangelical position is linked to a vintage view of Scripture (inspired and inerrant) and how to interpret it (literally). Explaining this connection, Norman Geisler writes:

> It is argued that if interpretation is an entirely separate issue from inerrancy, then all the debates about inerrancy boil down to a matter of interpretation. But since there are many different and legitimate ways to interpret a biblical text, then the inerrancy issue becomes one of how one interprets the Bible. In response, inerrancy and interpretation are not totally separate matters. Inerrancy implies a certain way to interpret the Bible. For even the statement that "the Bible is inerrant (without error)" involves an interpretation of some facts. Otherwise, how could one know it was without error, unless he knew what was true (that is, what corresponds to the facts).[51]

As one of the key framers of the Chicago Statement on Biblical Inerrancy quoted earlier, Geisler explained that the ICBI viewed the doctrine of inerrancy as not only a key identifier for anyone claiming to be "evangelical," but also as the necessary outflow of a literal or "grammatical-historical hermeneutic." Sharing this conviction with the other framers he said, "For one thing, there would be no doctrine of inerrancy were it not for the grammatical-historical hermeneutic by which we derive inerrancy

---

50. Frank Newport, "Fewer in U.S. Now See Bible as Literal Word of God," https://news.gallup.com/poll/394262/fewer-bible-literal-word-god.aspx#:~:text=The percent20majority percent20of percent20Christians percent20(58,an percent20ancient percent20book percent20of percent20fables.

51. Norman Geisler, "'It's Just a Matter of Interpretation Not of Inerrancy': Examining the Relation between Inerrancy and Hermeneutics," in *Vital Issues in the Inerrancy Debate,* ed. F. David Farnell (Eugene, OR: Wipf & Stock, 2015), 118.

of Scripture…. Without it there would be no 'evangelical' or 'orthodox' creeds or orthodox beliefs in accord with them."[52]

Quite simply, one who categorially denies the Bible's inerrancy and the grammatical-historical interpretation of it implicitly denies the Bible's authority and has no legitimate right to the label "evangelical." For a Christian to believe in the inerrancy of Scripture, which is the primary identity marker of an *evangelical* Christian, is to believe in and apply an inductive and consistent method that affirms the Bible speaks truth about the real world. The Bible is the highest authority there is, period. It must be since God breathed it out and carried men along as they wrote it (2 Tim. 3:16; 2 Pet. 1:21). This means the Bible doesn't merely *contain* God's Word or *become* God's Word in crises moments of faith (both neo-orthodox positions). Rather, evangelicalism contends the Bible *is* God's Word. As such, the supremacy of Scripture is the first marker for vintage evangelical identity and governs all positions that follow.

52. Norman L. Geisler, *Explaining Inerrancy: The Chicago Statements on Biblical Inerrancy, Hermeneutics, and Application* with *Official ICBI Commentary*, eds. R. C. Sproul and Norman L. Geisler (Arlington: Bastion Books, 2013), xxii.

CHAPTER 3

The Exclusivity of Jesus

Prioritizing the "Evangel" in Evangelicalism

It goes without saying that evangelicalism is all about Jesus.
Or does it? If someone who confesses a religious experience,
or attends a megachurch, or votes Republican can be classified
as "evangelical," does their view of Jesus really matter anymore?
Modern trends indicate that genuine belief in Jesus is tangential
to contemporary evangelicalism.

However, the exclusivity of Christ as Savior and Lord has been
an unquestioned identity marker for authentic evangelicalism
since its earliest development. The gospel of salvation in *Christ
alone* finds continuity with basic Protestantism beginning in the
sixteenth century. In fact, an argument can be made that the most
vintage iterations of evangelicalism carved their identity within
Protestantism precisely *because* of their convictions over the
evangel—the gospel message of Jesus Christ dying for unworthy
sinners (Rom. 5:8).

This core belief continued in the evangelicalism of the
seventeenth and eighteenth centuries and distinguished itself
historically as the premier theological conviction on how
someone gets right with God. Nick Needham points out that

early gospel preachers in Britain and America were "steeped in the 'godly literature' of the Reformation and Puritan eras" which placed a high premium on the exclusivity of Christ's atoning work for man's salvation. For these early evangelicals, there was one sustaining message that thundered from their pulpits: "Justification by faith alone in Christ alone, a Christ who is both very God and very Man, whose death was a penal substitutionary atonement for humanity's sin, and whose resurrection constituted Him as a living and present Saviour who outpoured His Spirit on His people, bringing them new birth and sanctification."[1] Just as there can be no true Christianity without Christ, there can be no true evangelicalism without the *evangel*. Such vintage faith is bold in its belief that the gospel alone is the power of salvation, not any human program, work, or ritual. The *gospel* is God's power for salvation (Rom. 1:16). It needs nothing to make it palatable and is not dependent on any theological system for its meaning. Early evangelicals realized that the "sacraments" of both Roman Catholicism and Eastern Orthodoxy obstructed the exclusivity of the pure gospel which required simple repentant-belief in Christ for forgiveness and eternal life (Luke 24:47; John 20:31; Acts 20:21). Indeed, when the crowd asked Jesus, "What must we *do*, to be *doing* the works of God?" Jesus answered in clear language of faith, barring any notion of works-righteousness so common to religious systems: "This is the work of God, that you *believe in him whom he has sent*" (John 6:28–29, emphasis added). Exclusive belief in Jesus Christ is absolutely fundamental for evangelical identity. Therefore, the gospel, which is the saving message of Jesus Christ—a message anchored in the inerrant Scriptures—serves as the second marker for a vintage faith.

In Pursuit of Jesus Alone

Despite the onslaught of criticism toward modern evangelicalism, scholars recognize that the exclusivity of Christ for salvation is a

---

1. Nick Needham, *2000 Years of Christ's Power* (Fearn, Ross-shire: Christian Focus, 2023), 5:87.

non-negotiable for real evangelicalism. "But above all," Campbell rightly points out, "the central feature of historic evangelicalism is its advocacy of vibrant personal faith in Jesus."[2] It's safe to say that all would agree with this statement. For Campbell, such a crucial position lies at the center of his grouping termed "theological evangelicals."

As I argue in this book, there is no other legitimate evangelicalism. In other words, real evangelicalism is *entirely* theological which results in evangelical behavior. It is not a social-group, cultural fad, or voting constituency for pollsters to target. Vintage evangelicalism, as I call it, exists by way of a core set of beliefs or positions. Outside of those convictions (totaling five in this book), any related ideas are peripheral to the discussion. Still, Campbell goes on to offer a sobering critique: "It's not the pursuit of Jesus that's failing contemporary evangelicalism but the failure to pursue Jesus in favor of other pursuits."[3] Tragically, Campbell's assessment is spot on.

Contrary to modern evan-jello-calism, the New Testament is relentless in its presentation of Jesus *alone* for salvation. The apostles viewed Christ as towering over every other figure in Scripture. Space limits an exhaustive exposition, but examples from two fountainheads of New Testament theology should suffice: the apostles John and Paul.

The Gospel and Faith According to John and Paul

The Gospel of John is particularly unique. It features elements not found in the other three Gospel accounts (called the Synoptics). For example, John structures his contents around seven signs that Jesus performed, as well as seven self-predicated "I Am" (*egō eimi*) statements Jesus made, all of which point to his divine nature and are found only in John's Gospel.[4] In addition to Jesus's self-

---

2. Constantine R. Campbell, *Jesus v. Evangelicals: A Biblical Critique of a Wayward Movement* (Grand Rapids: Zondervan Reflective, 2023), 9.

3. Ibid., 9.

4. Andreas J. Köstenberger, *Signs of the Messiah: An Introduction to John's Gospel* (Bellingham: Lexham, 2021), 33.

predicated statements ("I am *something*"), John records seven other *egō eimi* declarations without a predicate (simply, "I Am") that Jesus used of himself harkening back to statements of deity in Exodus and Isaiah in the Septuagint, as well as seven more with various modifiers—totally twenty-one unique *egō eimi* statements from Jesus in John's Gospel.[5]

One of Jesus's *egō eimi* self-predicated declarations is unequivocal regarding the exclusivity of himself for salvation. On the night of his arrest, Jesus announced to his disciples: "I am the way, and the truth, and the life. No one comes to the Father except through me" (John 14:6). The thrice repeated article ("the") in the sequence enforces Jesus's intention of being definitive. There is no secret knowledge or human philosophy to obtain for matters of ultimate importance—Jesus is it. He then doubles down on how one gets to the heavenly realm where his Father resides, in other words, how one obtains salvation: "except through me." It is only through believing in Jesus alone does one gain eternal life.

The exclusivity of Jesus for salvation is a theme presented, not only toward the end of John's Gospel, but also at its beginning. What scholars refer to as the book's "prologue," John states, "But to all who did receive him [Jesus], *who believed in his name*, he gave the right to become children of God" (John 1:12, emphasis added). To become a child of God, which guarantees access to eternal life, is through exclusive belief in Christ. In fact, more than any Gospel writer, John uses the word translated "believe/trust" (*pisteuō*)—a ridiculous ninety-eight times! What's more is that the word is a verb in each instance, never a noun, suggesting an *action-oriented* belief rather than a static, intellectual assent. This is what I referred to earlier as simple, "repentant-belief."

---

5. Robert M. Bowman Jr., and J. Ed Komoszewski, *The Incarnate Christ and His Critics: A Biblical Defense* (Grand Rapids: Kregel Academic, 2024), 509, break down the twenty-one instances of *egō eimi* in John into three groups: no predicate (e.g., John 4:26; 6:20; 8:58); a following predicate noun (e.g., 6:35; 8:12; 11:25); and a predicate expressed with an adverb, phrase, or articular participle (e.g., 7:34; 8:18; 17:14).

Such faith, according to John (and other NT authors), is a genuine trust that involves a change of the mind toward Jesus and away from sin, followed by a life that expresses that change. Everything John writes is meant to lead the reader to swear their allegiance to Christ alone for salvation. His purpose for writing the entire account couldn't be clearer: "But these are written so that you may believe that Jesus is the Christ, the Son of God, and that by believing you may have life in his name" (20:31).[6]

Of course, John is not alone in presenting faith in Jesus as the only way to be saved. The gospel is a premier theme for Paul as well. In what many consider his magnum opus, the apostle wrote to the Roman church and presented the gospel as the overall theme of the letter: "For I am not ashamed of the gospel, for it is the power of God for salvation to everyone who believes, to the Jew first and also to the Greek" (Rom. 1:16). The present tense form of the verb "is" (*estin*)—for it *is* the power of God for salvation—governs the rest of the verse, signaling that the gospel of salvation is *always* for both Jewish people and non-Jewish people.[7] This means that it is *not* the case that at *one time* Israel benefited from the gospel as Jesus came to that nation first and *now* the gospel's power has transferred for everyone else, leaving Jews behind. Rather, by its very nature coming from God, the gospel's power is not limited by ethnic or time restraints; it is *always* for "everyone who believes." Indeed, as Paul follows up, "For in [the gospel] the righteousness of God is revealed *out of* [ek] faith [and] *into* [eis] faith, as it is written, 'The righteous shall live by faith'" (v. 17, emphasis added). Paul's use of different prepositions is interesting and has kept scholars debating over their exact meaning.[8] According to their most literal

---

6. Another plausible translation for the third clause is "… the Christ, the Son of God, is Jesus." See D. A. Carson, "The Purpose of the Fourth Gospel: John 20:31 Reconsidered," *Journal of Biblical Literature* 106 (1987), 639–51.

7. See Arnold G. Fruchtenbaum, *The Book of Romans*, Ariel's Bible Commentary (San Antonio: Ariel Ministries, 2022), 37.

8. See Douglas J. Moo, *The Letter to the Romans*, The New International Commentary on the New Testament 2nd ed. (Grand Rapids: Eerdmans, 2018), 78–82.

translation—"out of" and "into"—the idea suggests that the gospel of Jesus is all about faith for everyone—*from* Jew *to* Gentile.

The gospel has a wonderfully exponential affect as it moves from one person who believes and is justified, to another person who believes and is justified. Its righteous truth is shared "out of" [*ek*] one person and "into" [*eis*] another. Quoting from Habakkuk 2:4, Paul demonstrates the idea of justification by faith is not new, and that the justified person in the church era—the one who God views as "innocent"—is through faith in the gospel of Christ alone. Fruchtenbaum sums it up well: "The principle of salvation by faith was and is true for every dispensation. Salvation was and always is by grace through faith. While the content of faith has changed from age to age depending on progressive revelation, the means of salvation has never changed."[9]

Paul is often considered the "apostle of faith" for good reason. He uses the root word for faith (*peithō*) over two hundred and fifty times throughout his writings, the majority of which appear in Romans. The idea of faith in the gospel is paramount for the apostle, and accordingly, for evangelicalism as well. Christians are justified by faith resulting in peace with God (Rom. 5:1; cf. 4:3). Jesus's sacrifice is received by faith (Rom. 3:25). Paul wrote that "If you confess with your mouth that Jesus is Lord and believe in your heart that God raised him from the dead, you will be saved" (Rom. 10:9). As the apostle saw it, the *evangel* is everything (cf. 1 Cor. 1:23; 2:2). This is because belief in Jesus is the only way to be made right with God. "Faith comes from hearing," Paul declared "and hearing through the word of Christ" (Rom. 10:17).

There is no question that belief in the exclusivity of Jesus as the means or way for eternal redemption (i.e., the *evangel*) was a fundamental priority for both John and Paul. Likewise, belief in the exclusive *evangel* is fundamental for genuine evangelical identity.

The Biblical Meaning of Conversion

The word "conversion" doesn't always invoke positive feelings. Often it's used in the negative context of being "brainwashed," as in

---

9. Arnold G. Fruchtenbaum, *The Book of Romans*, 41.

THE EXCLUSIVITY OF JESUS

converting to a dangerous cult. Followers of horrible false-prophets Jim Jones, David Koresh, or the Mormon-pedophile-polygamist Warren Jeffs are described as *converts* to these monsters. Yet, the word itself is neutral. It carries the idea of motion and simply means being a new devotee to a party or association. There can be political converts (changing *from* Democrat *to* Republican), musical converts (changing *from* non-Swifty *to* Swifty), or new religious converts (changing *from* no or a certain kind of theology *to* another theology). Obviously, this latter form is most prevalent in the New Testament.

Several words get translated "conversion" and its cognates from the Greek New Testament. Most times the idea of turning *from* something *to* something is meant. Other times *chronological priority* is what is stressed. And still other times it's the idea of *newness* that's being emphasized. In each appearance, however, whichever word is used, it speaks of those who have placed their faith in Christ. For instance, during their first missionary journey, Paul and Barnabas preached the gospel to a Jewish synagogue in Antioch in Pisidia. Luke writes, "After the meeting of the synagogue broke up, many Jews and devout *converts* [*prosēlytōn*] to Judaism followed Paul and Barnabas, who, as they spoke with them, urged them to continue in the grace of God" (Acts 13:43). The context here suggests that these were people who came over *from* polytheism *to* the Jewish religion and were now believers in Jesus.[10] Later, when Paul and Barnabas left Antioch to participate in the first-ever church council in Jerusalem, "they passed through both Phoenicia and Samaria, describing in detail the *conversion* [*epistrophē*] of the Gentiles, and brought great joy to all the brothers" (Acts 15:3). The word here is used to identify non-Jewish believers in Jesus who had turned *from* paganism *to* Christianity.

---

10.   Walter Bauer, William F. Arndt, F. Wilbur Gingrich, and Frederick W. Danker, *A Greek-English Lexicon of the New Testament and Other Early Christian Literature*, 3rd ed. (Chicago: University of Chicago Press, 2000), 880. From here on abbreviated, BDAG.

Other places where "conversion" occurs stresses the idea of either *chronological priority* or the *newness* of one's faith in Christ. As to the former, Paul ends his first letter to the Corinthians with, "Now I urge you, brothers—you know that the household of Stephanas were the *first converts (aparchē)* in Achaia, and that they have devoted themselves to the service of the saints" (1 Cor 16:15). Here, the word pictures Stephanas's home as the initial harvest of believers in Christ in Achaia, a kind of "first fruits" of Christians[11] (see also Rom 16:5 and 2 Thess 2:13). As to the latter, in one of Paul's final letters, he gave instructions to his protégé Timothy about the qualifications of pastors. Among other requirements, an overseer "must not be a *recent convert [neophyton]*, or he may become puffed up with conceit and fall into the condemnation of the devil" (1 Tim 3:6). The idea of *newness* is stressed here, which pictures a "newly planted" believer in the Chistian community.[12] Paul's point was that men who were untested and new to following Jesus should refrain from jumping into the pastorate as they have a particular tendency to become prideful.

Evangelical Conversion

The idea of being converted to Christ is part and parcel for vintage faith. In his definition for "evangelicalism," John Hannah included: "At the core of the movement are a set of religious values that center on the necessity of personal conversion and the spreading of the gospel."[13]

Evangelicalism has had a string of scholars who use the term "conversionism" in their metrics to identify what makes someone evangelical. As touched on earlier, David Bebbington is the most noteworthy to include the phrase in his quadrilateral of evangelicalism, which has since been adapted by other evangelical

11. BDAG, 98.
12. Ibid., 669.
13. John D. Hannah, *Our Legacy: The History of Christian Doctrine* (Colorado Springs: NavPress, 2001), 369.

scholars.[14] For genuine evangelicalism, conversion is not a rite of passage nor the prize one gets after performing so many duties. Rather, an evangelical conversion is spiritual, personal, and necessary. It is the dual-sided act of repenting and believing. Roger Olson explains:

> Anyone who studies evangelical movements as revivals of authentic Christian faith and renewals of the church within Protestantism has to recognize this as their most common feature [i.e., the need for conversion]. It can be expressed in various ways and has no definite formula or outward expression, but it always involves the appeal to personal decision to live a new life for Jesus Christ through inward transformation by the Holy Spirit in response to repentance and faith.[15]

Conversion to Christ is absolutely necessary for vintage evangelicalism. This goes beyond a mere profession of faith. As the biblical examples demonstrate, to *convert* is to change to a whole new way of life. The move is from one worldview or allegiance to another worldview or allegiance. A person's life is changed and it's obvious to everyone around them. Paul commended the newly converted Thessalonians on how they "turned [converted] to God from idols to serve the living and true God" (1 Thess 1:9). The motional sequence of the turn is interesting as it begins with God pulling the wayward sinner *to himself* and *away from* useless idols. The order is important. One can imagine someone turning *from* idols and stopping there. In such cases, "repentance" is technically completed since a change of thinking occurred from previous devotion to idols and then simply ended. However, an evangelical conversion requires not merely turning from something but

---

14. See Mark A. Noll, David W. Bebbington, George A. Rawlk, eds., *Evangelicalism: Comparative Studies in Popular Protestantism in North America, the British Isles, and Beyond, 1700–1990* (New York: Oxford University Press, 1994).

15. Roger E. Olson, "Postconservative Evangelicalism," in *Four Views on the Spectrum of Evangelicalism* (Grand Rapids: Zondervan, 2011), 170–71.

turning to someone. Though the logical sequence goes *from—to*, for the one actually converting, the process is experienced at the same time. Chafer observed, "To believe on Christ is one act, regardless of the manifold results which it secures. It is not turning from something to something; but rather turning to something from something."[16]

This is what Paul referred to as repentance and faith, which carries equal grammatical weight in Acts 20:21. Though both are experienced simultaneously, Paul's sequence to the Thessalonians is that faith toward Christ is the initial pull that immediately turns the sinner away from idols. These are not two separate acts, as if a partial conversion is possible. There is no such thing as an evangelical who repents but refuses to believe in Christ. Likewise, there are none who believe in Christ while refusing to repent. Rather, a genuine evangelical conversion is a solitary act of faith and repentance *together* or, as I refer to in this chapter, repentant-faith.

Another factor in conversion is important: it is not an isolated phenomenon. Though it is certainly a personal experience—placing one's faith in Jesus for eternal life—this does not mean that conversion is a *privatized* or *individualistic* matter. Such an idea is common to American life, as privatization is almost a sacredly held belief among American evangelicals. Though more will be said later when discussing the "x-factor" of evangelical community and fellowship, for now it is worth pointing out something Paul says in his only letter to Titus: Jesus redeemed and purified "a people" (*laos*) collectively, meaning the church as a whole (Titus 2:14). Still, conversion is personal at its core and the church is obviously made up of *converted individuals.*

Scripturally speaking, conversion is not merely a turning from sin, nor just a change of mind about Christ. It incorporates an entirely new established relationship with the Godhead. Jesus uses the words "born again" in his conversation with Nicodemus.

16. Lewis Sperry Chafer, *Systematic Theology* (Dallas: Dallas Seminary Press), 3:374.

It is a truly spiritual "re-birth," a completely new life brought on by the Spirit who regenerates lost sinners (John 3:1–7). The order of what occurs first at conversion—regeneration *or* faith—differs according to evangelical traditions and continues to keep them in debate. Whether the Spirit regenerates a person *in order to* believe in Christ, or whether a person believes in Christ and is *then* regenerated or born again by the Spirit lies outside the scope of what's presented here. Both Calvinism and Arminianism are thoroughly evangelical traditions, and this book is concerned only with evangelicalism itself.

That said, a biblical case can be made for both options, which find support in Romans. Paul wrote that "faith comes by hearing" (not by "regeneration") in Romans 10:17, suggesting personal faith *results* in regeneration or being born again. And yet, in what many call the "golden chain of salvation," Paul writes that those whom God predestined he also called, and those whom he *called* he also justified" (Rom. 8:30). If "called" here is synonymous with the act of being born again or regenerated by the Spirit—that is, an *effectual calling*—than a strong case exists for regeneration *resulting* in one's personal faith to be justified. If such is the case, that divine calling is the element needed *in order to* believe in Christ and be saved. Arguments for both positions notwithstanding, what is clear is that an evangelical conversion results in an entirely new life.

Paul uses "new creation" language when describing the converted soul: "Therefore, if anyone is in Christ, he is a new creation. The old has passed away; behold, the new has come" (2 Cor. 5:17). An evangelical conversion implies motion, a turning from *something* to *someone*, or as Paul's earlier sequence goes—*to* someone *from* something(s) (1 Thess. 1:9). Whatever the exact directional succession, the idea of turning is baked into the word repentance. The converted evangelical has changed their thinking first and foremost about Jesus Christ—who he is, what he did, and what he does. They then begin to change (or reform) their beliefs about sin, life, death, the Scriptures, and so on, and their life reflects this continual change. Their thinking grows in alignment with the Bible, which is God's thoughts in written form, as they grow in their biblical literacy. An evangelical conversion is one from apathy or non-belief to thriving belief in Jesus and all that the Bible says about him.

This means, a vintage evangelical conversion assumes a constellation of other doctrinal beliefs about salvation. This has always found agreement among evangelicals. Authentic conversion entails presupposing Jesus Christ as Lord, Savior, and God, and that only the Holy Spirit, who is God, can cause salvation to happen—"even if the person being converted doesn't yet fully understand this."[17] A true conversion takes place when the once un-reconciled sinner is imparted spiritual life by the Holy Spirit (2 Thess. 2:13). That person becomes reconciled to God through their repentant-faith in Christ (Acts 20:21; Rom. 5:10). Their life changes as a result, as they now live for Christ who died for them. A genuine conversion is a personal and spiritual re-birth—from being one of the walking dead to living among the saints. Theologically speaking, Christ is now their life. The apostle declared: "For you have died, and *your life is hidden with Christ* in God. When *Christ who is your life* appears, then you also will appear with him in glory" (Col. 3:3–4, emphasis added). Christian conversion goes from following other things or people to following Jesus wholeheartedly—and is a non-negotiable for vintage evangelical faith.

The Great Vicarious Exchange

One of the most important truths about Christ's death is that it was a vicarious atonement. That is, Jesus acted on behalf of others (Mark 10:45). He died on behalf of sinners, and consequently, repentant sinners died on the cross vicariously through Jesus. Evangelicals believe that when Jesus died, they died. When Jesus rose, they too rose to newness of life (Rom. 6:3–4). This great exchange—Jesus's life for ours—is the glorious teaching of New Testament salvation as well as classic Protestantism.

17. Olson, "Postconservative Evangelicalism," 171.

The idea of vicarious atonement is powerfully captured in Galatians 2:20 when Paul explains: "I now live by faith in the Son of God, who loved me and gave himself *for* me." But Paul knows he's not the only benefactor of Christ's death. The same concept appears in 1 Corinthians 15:3 where the apostle applies Jesus's vicarious atonement to all Christians, declaring that: "Christ died *for* our sins according to the Scriptures." The word translated "for" in both places is the Greek preposition *hyper*, which denotes substitution (cf. Philemon 13). The word can literally be translated "in behalf of."[18] Christ died as a *substitute* for those God chose to save. Evangelical theologian Paul Enns refers to this as the supreme work of Christ achieving man's salvation. He explains, "Primarily, it involves the death of Christ as a substitutionary atonement for sin in securing man's release from the penalty and bondage of sin and meeting the righteous demands of a holy God."[19]

Jesus's death is called a "propitiation" since it appeased God's wrath (1 John 2:2). Thus, the holiness and justice of God, as well as his love toward mankind are both upheld to their rightful places in the vicarious atonement of Christ. In the great exchange on the cross, Christ's righteousness was imputed to the repentant sinner's account, while their sin was imputed to Christ's account. Paul says, "For our sake he made him to be sin who knew no sin, so that in him we might become the righteousness of God" (2 Cor. 5:21). We are saved by the death of Christ, as forgiveness is only through the shedding of blood (Heb. 9:22). Because Jesus's death makes those who are his righteous by virtue of *his* righteousness, their personal salvation is secured forever in him.

The reason why I chose to title this section "vicarious" instead of "substitutionary" is because Jesus is more than a mere substitute for humans. The word "substitute" alone for the death of Christ can imply there was an even exchange. While Christ was certainly a representative of humans (Rom. 5:17), he was not equal to them.

---

18. BDAG, 1030.
19. Paul Enns, *The Moody Handbook of Theology* (Chicago: Moody, 2014), 341.

Jesus's sinlessness alone separates him from everyone else and makes his death infinite in value. No one's death could ever be as equally propitiatory as Christ's death (see Heb. 7:26–28). Jesus's death was a definite and vicarious act of sacrifice, unrivaled in value and unlimited in power.

Repentant-Faith and Works

The concept of faith in God for salvation has always been emphasized in evangelicalism. Both the Old and New Testaments testify to the need for faith (or faithfulness) for redemption. The Protestant doctrine of justification by faith alone finds its origin in the Hebrew Scriptures which state, "Abraham believed in Yahweh and it was accounted to him as righteousness" (Gen. 15:6).

During the exodus, only those who believed that the lamb's blood would deliver their firstborn from death (as shown in their applying it to their doorposts) were delivered (Exod. 11–12). As the prophet Habakkuk said, "The righteous will live by his faith/faithfulness" (Hab. 2:4),[20] which the New Testament repeats three times (Rom. 1:17; Gal. 3:11; Heb. 10:38). Indeed, as mentioned earlier, John purposed his entire Gospel account on the idea of faith for eternal salvation (John 20:31).

The *object* of the gospel has remained the same (God) as well as the *means* by which to access it (faith). The *content* of the gospel, however, has changed throughout the various administrations of God's sovereign rule. In his letter to the Galatians, Paul said, "And the Scripture, foreseeing that God would justify the Gentiles by faith, *preached the gospel [proeuēngelisato]* beforehand to Abraham, saying, 'In you shall all the nations be blessed'" (Gal. 3:8). The gospel to which the apostle referred goes back to the blessings of the Abrahamic covenant, that not only guaranteed

---

20. The Hebrew noun *'ĕmûnâ* denotes "trustworthiness," "faithfulness," and "steadfastness." See Ludwig Koehler, et al, *The Hebrew and Aramaic Lexicon of the Old Testament*, trans. Mervyn E. J. Richardson, 2 vols. (Leiden: Brill, 2001), 63. From here on, this will be abbreviated as *HALOT*.

a Jewish lineage and land but also blessings for the entire world through that lineage (Gen. 12:3). Yet this is a different sounding "gospel" than what evangelicals are accustomed to preaching, which is the message of Christ dying and rising for the forgiveness of sins along with the need to believe in such wonderful news for eternal life (Luke 24:46–47; 1 Cor. 15:3–4). Why are these two gospel messages different?

There is no contradiction between these two messages. It just demonstrates how multifaceted the "gospel" truly is, like a diamond that sparkles with each turn. At the core of each gospel promise is Christ, whether implicit or explicit. Christ's death on the cross was always the basis for eternal life, even through the various iterations of the gospel throughout progressive revelation. Whereas at one time God's people believed in Yahweh and *expressed* that belief in obedience to the Mosaic law (e.g., sacrificial system), now God's people believe in Yahweh *through his Son* and express that belief in church ordinances like baptism and communion, as well as through loving one another as Christ commanded along with other New Testament injunctions (see John 13:34–35). As John said, "No one who denies the Son has the Father. Whoever confesses the Son has the Father also" (1 John 2:23). In the current administration of God's government, faith in him as a "higher being" is not good enough; salvation requires faith in God *through explicit and genuine confession of his Son.* This confession of Jesus is a clear development in the gospel message, which progressed alongside of revelation as God breathed out his Scriptures. Salvation has always been by God's grace through faith, in every administration. The content of that message, however, along with how faith in it is to be expressed by the believer, has clearly changed throughout the history of redemption.

Vintage evangelicalism understands that faith in Christ is the only requirement that is required for salvation. However, as the earlier discussion on repentance stressed, a true saving faith is not one of mere intellectual assent. After all, even the demons believe—and shudder (James 2:19)! Satan and the demonic realm believe in God their Creator and even that Jesus is Lord. Ironically, some of the highest Christological confessions in the Bible come from demons, even before humans understood Jesus's identity (Mark 1:23–24; Matt. 8:29; Luke 4:33–34; cf. Acts 16:16–18).[21] So what is the difference between the two "faiths"? Something vital must distinguish "demonic faith" from true saving faith. I would argue it is the grace of *repentance*, which results in a life of joyful obedience to the Lord. Such saving faith is available for humans, not demons.

In one sense, the idea of works has always been an enemy to faith. In Paul's epistle to the Galatians, he admonishes the Galatian Christians for being duped into a works-righteousness brought on by legalists (Gal. 1:6–7; 3:2–3). It appears a similar situation happened to the Colossian church several years later (Col. 2:16–23). In response to the notion that performing certain religious duties can merit favor with God, Paul emphatically declared, "those who are of *faith* are blessed along with Abraham, the man of faith" (Gal. 3:9). It is telling that every religion in the world, save biblical Christianity, emphasizes personal works in order to appease their deity. It seems that grace through faith is reserved for Christianity alone. Still, works are not entirely absent from the picture. When it comes to the Christian's works, they are related to salvation, but a specific order is upheld: faith *then* works.

Paul made such an argument throughout Romans 4 when proving that Abraham was justified by faith—well before he performed any religious duties. It is a New Testament certainty that good deeds have no bearing on producing personal salvation whatsoever. The Christian's good works, that is, a life of obedience and love, are a *result* of faith, not its antecedent; works are the cart, while faith is the horse. James wrote that a Christian shows his or her faith by their works (James 2:18), and Paul later wrote that we are saved "for good works prepared beforehand that we should walk in them" (Eph. 2:10). This latter verse makes it plain

---

21. An insightful article is, Jospeh L. Kimmel, "Demons Seeking Identity? The Psychic Life of New Testament Exorcisms," *Journal of Biblical Literature* 143.1 (2024): 85–104.

that good deeds are inevitable in one's salvation, and the former shows that good deeds are the proper expression of one's salvation.

Unmistakenly, the life of vintage or genuine faith is a life of *love in action.* "By this we know love," explained the apostle John, "that Jesus laid down his life for us, and we ought to lay down our lives for the brothers. But if anyone has the world's goods and sees his brother in need, yet closes his heart against him, how does God's love abide in him? Little children, *let us not love in word or talk but in deed and in truth*" (1 John 3:16–18, emphasis added). Therefore, repentant-faith, love, and works form an unbreakable bond of genuine evangelical identity.

Vintage faith prioritizes the evangel—the exclusivity of Jesus alone for salvation. A genuine evangelical conversion is personal and life changing, resulting in a faithful life of joyful obedience for the glory of God. This pursuit of Jesus alone for eternal life, therefore, which results in a life that has clearly changed, is what I argue is the second fundamental marker for true evangelicalism.

CHAPTER 4

Zealous Evangelism

Transformed Lives Transform Culture

If we are to recover the "fundamentals" of evangelicalism's vintage form, its legacy of activism in evangelism, missions work, and challenging societal ills needs to be recovered as well. At the heart of evangelical activism is the belief of personal human depravity (see Rom. 3:9–18). Sin has corrupted the entirety of each person—their character, their communication, and their conduct.[1] The human plight of being helpless outside of God's mercy in Christ is what necessitates evangelism, and why evangelicals are so zealous about evangelizing.

It's not surprising that mankind's depraved nature appears nowhere for discussion in either Du Mez's *Jesus and John Wayne* or Sharp's *The Other Evangelicals*. Both books support LGBTQ+ and other such progressive sentiments as being "evangelical," despite the stinging connection Paul makes between idolatry and homosexuality in Romans 1:18–32 and elsewhere. Instead, social activism is their priority. Though today there is a pull to denounce systemic sins, a vintage faith understands sin to be a personal

---

1. Alva J. McClain, *Romans: The Gospel of God's Grace* (Winona Lake: BMH, 1989), 96–97.

aberration. Corrupt systems are merely symptomatic of corrupt people. It is people, not systems, who need redemption.

When Jesus said that he "came to seek and save the lost" (Luke 19:10), his context was not to redeem culture. It was for the personal redemption of Zaccheaus, a corrupt tax-collector, who demonstrated repentance for exploiting the poor (see v. 8). Luke records Jesus's words in very personal terms, not in abstract or conceptual ideas signifying cultural or systemic redemption. "Today salvation has come to *this house*, since *he* [Zaccheaus] also is a son of Abraham" (v. 9). Christ had graced Zaccheaus by coming to the man's house and affirming his personal salvation there. From that point, the culture is changed. Zacchaeus gave back to those he defrauded "four times" the amount he stole from them, helping boost his immediate economy. But he needed personal redemption first. The restorative order goes: people *then* programs.

The same idea is what lays behind what evangelicals refer to as the "Great Commission" at the conclusion of Matthew's Gospel. Jesus *commissioned* his remaining disciples to make disciples from all nations, not merely Israel (Matt. 28:19). To be clear, the commission to "make disciples" (*mathēteusate*) goes beyond personal evangelism, as in merely sharing the message of Jesus in hopes of obtaining a profession of faith, at which point the task is done. Matthew's commission involves *baptizing* believers in the name of the triune Godhead and *teaching* them all that Jesus taught.[2] We might call this personal discipleship today, which always has indelible effect on culture. In any event, the commission necessitates the initial need to "go," seeking out the lost and proclaiming their need for salvation in Christ alone.

Mark uses more expansive language with proclaiming the gospel to "all the world" and to "the whole creation"

---

2. I lean more toward the participles "baptizing" and "teaching" being *instrumental*, i.e., expressing *the means by which* disciples are made over them being *resultant* participles, suggesting how a disciple *expresses their* faith, e.g., through baptism (even though that may be the reality). Furthermore, the act of *teaching* implies the recipient's ability to comprehend biblical doctrine.

(Mark 16:15).[3] Rather than through legal policies or politicking, it is *transformed lives* who transform society. This sequence emulates Jesus who came to seek and save lost individuals. A genuine evangelical, therefore, not only believes in the gospel but is also passionate to preach and teach it to others, as well as mentor disciples in the truth. It is this idea of zealous evangelism that marks the third fundamental for recovering an authentic vintage faith.

The Evangelical Priority of Gospel over Law

In his analysis of the fundamentalist-modernist culture wars surrounding the (in)famous Scopes "monkey trial" in the 1920s, Madison Trammel overturns the popular narrative that fundamentalists were ever culturally ambivalent—contrary to Carl Henry's claim in his classic work *The Uneasy Conscience of Fundamentalism.*[4]

Turns out the Scopes trial did not embarrass conservative evangelicals—a group then called "fundamentalists"—at the time, nor did it force them into anti-cultural or anti-intellectual retreats as is often assumed. When they did confront societal evil, they did so driven by the conviction of human depravity and the need for personal redemption. According to Trammel, these fundamentalist/evangelicals did not believe, "righteousness could be achieved by legislation, as proponents of the social gospel did. Instead, they believed good laws might mute sinfulness. The gospel defeated it."[5] The logic is that salvation transforms individuals who, when born-again, can help transform society by their renewed thinking (see Rom. 12:2).

---

3. Engaging the debate over the authenticity of Mark's longer ending is beyond the scope of this chapter. It should be obvious the point made is that believers are to preach the gospel to everyone everywhere.

4. Madison Trammel, *Fundamentalists in the Public Square: Evolution, Alcohol, and Culture Wars after the Scopes Trial*, SHST (Bellingham: Lexham Academic, 2023), 128–29.

5. Ibid., 124.

The classic evangelical law-gospel distinction becomes apparent here. Laws never save anyone; only the gospel does. However, laws are clearly necessary for a society to exist and even thrive. Still, every society is comprised of individual people who need the gospel to think rightly. This highlights the relationship between law and gospel, but there is a priority: the gospel saves *people* who can then influence *societies* for God's glory. The former is essential; the latter is secondary. Therefore, the starting point is for people to hear the gospel, which necessitates an active life of evangelism.

Different Missionary Mandates

There is an important distinction in God's people(s) that shouldn't be missed as it relates to evangelism. Israel and the church have different mandates to make salvation known to the world.

Trammel highlights what early twentieth-century conservative evangelicals believed: "Salvation transformed individuals, but it did not transform the earth; worldly salvation was intended for the Jewish people in the end times. Fundamentalists never proposed an earthly utopia as the end goal of their activism."[6] The reality of the statement deserves some pushback as the previous chapter citing Romans 1:16 emphasized that personal salvation is *always* to the Jew first followed by the "Greek" (that is, Gentile). The gospel should continually be preached to Jews as well as to non-Jews. Nevertheless, the general tenor of the point is spot-on.

These early American evangelicals understood that an earthly utopia apart from Jesus reigning physically in Jerusalem was an impossibility. Despite overly ambitious promises of hope, healing, and peace that today's politicians are prone to offer, no system of laws can ever legislate salvation or everlasting peace. The messianic kingdom still to come, when Israel is restored "for the Jewish people in the end times," as in the quote above, will alone accomplish such a dream for the world in accordance with prophecy (Zech. 14:4–9; Matt. 19:28). Jesus will reign physically

---

6. Madison Trammel, *Fundamentalists in the Public Square*, 124.

from Jerusalem, which will serve as the holy capital from which all blessings flow to the earth.

Still, in the only section of Romans where the word "Israel" appears, Paul interweaves texts from Isaiah to make the case that his fellow Jews, alongside Gentiles, need the gospel (see Rom. 9–11).[7] As he points out, this demands active Christian evangelism, to go and preach the gospel—even to Israel:

> How then will they call on him in whom they have not believed? And how are they to believe in him of whom they have never heard? And how are they to hear without someone preaching? And how are they to preach unless they are sent? As it is written, "How beautiful are the feet of those who preach the good news!" But they have not all obeyed the gospel. For Isaiah says, "Lord, who has believed what he has heard from us?" So faith comes from hearing, and hearing through the word of Christ (Rom. 10:14–17).

Contrary to misconceptions suggesting that individual Jews are redeemed because they are ethnically Jewish, the truth is they need to believe in the gospel like everyone else. Eternal life is obtained only through repentant-faith in the gospel of Christ. That said, Paul is equally clear that based on God's election of the Jewish patriarchs, ethnic Israel will always have a remnant on earth including the nation's future restoration (Rom. 9:4, 11:25–29). This means that when we talk about "salvation," a distinction must be made: individual redemption and national redemption. The former regards *personal* eternal life; the latter regards continuous *national* witness on earth. One deals with individual justification by faith; the other deals with ethnic covenant.

It is no accident that there remain Jewish people to this day despite every attempted extermination of their race—from Haman's failed plot to Hitler's Third Reich. Jews who do *not* believe in Jesus are "saved" only in the sense of serving as a continual

---

7. The word Ἰσραήλ (*Israēl*) appears twelve times throughout this distinct block of Romans directly addressing the nation (Rom. 9:6, 27, 31; 10:19, 21; 11:2, 7, 11, 25, 26). The cognate Ἰσραηλίτης (*Israēlitēs*) appears an additional two times (9:4; 11:1).

tangible witness of Yahweh's faithfulness to his Word concerning Israel (see Jer. 31:35–36). Paul makes the argument that even if he alone were left, God's promise never to forsake the Jewish people remains (Rom. 11:1). Israel as a people will remain on earth, it will be "saved" from her enemies and redeemed nationally with borders as promised in the Abrahamic covenant (Gen. 15:17–20; cf. Deut. 30:1–5; 34:4). Non-believing Jews, however, just like non-believing Gentiles, are in desperate need for Christ and individual salvation in him alone. One day, all Jewish people will be eternally saved and "know the Lord" as promised in the New Covenant (Jer. 31:31–34; Heb. 8:8–12). But this requires God's grace and personal trust in Jesus who was pierced (see Zech. 12:10).

The distinction between church and Israel has important implications to draw out as it relates to evangelism and God's mission for his people. In previous economies, God's people were to be a fixed place on earth. The nations were to come to *them.* Yahweh was present among his people and manifested in tangible ways such as fighting for them in battles, giving them his oracles, the Tabernacle, the Temple, national festivals, and so on. Paul says, "They are Israelites, and *to them* belong the adoption, the glory, the covenants, the giving of the law, the worship, and the promises" (Rom. 9:4). Israel was a fixed place on earth that was to be a beacon of Yahweh's light to the world's nations shining his love and faithfulness on his people, a reality that will resume after Christ's return (Isa. 60:3). In other words, their mission was to be a blessing to the world as a constant immovable witness of God's faithfulness, including the patriarchs and land from which would produce the Jewish messiah (see Gen. 12:2–3). Even the Son of God came only to *Israel* and remained only there during his entire earthly ministry (Matt. 15:24).[8]

---

8. An insightful work calling attention to Jesus's and the disciples' missionary differences to Israel and all nations is James I. Fazio, *Two Commissions: Two Missionary Mandates in Matthew's Gospel* (El Cajon: SCS Press, 2015).

The church has a different mandate. Whereas previously nations were to go *to* Israel to know salvation, the church went out *from* Israel to make salvation known to the nations. While Israel's borders can be pinpointed on a globe, the church by its nature is global. Unlike Israel, no local church from the New Testament remains today. That fact should give pause to pastors who feel their job is to build a church that will serve as an immovable form of nationalism. It also pushes back on the idea that a local church is supposed to stay put and produce an endless line of generational Christians. There is nothing inherently righteous about lodging in the same church for a lifetime. Rarely does a local church hit its centennial birthday, still faithful to its original vision and mission statements. Instead, it eventually deviates and/or dies.

For example, the church at Ephesus is mentioned more than any other local assembly in the New Testament. Its launch and operational ministry read like a who's who list of pastors and teachers! It was founded by the apostle Paul. It was pastored by Paul's protégé Timothy, who is the recipient of two inspired letters. It hosted Apollos, "a man mighty in the Scriptures," as a guest teacher. Even John, an original member of the Twelve, oversaw the Ephesian church toward the end of his life. Everything about this church would make one project that it was poised to endure until the return of Christ. Yet, they had a serious problem. While excelling in doctrine and celebrity pastors, they turned cold and loveless. Paul ends his letter to them emphasizing the theme of love: "Grace be with all who *love* our Lord Jesus Christ with *love* incorruptible" (Eph. 6:24). By the time John wrote his apocalypse three decades later, this same church "abandoned the *love* [they] had at first" (Rev. 2:4). Though Jesus commended them for their doctrine and ability to spot early cults like the Nicolaitans, he promised to remove their lampstand if they didn't repent of their lovelessness (vv. 5–6). Since this church no longer exists, it's safe to assume that Jesus in fact did turn out their lights. They became a holy huddle to themselves, no longer taking the love of the gospel outside their walls to make disciples.

There is a sobering lesson here. It is *Jesus* who ultimately turns out the lights of churches, not Satan or the world. His messages to the seven churches in Revelation 2 and 3 make this abundantly clear. The reason is because Christians are under a different missionary mandate than Israel—they are called to go—and keep going with the gospel (Matt. 28:19). God has creative—even scary—ways to get Christians to *move* and make disciples of the nations. It took the martyrdom of Stephen for the earliest believers to eventually pick up and take the gospel outside of their comfort zone in Jerusalem (Acts 11:19). The church, not Israel, produces evangelists and missionaries (Eph. 4:11; 2 Tim. 4:5). Indeed, the biblical distinction between national Israel and the church calls into question popular American evangelical methods that reflect empire building instead of birthing small and temporary assemblies zealously reaching the lost.

The Gospel Commission

Each of the Synoptic Gospels end with a variation of the same commission for followers of Jesus to evangelize the world and make disciples (Matt. 28:19; Mark 16:15; Luke 24:46–47). Luke's Gospel concludes with Jesus's promise of the Father that the Holy Spirit will come to empower the disciples' witness, which Acts picks up with their commission to be witnesses beginning in Jerusalem and expanding out to all of Judea and Samaria and finally to the ends of the earth (Acts 1:8). Luke–Acts has an interesting radial effect as the gospel goes to Jerusalem and pivots back to the whole world.[9]

In Luke, Jesus begins in Nazareth of Galilee in the north and moves toward Jerusalem in the south where he is crucified. In what scholars call the "travel narrative" beginning in Luke 9, Jesus "set his face to go to Jerusalem" (v. 51) which he does not reach until ten chapters later. Once there, Jesus remains until his crucifixion—the gospel in its most dramatic presentation. In

---

9. David L. Turner, *Interpreting the Gospels and Acts: An Exegetical Handbook* (Grand Rapids: Kregel Academic, 2019), 136–43.

Acts, the earliest church spreads the goods news of Jesus's death for sins from Jerusalem outward before reaching the Roman empire where it ends with Paul under house arrest preaching Christ (Acts 28:31). See figure 1, which pictures the centripetal and centrifugal movement of the gospel in Luke's dual accounts.

Luke: Salvation accomplished in Jerusalem   *Acts: Salvation increases from Jerusalem*

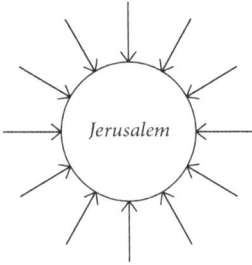

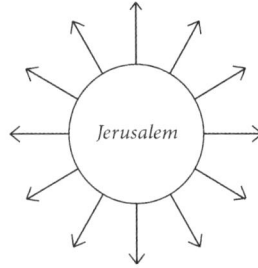

Figure 1

While John's Gospel has no equivalent commission with the Synoptics, it does contain an interesting flow of Jesus's earthly ministry that foreshadows the disciples' later global mission. The structure is intentional and sourced in Jesus's mission. As evangelical scholar Andreas Köstenberger points out, "It is the mission of Jesus, not that of his followers, that is central in John. Every other mission is derivative of the mission of Jesus: the mission of the Baptist, the Spirit and the disciples."[10] The church's missionary mandate in John is captured in Jesus's language of "sending," which is the verb form of "apostle" (*apostellō*) along with the verb *pempō*. As Jesus was *sent* from the Father into the world, he is *sending* his disciples into the world (17:18), and as the Father *sent* Jesus, Jesus is *sending* them (20:21).

John begins his account of Jesus, not in Galilee like the Synoptics, but toggling between Judea and Jerusalem and Galilee

---

10. Andreas J. Köstenberger with T. Desmond Alexander, *Salvation to the Ends of the Earth: A Biblical Theology of Mission*, NSBT 53, 2nd ed. (London: Apollos; Downers Grove: IVP Academic, 2020), 207.

(John 1–3). Beginning in John 4, Jesus expands his ministry by leaving Jerusalem and ministering to the Samaritan woman (4:1–45), followed by a Gentile official (vv. 46–54). The structure of Jesus's ministry in John serves as a precursor to the very commission he would give his disciples in Acts of expanding out from Jerusalem and Judea, Samaria, and the "ends of the earth." In fact, this latter global expansion is echoed in the Samaritans' confession that Jesus is "the Savior of the *world*" (v. 42, emphasis added). Thus, in John's Gospel there is no explicit "great commission" passage. What's there instead is Jesus modeling for his disciples what evangelism looks like by his ministering to Jews (Jerusalem), mixed-Israelite ethnicities (Samaria), and then to Gentiles (the ends of the earth).

Spirit-Empowered Boldness

To evangelize is simply to be a public witness for Christ, for his gospel, and for his glory. A formal definition is to "spread…the gospel, or good news, by means of proclamation or announcement."[11] Evangelism is one of the earliest identity markers for Christians. The reason is because embedded into the idea of evangelism is *boldness*. It takes a valiant courage given by the Holy Spirit to preach the name of Christ to those who are an enmity with God—and people notice. One cannot witness effectively without being filled with the Spirit, which demands prayer and submission to his will.

In the earliest days of the church, the Jewish temple leadership did what they could to stop the Jewish disciples from preaching in the name of Christ. In fact, the text says these religionists became "greatly annoyed" (*diaponeomai*) at Peter, John, and the other disciples "because they were teaching the people and proclaiming in Jesus the resurrection from the dead" (Acts 4:2). The very

---

11. Daniel G. Reid et al., *Dictionary of Christianity in America* (Downers Grove: InterVarsity, 1990), s.v., "Evangelism and Evangelists." The entry continues: "New Testament Greek verb *euangelizomai* means to announce the *euangelion*, or good news. New Testament evangelism is defined by its content or message, and not by its methods or results."

leaders who had just months before condemned Jesus to death now interrogated Peter, eventually commanding him and John to stop preaching in the name of Christ (v. 18). But Peter was "filled with the Holy Spirit" and boldly thundered the gospel to them and the bystanders, preaching that salvation does not exist in or by anyone other than Jesus (v. 12).

The disciples did not possess formal apologetics degrees or certificates in evangelistic strategies. In fact, they were known not to possess any formal rabbinic training at all; they were "uneducated men" (*agrammatoi*), according to the religionists.[12] However, what the disciples did have was boldness; that was the proof they knew Christ. "Now when they saw the *boldness* of Peter and John, and perceived that they were uneducated, common men, they were astonished. And they recognized that they had been with Jesus" (Acts 4:13). The Greek word is *parrēsia*, which translates as "boldness," "confidence," "courage," even "fearlessness."[13] Another leading lexicon adds: "freedom of speech," "power," and "liberty of action."[14] The disciples were known for their *bold power*, not for any letters following their names or for prefixes at the beginning of their names. Their *parresia* is what blew the minds of the religious enemies who had recently condemned Jesus to crucifixion and could have delivered the same fate for Peter and John. Instead, these gospel-enemies were literally "astonished" (*thaumazō*) at the fearlessness in the disciples' preaching Christ to them and to everyone around them. Such power is what happens when evangelicals filled with the same Spirit go and evangelize the lost, whether locally or overseas, whether to friends or to enemies. Being filled with the Holy Spirit, coupled with a brokenness for the lost and love for Christ, fuels bold and powerful evangelism (see Acts 4:31).

---

12. Literally "un-lettered," which is likely a reference, not to a lack of literacy, but of formal training in the law under a recognized rabbi.

13. BDAG, 781.

14. Franco Montanari, et al., *The Brill Dictionary of Ancient Greek* (Liden: Brill, 2018), 1592.

Biblical Activism

The idea of evangelism being a fundamental of genuine evangelicalism is captured in what Bebbington famously called "activism" in his quadrilateral. What he described as comprising the "regular hallmarks of the evangelical movement," his metric consisted of devotion to the Bible, proclamation of the cross, and zeal for conversions—all of which necessitated "unbound activism."[15]

Biblical activism includes evangelism—spreading the gospel far and wide—which affects change in society and culture at large. "The quest for souls has constantly driven [evangelicalism's] adherents into fresh evangelistic initiatives," observed Bebbington. Reflecting on the "sheer energy" of prominent evangelicals in Britain he says: "Their dynamism has spilled out in many directions—into the overseas missionary movement, into organized philanthropy, into social reform.[16] Because evangelicals have historically identified as evangelists and missionaries, recovering a biblical "activism" is essential for recovering what this book argues is a vintage faith.

Though the word "evangelist[s]" occurs just three times in the New Testament (referenced below), the concept of preaching Christ and making disciples is one of the great presuppositions following the Gospels. The Acts of the Apostles and the epistles that follow are all founded on the idea of going and preaching and planting. If this were not the case, there would be no church at Corinth or Colossae or Thessalonian or any other assembly to whom Paul wrote. Still, on three occasions the word *euangelistēs* (evangelist) does make an appearance. The first is in Acts, which identifies Phillip, one of the church's original deacons, as an "evangelist" (Acts 21:8). Elsewhere, Paul lists "evangelist[s]" as one of the offices of the local church (Eph. 4:11). And finally, in his last letter, the apostle called his delegate Timothy to "do the work

---

15. David W. Bebbington, *The Evangelical Quadrilateral: Characterizing the British Gospel Movement* (Waco: Baylor University Press, 2021), 1:39.

16. Ibid.

of an evangelist," as part of his pastoral ministry (2 Tim. 4:5). In each place, the context is one who proclaims the good news of salvation in Christ.

To preach the gospel to both the lost and converted is a central task for all evangelicals. The lost need to hear the words of Christ to be saved, and the saved need to hear the words of Christ to be encouraged and strengthened. Out of evangelism grows missions work which should never be divorced from the local church. All three of Paul's missionary journeys in Acts included planting churches and strengthening churches. The evangelists and missionaries in John's final epistle testified before "the church" and were supported in their work by Gaius and his church (3 John 5–8). In fact, John calls to task selfish church leaders like Diotrephes who refuse to support those "who have gone out for the sake of the name" (vv. 7–10). This passion of church-supported evangelism and missions is shared by classic evangelicalism.

This means evangelism and missions go hand in glove. To preach Christ to lost souls while neglecting their need for assembling with other believers is not biblical activism. Though modern day missions work is often done by agencies detached from a local church body, that idea lays outside of what is portrayed in the Book of Acts and New Testament letters. It's not that such agencies dishonor Christ by sending teachers and preachers to parts of the world lacking a witness for Christ. Far from it. Sending qualified workers to share the gospel of Jesus and salvation in him alone or in supporting roles to make it happen is *always* a noble task. But doing so apart from planting or strengthening a local church is a method foreign to New Testament missionary endeavors.

Unfortunately, too many evangelicals adapt methods of over-contextualization, cultural accommodation, and other missiological strategies that look outside of Scripture for help. Some believe the propositions of Scripture are not accommodating enough to meet the spiritual needs of target audiences sufficiently. This, however, reflects a lower view of Scripture than historic, vintage evangelicalism allows because it doubts the Bible's authority and sufficiency in making disciples in every culture and generation (see chapter two).

In his doctoral dissertation, evangelical missionary Chris Burnett argues that the biblical text contains all the divinely given spiritual knowledge that sinners must hear and believe to be spiritually transformed. In what he calls a "missiological propositional assertion," Burnett's model provides an alternative to culturally accommodating missiological approaches common among evangelicals today simply by taking the Bible's propositions to go and make disciples to all nations at face value.[17] If one is defining missions in terms of short-term projects like digging wells or repairing roofs on houses, then the Bible will not give clear direction. Such humanitarian acts are morally ethical, of course, but often replace the necessity of gospel proclamation. However, if missions work is defined by preaching the gospel and making disciples for local assemblies, the Bible is all that is needed. The link between a high view of Scripture and evangelism and church planting as presented here is unavoidable. It takes believing in the words of Scripture in its most natural sense—for example, that power really is available through the Holy Spirit yielding boldness to go and make disciples of all nations—and that these propositions are indeed authoritative, infallible, inerrant, and sufficient.

Suffering and Evangelism

Being filled by the Holy Spirit through prayer and submission results in the power needed to witness to a hostile world. Persecution and even martyrdom is a reality promised in the New Testament. The disciples as a group were promised they would be persecuted in various ways throughout John 14–16. Just before his arrest, Jesus reminded his disciples:

---

17. Christopher Ryan Burnett, "Defining Biblical Missions through 'Missiological Propositional Assertion'" (PhD diss., The Master's Seminary, 2022), esp. 258–316. See also Mark Tatlock and Chris Burnett eds., *Biblical Missions: Principles, Priorities, and Practices* (Nashville: Thomas Nelson, 2025).

If the world hates you, know that it has hated me before it hated you. If you were of the world, the world would love you as its own; but because you are not of the world, but I chose you out of the world, therefore the world hates you. A servant is not greater than his master. If they persecuted me, they will also persecute you. If they kept my word, they will also keep yours. But all these things they will do to you on account of my name, because they do not know him who sent me (John 15:18–21).

The truth is that sometimes what enemies will do to Christians who evangelize includes the extremities of persecution and martyrdom. The New Testament does not try and hide this fact; instead, it promises it. On the same night, Jesus told the disciples: "They will put you out of the synagogues. Indeed, the hour is coming when whoever kills you will think he is offering service to God" (John 16:2). However, by the Spirit, followers of Jesus are to testify about Christ regardless of sufferings they encounter. Thankfully, the evangelical (and any other genuine Christian) is not left to their own devices or strength to evangelize those who are hostile. Jesus provides supernatural power in the endeavor. "When the Helper comes," promised Jesus, "whom I will send to you from the Father, the Spirit of truth, who proceeds from the Father, he will bear witness about me. And you also will bear witness, because you have been with me from the beginning" (John 15:26–27). This "helper" or "advocate" (*paraklētos*) is none other than the Holy Spirit himself who has come and empowers believers to witness for Christ.

Evangelicals understand that hatred toward believers is really rooted in a hatred toward God. "The appropriate response for the believer," relays Glenn M. Penner, "is to witness through proclamation and example to the hostile world, sacrificially bearing a message of love and reconciliation in the power of the Spirit (15:27)."[18] The New Testament demands a perspective that never allows believers to view afflictions as complaints

---

18. Glenn M. Penner, *In The Shadows of the Cross: A Biblical Theology of Persecution and Discipleship* (Bartlesville: Living Sacrifice, 2004), 152.

over life's troubles but as one always glorifying God in Christ (cf. Phil. 4:11–13). Such became the apostle Peter's perspective, which resulted from a life that exemplified faithful suffering.

Reflecting Jesus's earlier promises to him and the disciples about suffering persecution, Peter would come to write: "But rejoice insofar as you share Christ's sufferings, that you may also rejoice and be glad when his glory is revealed. If you are insulted for the name of Christ, you are blessed, because the Spirit of glory and of God rests upon you" (1 Pet. 4:13–14). As evangelical commentators Tim Miller and Bryan Murawski explain, "To the degree that [Christians'] suffering is based on their obedience to Jesus, they should rejoice to the same degree."[19] Suffering in obedience to Christ and his commission is actually a blessing, demonstrating the presence of the Spirit. They go on to conclude: "The logic of the passage works this way: 'by suffering persecution you show the same spirit that resided with Jesus resides with you, since he was likewise persecuted for righteousness.'"[20] The lesson is clear for the global church: because Jesus suffered for the glory of God, those who trust in Christ suffer for God's glory. Even in death, a Christian's witness is on display.

Contrary to the actions of Judas, Peter serves as a perennial example for all Christians, teaching that commitment to a life lived following Christ is always the correct choice. A believer who chooses to live and minister despite possibilities of persecution and death ironically enables other Christians to have greater courage and joyful service for Christ. A biblical theology of suffering refuses to accept any thought that suggests holding on to this temporal life should be one's aim as if it is the only life that matters. Rather, as Jesus declared and demonstrated, the one who willingly dies for the glory of God "bears much fruit" (John 12:23–24).

---

19. Timothy E. Miller and Bryan Murawski, *1 Peter: A Commentary for Biblical Preaching and Teaching*, Kerux Commentaries (Grand Rapids: Kregel Ministry, 2022), 255.

20. Ibid., 256.

Because the world hates Jesus and those who follow him, suffering unto glory is the inevitable reward for sharing a message the world so desperately needs. This "joyful suffering," explained Schlatter, "arose from the service [the disciples] owed to humanity, since they did not receive what Jesus gave to them merely for themselves but for the world. Therefore, it was their holy duty to make what they received effective for others."[21] Cast in such light, the idea of glory by suffering in evangelism demonstrates that God ordains personal suffering for Christians out of his love for them and empowers them by the Spirit to be a bold witness for Christ—regardless of the situation.

Evangelism and the Sovereignty of God

Missions and evangelism are two sides of the same coin for a vintage faith. To evangelize the lost is to engage in the mission commanded of all believers, and to plant churches and disciple believers into Christian maturity within those churches necessitates evangelism. But a classic tension arises. If God is in charge of all who get saved, why bother evangelizing?

The Bible teaches two soteriological truths—God is sovereign over every believer's salvation *and* believers have a responsibility to share the gospel for people to be saved. Paul taught that saving faith comes from hearing the gospel (Rom. 10:13), and that everyone who calls on the name of the Lord will be saved (v. 17). Clearly, the implication is that one must preach the gospel in order for people to call on the Lord for salvation. And yet the same apostle taught elsewhere that God chose (or "elected") those who come to believe in Jesus from the foundation of the world and predestined them for adoption though Christ (Eph. 1:4–5). Clearly then, God sovereignly determines everyone who will come to believe in Christ and be saved. But how can both propositions be "clear" truths?

---

21. Adolf Schlatter, *The History of the Christ: The Foundation of New Testament Theology*, trans. Andreas J. Köstenberger (Grand Rapids: Baker, 1997), 242.

Because the Bible cannot contradict itself as God's inspired and inerrant Word (see chapter two), both ideas must be true despite the tension. The late evangelical theologian J. I Packer confronted this very pressure in his classic treatise *Evangelism and the Sovereignty of God*. In what he called an "antinomy," meaning an *apparent* contradiction that was in actuality a tension with two undeniable truths, Packer believed that a correct understanding of God's sovereignty served as a powerful incentive to evangelize rather than a barrier to it. "The doctrine of divine sovereignty would be grossly misapplied if we should invoke it in such a way as to lessen the urgency, and immediacy, and priority, and binding constraint, of the evangelistic imperative," he wrote.[22] As it turns out, there is no actual incompatibility or genuine contradiction. The biblical facts are: (1) believers in Jesus are to evangelize the lost with gospel of salvation; and (2) God is the one in control over all efforts and results. There may be a tension, but it is one that is complementary not contradictory; both are true, neither is exclusively mutual. As such, rather than throwing one's arms up in defiance to the task, the antinomy, when properly understood, should breed confidence in the evangelical to evangelize— knowing that *the Lord* knows who are his (2 Tim. 2:19). Packer was forthright: "God did not teach us the reality of His rule in order to give us an excuse for neglecting His orders."[23]

The dual biblical truths of God's sovereignty and man's responsibility has inspired cross-cultural missions work as a fundamental element of vintage evangelicalism since its earliest days. A great example is the "father of modern missions," British Baptist pastor William Carey (1761–1834). In 1799, Carey converted from Anglicanism to a Calvinistic, Baptist, and Non-Conformist persuasion after he was convinced that Calvinistic soteriology did not preclude evangelistic responsibility.[24] As

---

22. J. I. Packer, *Evangelism and the Sovereignty of God* (Downers Grove: InterVarsity, 1973), 34.

23. Ibid., 34.

24. John D. Woodbridge and Frank A. James III, *Church History:*

Carey came to understand, God is sovereign over all affairs and predetermines even those he elected for salvation but chooses to use people to bring about his predetermined results. This meant that although every elect person is already written in the Lamb's book of life (Rev. 13:8; cf. Phil. 4:3), they still needed to hear the gospel *during their life time* and trust in Christ.

Carey, who was the first evangelical missionary to India, founded what eventually became the Baptist Missionary Society based on the principle of Christian responsibility to reaching God's elect all over the world and disciplining them in accordance with Matthew's Great Commission. Though a mysterious tension, Carey saw no conflict between God's sovereignty and the evangelical's responsibility to evangelize the lost. God's election is the guarantee that those chosen from the foundation of the world, according to the councils of his will, *will* come to saving repentant-faith in Jesus at some point before they die. Christians just need to be obedient to the task and go preach the gospel to everyone without restraint. God determines the results (election) *as well as* the means (prayer and evangelism). From Carey came the now-famous dictum, "Expect great things from God, attempt great things for God," which was based on Paul's words in Ephesians that God can do far more than we can ever ask or think (Eph. 3:20).

Through his passion to evangelize the "heathen" that God had previously elected for salvation, Carey convinced Christian leaders in England that foreign missions was an evangelical duty. He taught that the missionary can take comfort in the fact that ultimately a person's salvation rests in God's sovereignty. According to evangelical historians John Woodbridge and Frank James, "Influenced by Carey's arguments, its leaders rejected the notion that the Calvinistic doctrine of election relieved Reformed Christians of their obligation to pursue foreign mission

---

From Pre-Reformation to the Present Day: The Rise and Growth of the Church in Its Cultural, Intellectual, and Political Context (Grand Rapids: Zondervan, 2013), 2:586.

activity."[25] Of course, Calvin wasn't the first to see the tension relieved. Augustine taught in the fifth century that because we don't know who belongs in the group predestined for salvation, we should preach the gospel to everyone—comforted with the knowledge that some of them are elect and will come to believe in our message.

Maintaining the biblical balance of God's sovereignty and human responsibility helps re-orient evangelism in terms of simply obeying the command to preach the gospel and *not* in the effect it has on hearers. As Packer observed, "Man's responsibility for his actions, and God's sovereignty in relation to those same actions, are thus…equally real and ultimate facts."[26] Indeed, Paul taught, the evangelist merely plants and waters—but it is God who causes the growth (1 Cor. 3:7). Ultimately, God saves according to his mercy and grace even despite our poor presentations. Historic evangelicalism understands that obedience to the Great Commission is a great responsibility and privilege in which Christians play a role in the drama of salvation.

The gospel is always central to the task as justification and sanctification in Christ shatters all cultural barriers. This means a "gospel mission" is anything but ethnocentric. It is meant to reach all cultures and ethnicities as all people are image bearers of God. "The target of the gospel mission," relays evangelical scholar Jason DeRouchie, "is to see people saved and satisfied from 'among *all* the nations.' The good news that the reigning God saves and satisfies believing sinners through Christ's life, death, and resurrection is for the Libyan and Bolivian, for the expats in Dubai and the mountain tribes in the Himalayas, for the Latinos in Miami and for the poor in rural Minnesota."[27] Such a view should encourage the evangelical to a lifestyle of evangelism knowing a person's salvation is not determined in their methods,

---

25. Ibid., 2:587.

26. J. I. Packer, *Evangelism and the Sovereignty of God*, 93.

27. Jason S. DeRouchie, "What is a Biblical Theology of Mission?" in *40 Questions about Biblical Theology*, eds. Jason S. DeRouchie, Oren R. Martin, and Andrew David Naselli (Grand Rapids: Kregel Academic, 2020), 274.

strategies, or buzz words. The evangelical can be zealous about evangelism because he or she knows that God has determined all who come to salvation eventually will, and that he allows them to participate in such a magnificent plan.

CHAPTER 5

Participating in Theological Education

The Need to Grow in Knowledge

Virtually all evangelicals know something of the American evangelist Dwight Lyman (D. L.) Moody (1837–1899). He became the most famous open-air preacher in the world and set the pace for future evangelical leaders who were all in on both the gospel and education. But not all know that Moody himself never attended college or seminary. He never graduated high school or even elementary school. This may be surprising since the Bible institute movement can be traced to Moody and his zealous contribution to Christian education.

Moody serves as a fine example of the indelible link between the vintage faith and participating in theological education. Because he never formally obtained an education further than the equivalent of fifth-grade, Moody became painfully aware of his lack of theological training as he grew older and accrued opportunities to evangelize large crowds. The need for evangelicals to participate in theological education became evermore apparent for the famous evangelist who would go on to establish America's foremost Bible institute in Chicago in 1886—The Moody Bible Institute (originally called the Chicago Evangelization Society).

Theological education became a relentless conviction for Moody, evidenced earlier when he founded Northfield Seminary for Young Women and the Mount Hermon School for Boys in 1879–81 respectively, both with the intent to educate the poor and minorities who lacked a Christian education.

In a critical, biographical chapter, historian Donald Akenson discusses D. L. Moody's founding various schools and summer "colleges," even on his own Massachusetts estate. He then makes the link argued in this chapter. According to Akenson, "[Moody] saw education and evangelicalism as ideally intertwined."[1] This dual conviction of evangelical belief and theological education is not only historic for the vintage faith but is logical as well. As traced so far in this book, a true evangelical is governed by the authority of Scripture, a love for Christ, and a passion to reach the lost. It makes sense that to commit to these ideas necessitates a constant growing in one's knowledge of God and the universe that he created filled with people who need redemption.

Admittedly, the need to participate in theological education isn't usually thought of as a "fundamental" for evangelical identity. In fact, it is probably here and the following chapter on church fellowship where this book differs from other works that propose a *sine qua non* for the vintage faith. But I do believe that because genuine evangelical identity begins with a love for Christ and Scripture, it follows that evangelicals want to grow in their knowledge of both. And growing in such knowledge often results in a desire to know more about things addressed in Scripture like science, metaphysics, nature, animals, etc. As laid out in chapter two, a Christian's relationship with God is directly proportionate with their relationship to God's Word. When evangelicals dedicate themselves to learning the Scriptures, they ultimately grow in grace and in their knowledge of God. In other words, they grow in their theology—the fourth fundamental comprised of what this book argues is a vintage faith.

---

1. Donald Harman Akenson, *The Americanization of the Apocalypse: Creating America's Own Bible* (New York: Oxford University Press, 2023), 234.

Formal Theological Education

Christians are commanded to increase their theological knowledge. Paul prayed that the Colossian church would be filled with all "knowledge and spiritual wisdom and understanding God's will," and that they continually "increase [*auxanomenoi*] in the knowledge of God" (Col. 1:9–10). The very last thing Peter wrote included a present active imperative: "But grow [*auxanete*] in the grace and knowledge of our Lord and Savior Jesus Christ. To him be the glory both now and to the day of eternity. Amen." (2 Pet. 3:18). Continual growth in the knowledge of God and Christ demands a commitment to theological education primarily through the Scriptures, prayer, and fellowship. These three are part and parcel of the normal Christian life.

But one's knowledge of Christianity also develops through formal theological training that extends past the resources most local churches can offer. This includes learning the Bible's original languages, linguistics, textual criticism, hermeneutics, church history, and the various theological disciplines (biblical theology, historical theology, systematic theology, practical theology, etc.). It is not impossible for churches to provide such in-depth training, but it is rare for a local church to be able to offer resources that often demand credentialed teachers with expert pedagogy. Because of this, such training is best sought in institutions like Bible institutes and colleges, Christian universities, and seminaries that hold to the highest view of Scripture and understand that their role is to support (not consume or replace) the local church.[2]

This high view of Scripture is a non-negotiable to qualify any theological education as a genuinely *evangelical* education. Sadly, there are a lot of accredited "Christian" seminaries that are anything but evangelical or genuinely Christian. Some theological schools hire professors who are so extreme in their ecumenism they begin classes by praying to and bowing down to foreign

---

2. See the excellent essays in David S. Dockery and Christopher W. Morgan, eds. *Christian Higher Education: Faith, Teaching, and Learning in the Evangelical Tradition* (Wheaton: Crossway, 2018).

RECOVERING A VINTAGE FAITH

Gods. One historically liberal seminary in New York boasts in its faculty being "double-belonging," since they identify as "Christian Buddhists."[3] Another progressive seminary in Chicago mocks the Lord's return by handing out condoms at LGBT+ pride festivals with the slogan, "Take Two (for second coming!)" printed on them.[4] The identity that these institutions crave calls to mind scenes of God's glory departing from the temple because of the horrific abominations committed by Israel's very own teachers and leaders in that holy space (Ezek. 8:5–18).

However—and this should be obvious—not all seminaries are bad. In fact, many (most?) are quite good and understand their role as historically providing in-depth rigorous training for future pastors, chaplains, missionaries, and professors. This very idea is embedded in the mission statement of Southern California Seminary where I currently teach, which enjoys an eighty-year heritage of "bringing glory to God by assisting local churches to equip believers of various cultures and languages to live and minister biblically based on the inerrant Word of God."[5] And of course we're not alone. Since its beginning, evangelicalism has emphasized the need for believers to grow in their theological knowledge.

---

3. Union Theological Seminary (Columbia University). See their YouTube page dated April 20, 2012 at, https://www.youtube.com/watch?v=vdWg98vDMZ4&list=PLEFyMJpwMeIQ8e0qqIoP_YEKVN_BuXNoD. With blatant insincerity this school claims in the video's description, "We are a school where nothing less than God is the subject of our study." Watching their video that is pervasive with extreme social-critical theory, it becomes apparent that in reality, everything *but* the God of Scripture is their ultimate subject of study.

4. Chicago Theological Seminary (University of Chicago). See, Manya Brachear Pashman, "Seminary's 'Second Coming' Condoms Offend Some Conservative Christians," *Chicago Tribune*, updated on August 19, 2019, https://www.chicagotribune.com/2015/07/30/seminarys-second-coming-condoms-offend-some-conservative-christians/.

5. Southern California Seminary, "Our Mission," https://www.socalsem.edu/.

Something to consider before pointing the finger of blame at seminaries for the amount of bad theology out there is this: the reality is the majority of pastors in the world have *no* formal theological training. According to the Center for the Study of Global Christianity, only 5 per cent of pastors in all Christian traditions worldwide have had theological training. That means out of the approximately five million active clergy in the world, only 250,000 of them are likely to have participated in theological training as in undergraduate Bible degrees or Master's degrees.[6]

These statistics put into perspective that on a global scale, the majority of bad theology in the world is not caused by liberal or apostate theological seminaries. Rather, the exact opposite is the case. The pervasive amount of poor theology comes from poorly trained or untrained pastors. The numbers bear out that the overwhelming majority of pastors in the world remain untrained in consistent hermeneutical method, biblical languages, church history, and the other disciplines provided by formal theological education. Does this mean untrained Christians cannot access books written on each of these topics and become well versed and self-trained in the material? Not at all. Such is common, in fact. However, more times than not, the authors of those books hold advanced degrees out of which they wrote their helpful works. Thus, even in the cases of those who never *directly* participate in formal theological education, they do so *indirectly* through the credentialed author whose works inform their learning.[7]

---

6. Center for the Study of Global Christianity at Gorden-Conwell Theological Seminary, "What Percentage of Pastors Worldwide Have Theological Training?" https://www.gordonconwell.edu/center-for-global-christianity/research/quick-facts/.

7. As an aside, one of the greatest benefits of attending Bible college or seminary is having professors assign good books that would otherwise remain unknown to the student. Also, usually missing in critiques that frown upon formal theological training is that included in most curricula of basic formal theological education are courses on critical thinking and theological research and writing. Theological writing is a skill that develops through seminary education, which is

Because churches will always reflect their leadership, when pastors are theological infants, their congregations will be as well. From my experience as a professor, this helps explain why some incoming students have been Christian for many years but still lack aptitude in basic biblical and theological knowledge. They have grown up in churches led by biblically and theologically illiterate pastors, resulting in their own lack of biblical and theological knowledge. The problem is reminiscent of what the writer of Hebrews said: "For though by this time you ought to be teachers, you need someone to teach you again the basic principles of the oracles of God" (Heb. 5:12).

There was a time when students enrolled in seminary, not as much to be spiritually formed, since that was to occur in their local churches, but for intellectual formation by way of academic theology. Times are now different. According to the former executive director of Association of Theological Schools (ATS), there has been such a drop in overall church membership in the US, matching a lack of engagement with the Bible, that students are coming to seminary hoping not to get *intellectually* formed, but the *spiritual* formation they should be getting at church.[8] This means that seminary professors now have the added responsibility of *pastoring* their students because local ministers often lack the skills necessary for both spiritual and theological formation. Richard Mouw, who formerly served as president of a historically evangelical seminary, defended the need for theological higher education:

> As a seminary president, I spend a lot of time explaining to people why they ought to support theological education. This kind of apologetic comes easy for me. I am convinced a healthy church

---

why most theological books, commentaries, reference works, articles, etc. are written by *graduates* of such training.

8. Douglas Estes and Daniel O. Alshire, "Facing the Future of Theological Education: Amid the Challenges, Daniel O. Alshire Sees Opportunities for Renewal," *Didaktikos: Journal of Theological Education* 5, no. 1 (Sep 2021): 17–23.

needs leaders who can read the Bible in the original languages, who can explain difficult passages in the Book of Revelation, who understand the heresies that threatened the church in the fourth century after Christ, who write books about the life of John Wesley, who can explain why Jehovah's Witnesses are wrong when they attack the doctrine of the Trinity . . . and on and on.[9]

Again, it's not that training at this level is impossible in well-staffed, healthy churches. But the reality is that most churches simply lack the resources, time, and energy, needed to devote to high-quality education in these matters, which is precisely why theological schools exist.

Seminary or Cemetery?

Isn't there something to the joke that replaces "seminary" with "cemetery"? A popular idea is that academic training in theology zaps one of all enthusiasm and love for God's Word. The seminarian goes from spiritual life to spiritual death due to the academics required, so the argument goes. Undeniably, such has occurred at times and is a real danger for those who choose to attend a critical or non-evangelical institution. Evangelical pastor-scholar John Piper recounts his awful experience during his doctoral studies at the University of Munich where he eventually wrote a dissertation on Jesus's love command:[10]

> What I saw in the theological educational system and state-church life in Germany confirmed most of what I did not want to become. Here were world-class scholars, whom everyone on the cutting edge in America were oohing and ahhing over, teaching in a way that was exegetically non-transferable, insubordinate toward the Scriptures, and indifferent to the life of the church.

---

9. Richard J. Mouw, *The Smell of Sawdust: What Evangelicals Can Learn from Their Fundamentalist Heritage* (Grand Rapids: Zondervan, 2000), 52.

10. See John Piper, *"Love Your Enemies": Jesus' Love Command in the Synoptic Gospels and the Early Christian Parenesis* (Cambridge: Cambridge University Press, 1979).

I attended university classes where nineteen-year-old ministerial students were soaked in every form of faddish criticism, while tools for mining the gold of Scripture were untouched and the taste buds for enjoying its honey were unawakened.[11]

Piper's experience is, unfortunately, not an isolated one. It is a common tale for those who have attended the most elite universities (and seminaries) in the world. Institutions that do not hold to fundamental evangelical beliefs like the authority of Scripture and the need for church fellowship *can* drain a Christian student of their passion for growing in grace and in the knowledge of the living Christ. In fact, Mouw acknowledged, "We evangelicals know that theological education has all too often had the effect of dampening spiritual ardor. Theological schools have sometimes fostered a clerical elitism that is out of touch with the spiritual needs of ordinary Christians."[12] But it doesn't need to be this way. Far from it.

Thankfully, in Piper's case, he was already grounded in his academic training at Wheaton College and Fuller Theological Seminary, which in the 1960s–70s, were both doggedly evangelical and intellectual.[13] He talks of his pre-doctoral, evangelical academic experience in terms of "immeasurable gifts" including "intellectual stimulation," and "emotional deepening, the stirring of imagination, [and] passion to write," resulting in an unquestioned passion expressed in terms only Piper can get away with: "By the end of three years, not only was I a romantic rationalist, but the romance and rational labor were now firmly focused on the Word of God. An absolute sovereign God of grace

---

11. John Piper and D. A. Carson, *The Pastor as Scholar and Scholar as Pastor: Reflections on Life and Ministry*, eds., Owen Strachan and David Mathis (Wheaton: Crossway, 2011), 41.

12. Richard J. Mouw, *The Smell of Sawdust*, 52.

13. While Wheaton College (est. 1860) still retains their evangelical convictions and academic rigor, Fuller Seminary (est. 1947) has, unfortunately, almost entirely lost their original evangelical vision as set out by its charter administration and faculty. See chapter nine for more.

was at the center."[14] The difference between Piper's pre-doctoral and doctoral education was squarely on the former's evangelical commitments to center all curriculum on God, his grace, and his word.[15]

Evangelical theological education is not merely about dedicated professors who lecture from a genuine evangelical conviction. There is a sense of community where learning also happens in fellowship with other like-minded students. "Another influence at Wheaton," recalls Piper, "was the students. Never had I been around so many intellectually engaged young people. It had a double effect. One was to pour gasoline on the fires lit by professors. The other was to remind me of my own weakness."[16] When a student becomes more and more conformed to the Word of God and bears their struggles, joys, temptations, excitement, etc. with other students, he or she becomes more self-aware and humble, in Piper's words, "weak." One of the unexpected beauties of formal theological training is experiencing the humility that Paul talks about when he commanded the Roman Christians not to think highly of themselves but rather sensibly, which requires a deep sense of self-reflective humility (see Rom 12:3).[17] Such is a regular occurrence when a student with a spirit to learn is surrounded by other students and professors who bring a wealth of experience and perspective that would never be gained alone.

---

14. John Piper and D. A. Carson, *The Pastor as Scholar and Scholar as Pastor*, 35, 41.

15. See the similar vision for seminary education in Ched Spellman and Jason K. Lee, eds. *The Seminary as a Textual Community: Exploring John Sailhamer's Vision for Theological Education* (Dallas: Fontes Press, 2018).

16. John Piper and D. A. Carson, *The Pastor as Scholar and Scholar as Pastor*, 31.

17. Another unexpected benefit of obtaining formal theological education is the number of vocational opportunities that such an education affords in areas like academia, congregational ministry, parachurch ministry, public service, and publishing and media. See Brandon C. Benzinger and Adam W. Day, eds. *What Can You Do with Your Bible Training? Traditional and Nontraditional Vocational Paths* (Eugene: Resource, 2023).

The False Dichotomy of Heart and Mind

Formal theological training is not favored by everyone. Some have advocated for a form of pietism over education; an inward focus on the heart and religious devotion. Historically, pietism was a reactionary movement in post-Reformation Germany against what was thought to be biblical dogmatism confined by a multiplication of theological definitions.[18] Its focus was on spiritual devotion, not on any one theological expression. This is still popular in many corners of Christianity.

There is a valid argument that the evangelical spirit in Europe and the United States has turned dry and arid due to domesticating its theology. Doctrines that at one time enflamed the soul with awe over the mysteries of God became cold and rigidly intellectual. So, pietism became an attractive alternative with its focus on individual feelings and striving for holiness. Yet evangelical scholar Os Guinness contends there should never be this either/or option in evangelicalism, as in heart *or* mind.[19] The divide between "head" and "heart," or "faith" and "reason," is a false distinction, though advocated by some pietists. With Guinness, I do not believe pietism is the answer that bridges a seeming gap between the longing of the soul and the intellect of the mind. Instead, these two are one and the same.

While a distinction does exist, it is not one between heart and mind. Rather, it is between living a grace-filled sanctified life (piety) and enforced rules that legislate one's piety at the expense of the mind's intellect (piet-*ism*). The former flows from growing in the knowledge of Scripture and the grace of Christ as advocated by Peter as well as in this chapter. This results in serving others and discipling them to do the same, both privately and publicly. The latter, however, is a privatized experience, one that inevitably

---

18. See Norman Sykes, "The Religion of the Protestants," in *The Cambridge History of the Bible*, ed., S. L. Greenslade (Cambridge: Cambridge University Press, 1963), 3:190–93.

19. Os Guinness, *Fit Bodies, Fat Minds: Why Evangelicals Don't Think and What to Do About It* (Grand Rapids: Baker, 1994), 30.

sets up inward competition among believers. As J. Daryl Charles argues, "Although *piety* is the bone fide expression of true religious devotion, *pietism* represents an inward turn, which if unmediated, results in a privatizing of faith and a distrust of the intellect."[20] Unfortunately, this false dichotomy of heart and mind infects a lot of evangelical pulpits today.

It is now commonplace for pastors to preach sermons that put everything down "on the bottom shelf." They do this either out of fear that some in the congregation may have to struggle with complex theological concepts or, more times than admitted, out of a lack of personal confidence since the pastor is formally untrained in exegesis, hermeneutical methods, church history, theological disciplines, and so on. Evangelical mega-pastors excel in preaching down to their people as if only those with a fourth-grade reading level populate their churches. Rather than offering exegetically informed biblical exposition and powerful theological reflection, they permeate their sermons with personal anecdotes and manufactured illustrations supported by Bible verses shoehorned in on occasion (usually out of context). Supplemented with a lengthy professionalized music experience, capturing emotions is what matters most in a lot of evangelical churches (a close second is having a children's ministry that rivals most theme parks).

The result is an evangelical culture of biblical and theological infants. "Given the tendency of those in American evangelical pulpits to encourage *distrust* of the intellect and to stress subjective experience over objective proposition," diagnoses Charles, "very often evangelicals have been their own worst enemy."[21] Charles traces this back to what he terms a "therapeutic model" popular in evangelicalism, focusing squarely on "a person's private feelings, emotions and psychological state."[22] The irony is tragic. A vintage evangelicalism is one devoted to learning *and* feeling.

---

20. J. Daryl Charles, *The Unformed Conscience of Evangelicalism: Recovering the Church's Moral Vision* (Dallas: Fontes Press, 2020), 102.

21. Ibid., 103.

22. Ibid., 27.

It seems contemporary evangelicalism focuses on the latter to the exclusion of the former. The truth is, when one grows in their theology, they grow in their zeal for God and his people. Biblical feelings, therefore, cannot be divorced from biblical education. Knowledge informs and guides feelings. It is not by accident the word "knowledge" and its cognates appear fifteen times throughout Peter's brief epistles along with emotionally charged ideas like love, hope, peace, joy, sympathy, and zeal.[23]

The Judeo-Christian Legacy of Reading and Writing

Christians in the majority world take for granted the ability to read and write. Because it's something we do daily without having to recall complicated grammatical rules and paradigms, we can lose sight of how significant it is to possess basic literacy skills. Come to find out, the art and science of reading and writing is baked into the history of evangelicalism.

In fact, Christianity as a whole was set apart from ancient pagan religions because it was founded on a message codified in a holy text that was read—the Bible. "Christians have always been particularly bookish people," explain evangelical scholars Charles Quarles and Scott Kellum. "The earliest periods saw an enormous amount of literary production. The early church sincerely appreciated quite a number of these works, some to the point of local canonicity."[24] The fact that certain writings were canonized (recognized as authoritative and collected as a group) implies the obvious prerequisite of these early Christians being able to read sophisticated literature. They had what scholars refer to as a "canon consciousness," in that they read what would come to be known as the New Testament and understood it as literature that was unlike other writings. This fact bumps the common narrative that virtually

---

23. The words "know," "knowing," "knowledge," and "known" appear at 1 Peter 1:18; 5:9; 2 Peter 1:2, 3, 5 [2x], 8, 16, 20; 2:9, 20, 21; 3:3, 17, 18.

24. Charles L. Quarles and L. Scott Kellum, *40 Questions About the Text and Canon of the New Testament* (Grand Rapids: Kregel Academic, 2023), 244.

all people in the ancient world were illiterate. Such a claim usually doesn't take into account the Judeo-Christian heritage of reading and writing, as even the most ancient Jews were commanded to read, write, and teach. Moses wrote:

> These words, which I am commanding you today, shall be on your heart. You shall teach them diligently to your sons and shall speak of them when you sit in your house and when you walk by the way and when you lie down and when you rise up. You shall bind them as a sign on your hand, and they shall be as phylacteries between your eyes. You shall write them on the doorposts of your house and on your gates. (Deut. 6:6–9).

This passage contains powerful insights.[25] The ancient Israelites were commanded to be "diligent" with God's Word.[26] A rhetorical merism is present in the text, which expresses the totality of a whole by use of two opposites (sit-walk / lie-rise). They were to know and repeat God's Word when sitting, walking, lying down, and when rising. In other words, *everywhere all day every day.* Additionally, they were to bind God's Word on their wrists, depicting easy retrieval. They were to attach God's Word on their foreheads, picturing a seeping into their minds. Moreover, they were to transcribe God's Word on their door posts and gates—a holy graffiti—signaling to everyone in their midst (as well as pagan neighbors) that they were devoted to God's Word. The biblical Jewish legacy is that of men and women of God who read the Word, study the Word, and even *write out* the Word! Such is a sacred diligence. Diligence with God's Word is not the legacy of ancient Israel alone. Reading and writing—*knowing*—the Scriptures has also been a legacy for the Christian church.

Earlier, Quarles and Kellum referred to Christians as "bookish people." This is confirmed by evangelical scholar Michael Kruger

---

25. For more, see my chapter "Recovering Biblical Literacy," in *Fight the Good Fight: Reclaiming Biblical Fundamentalism,* ed. Richard Bargas (Grand Rapids: IFCA Press, 2024), 41–63.

26. The Hebrew verb used for teach, שׁנן (*šnn*), is in the intensive piel stem suggesting a repeated or diligent teaching.

who explains just how *conscious* of the canon these early believers were, which required their ability to read and write: "Early Christians had a canon consciousness from a very early point as they read, copied, collected, and distributed those documents they viewed as central to their religious life and worship."[27] The fact that these Christians were engaging literature at such a productive volume shows they were a thinking and reading people. "They busied themselves not just with oral proclamation," argues Kruger, "but also, and perhaps primarily, with the *written text*. At their core, they were people of the book."[28]

The formation of the canon during the first few hundred years of the church demonstrates a few things. Along with the thousands of manuscripts copied and disseminated—requiring obvious intellectual prowess by those engaged in the process—the early church also took seriously an *expectation* of literacy among its members. How else can the impressive number of extant manuscripts be explained? Why copy and distribute them to such an extent if it was believed no one could read them? The amount of ancient biblical manuscripts dating to the first several hundred years of the church is unparalleled with other existing ancient literature. Just under six thousand ancient Greek NT manuscripts have been discovered to date, with the number increasing yearly.[29] And this number doesn't include the thousands more of its translation into early languages like Syriac, Coptic, Georgian,

---

27. Michael J. Kruger, *Canon Revisited: Establishing the Origins and Authority of the New Testament Books* (Wheaton: Crossway, 2012), 259.

28. Ibid.

29. Andreas J. Köstenberger, *Going Deeper with New Testament Greek, Revised Edition: An Intermediate Study of the Grammar and Syntax of the New* (Nashville: B&H Academic, 2020), 25, puts the count at more than 5,800, but this number needs to be nuanced. Jacob W. Peterson, "Math Myths: How Many Manuscripts We Have and Why More Isn't Always Better," in *Myths and Mistakes in New Testament Textual Criticism,* eds. Elijah Hixon and Peter J. Gurry (Downers Grove: IVP Academic, 2019), 48–69, offers a helpful discussion on how manuscripts are discovered and counted. With the inevitability of errors in counting, Peterson estimates a more conservative amount of approximately 5,100–5,300 Greek NT manuscripts to be in existence.

Latin, Ethiopic, and so on over the course of the first several centuries of church history.[30]

Some have posited that only church leaders, and not congregants, were literate and produced copies to read to their churches.[31] This explanation is offered in light of modern literacy studies that suggest only one in four people could read in the Roman empire (with some suggesting as little as one in ten).[32] While this theory is possible, it is not very probable given the enormous amount of literary output among Christians from the beginning. It would be odd if the volume of ancient manuscripts we possess were copied solely by, and intended exclusively for, church leaders. In fact, the New Testament itself implies an expected literacy among average believers.

For example, Paul wrote to the newly formed church in Thessalonica *before* there were any extant NT writings (with the possible exceptions of James and Galatians) and well before the canonization of the NT. In his first epistle to the Thessalonian church, Paul said, "I put you under oath before the Lord to *have this letter read to all the brothers*" (1 Thess. 5:27, emphasis added). These earliest of believers were to *read* the letter to every Christian at Thessalonica. But who are the plural "you" whom Paul is charging? Did Paul have in mind specific *leaders* of the church (as in the above theory)? I don't think he did as the closest antecedent is the plural vocative "brothers" (*adelphoi*) in v. 23, a Pauline word for general "believers" or "Christians" (hence *all the brothers* as the indirect object in v. 27). Surely this group or

---

30. For more see The Center for the Study of New Testament Manuscripts at https://www.csntm.org.

31. For example, Robert W. Yarbrough, "The Centrality of the Gospel in Romans: The Importance of Getting It . . . and Getting it Right," in *Paul's Letter to the Romans: Theological Essays*, eds., Douglas J. Moo, Eckhard J. Schnabel, Thomas R. Schreiner, and Frank Thielman (Peabody: Hendrickson Academic, 2023), 9–11.

32. See Robert W. Yarbrough, "The Centrality of the Gospel in Romans," 9–11. For support, Yarbrough relies on Justo L. Gonzalez, *The Bible in the Early Church* (Grand Rapids: Eerdmans, 2022), 60–61.

"brothers" would include everyone in the church at Thessalonica and not merely their overseers as addressed at the letter's outset: "To the church of the Thessalonians in God the Father and the Lord Jesus Christ" (1:1).[33]

In fact, a strong clue that Paul meant for everyone in the church to have access to his letter, thereby implying an assumption of literacy among them, is found several verses earlier in the same chapter. There, the apostle addresses the same "brothers" (inclusive of all in the church) but makes a distinction among them with a subdivision of their leaders: "We ask you, brothers [*adelphoi*], to respect *those who labor among you and are over you in the Lord and admonish you,* and to esteem *them* very highly in love because of *their work.* Be at peace among yourselves" (5:12–13, emphasis added). Nothing in these verses suggests that only the leaders could read, but rather that there is a certain group of leaders who labored / worked hard among them. It is the "brothers," ordinary believers along with their leaders, who were expected to be literate and copy Paul's letters.

The same is implied in Paul's letter to Colossae: "And when this letter has been *read* among you, have it also *read* in the church of the Laodiceans; and see that you also *read* the letter from Laodicea" (Col 4:16, emphasis added). As with Thessalonians earlier, Paul does not distinguish an audience of literate leaders in Colossians. Instead, the letter is addressed to "the saints and faithful brothers," which comprised one group—Christians (1:1). It is this group who is to read and copy the apostle's correspondence, which assumes a reasonable rate of literacy among them. Paul expected the same of the Ephesian letter which manuscript evidence shows was read and circulated among other churches. He also implies a developed literacy among individuals to whom he wrote. Timothy

---

33. Furthermore, the leader-only theory would require the church at Thessalonica to have a formalized leadership structure with elders and deacons, which was not disclosed until Paul's latter works (1 Tim. 3; Titus 1). However, his first missionary journey did include appointing elders in churches (Acts 14:23).

was "well acquainted with the sacred writings from childhood," most likely a reference to the Old Testament, which Paul said, "are able to make you wise for salvation through faith in Christ Jesus" (2 Tim. 3:15). Clearly, Timothy could read divine literature, as well as those in his household who taught him. Such literacy was an expectation of God's people, going back to the days of Moses. This makes sense since salvation was and is obtained through the *written text.*

Canonical Literacy Expectations

The biblical canon itself evinces key portions that either command or heavily imply the necessity of reading its literature—from the Law to the Writings, from the Prophets to the last book of the New Testament.

The Pentateuch (Genesis–Deuteronomy) ends with Moses prescribing both blessings and warnings for Israel, depending on whether they read and obeyed or discarded this portion of Scripture. A future restoration for Israel free of oppression and persecution hinged on them "Obeying the voice of the LORD your God, to keep his commandments and his statutes that are *written in this Book of the Law*" (Deut. 30:10, emphasis added). Yet, for any Israelite who chooses to serve the false gods of gentile nations, "The LORD will single him out from all the tribes of Israel for calamity, in accordance with all the curses of the covenant *written in this Book of the Law*" (29:21, emphasis added). To fail to read and to heed the words of the Law was to end in disaster while to read and obey them was to lead to life. This was all predicated on the idea of actually reading and obeying the words of Moses. Indeed, he earlier warned against adding or taking away from "the word" (4:2)—a promise repeated in the Writings (Prov 30:6) as well as the Book of Revelation (Rev 22:18–19). In between these books, various Prophets call attention to the necessity of reading and understanding their portions.

Joshua identified God's Word as "this *Book* of the Law," which believers were to "meditate on day and night." Clearly, Joshua expected a level of literacy of the written texts, "so that you may be careful to do according to all that is *written* in it" (Josh 1:8, emphasis added). The Psalter opens up by describing the blessed man as one who "delights in the Law of the Lord," on which "he meditates day and night" (Ps. 1:2). The notion of reading, reflecting, and writing continues throughout the Hebrew Bible, implying an expectation of literacy among God's people. For instance, the prophet Habakkuk was told to "*write* the vision; make it plain on tablets, so he may run who *reads* it" (Hab. 2:2). The final book of the OT closes with the injunction to remember God's earlier revelation that Moses wrote, "the statutes and rules that God commanded" for all Israel" (Mal. 4:4). Michael Shepherd observed, "At every major juncture in the composition of the Hebrew Bible (Moses–Prophets, Prophets–Pss, Dan–Chrn) the message is the same: read Scripture to find revelation of the future work of God in Christ."[34]

In addition to the Pauline references discussed earlier, the New Testament is just as vocal in its expectation for believers to read. At the end of Luke's Gospel, Jesus did not reveal his post-resurrected self by a sensational miracle, which would have been more than enough demonstration to the two disciples on the road to Emmaus. Rather, "And beginning with Moses and all the Prophets, he interpreted to them in all the Scriptures the things concerning himself" (Luke 24:27). There is little doubt that Jesus expected the two men had actually *read* their Old Testaments for he calls them "foolish ones," pointing out that they were "slow of heart to believe all that the prophets have spoken!" (v. 25). As they themselves confirmed to each other, "Did not our hearts burn within us while he talked to us on the road, while he opened to us the Scriptures?" (v. 32).

Finally, the biblical canon closes with promises of blessings for those who *read* and *heed* the Book of Revelation. On one end John writes, "Blessed is the one who reads the words of this prophecy" (Rev. 1:3; cf. Jesus's similar words at 22:7 that adds "keeps" and "book"). On the other end, John closes out the canon with

---

34. Michael B. Shepherd, *Textual World of the Bible*, SBL, 156 (New York: Peter Lang, 2013), 90.

warnings about the "words" of the prophecy, promising curses for anyone who "adds to them," or "takes away from them, which are described in this book" (22:18–19). Revelation's promises for those who read and dismiss its prophecy connect to each of the other biblical injunctions of reading and heeding Scripture. The book's placement at the end of the canon suggests its promises extend to *all* of the Bible. Thus, the entire canon anticipates an audience of readers further than the immediate recipients of each biblical writing.

Canon Consciousness

The idea of a "canon consciousness" was mentioned a few times above as a way to imply the earliest Christians' ability to read and write. This deserves more attention. The basic idea is that the formation of the canon itself demanded a conscious recognition of divinely inspired literature as compared and contrasted with other writings that were known, read, and even respected. At minimum, the process required the skill of critical thinking and discernment, itself likely reliant upon an advanced level of education. Scholars offer compelling arguments for a canon-consciousness, demanding a high level of literacy from as early as the first century.

Ched Spellman argues that the earliest Christians recognized the special normative aspect of prophetic and apostolic writings and were conscious of their internal authoritative, divine nature.[35] In fact, as Paul's reference to previously known "sacred writings" (2 Tim. 3:15), Peter's identification of Paul's letters as "Scripture" (2 Pet. 3:16), and Paul's quotation of Luke's Gospel as authoritative (1 Tim. 5:18) demonstrate the biblical authors themselves were conscious of texts already recognized as stable and authoritative among the believing community. Abner Chou refers to the prophets and apostles having an "authorial logic,"

---

35. Ched Spellman, *Toward a Canon-Conscious Reading of the Bible: Exploring the History and Hermeneutics of the Canon*, NTM 34 (Sheffield: Sheffield Phoenix Press, 2020).

whereby they consciously formed a web of divinely inspired texts, each biblical writer continuing their part for the next biblical writer to advance further.[36] That most of the biblical writers were not trained priests, rabbis, or professional scribes, but more often farmers, fishermen, and other non-academic trades, enforces the value ancient average Jews and Christians placed on the ability to read texts. This emphasizes a simple yet profound point: the biblical *authors* were also careful *readers*.[37]

Such a phenomenon demands a view toward literacy that non-Christian cultures simply did not have. Larry Hurtado confirms as much when commenting on the extant manuscripts available. He observes that of the hundreds of portions, fragments, and full manuscripts discovered that date to the first several centuries of the church, "enough survives to tell us that collectively early Christians produced, copied, and read a noteworthy range of writings."[38] He adds, "With all due allowance for the limitations in the likely extent of literacy in this period, the impression given is that early Christianity represented a religious movement in which texts played a large role."[39]

Though all scholars recognize that much of the ancient world was illiterate, many also recognize that the Judeo-Christian heritage was itself set apart due to its inherent nature of being a religion centered on written texts. "While Christians were certainly not the only members of ancient society who made significant use of literature," contends Benjamin Laird, "their affinity for written texts was one of their defining characteristics."[40] In polytheistic religions contemporary with ancient Christianity, there existed a

---

36. Abner Chou, *The Hermeneutics of the Biblical Writers: Learning to Interpret Scripture from the Prophets and Apostles* (Grand Rapids: Kregel Academic, 2018), 13–45.

37. Ched Spellman, *Toward a Canon-Conscious Reading of the Bible*, 52.

38. Larry W. Hurtado, *The Earliest Christian Artifacts: Manuscripts and Christian Origins* (Grand Rapids: Eerdmans, 2006), 4.

39. Ibid., 24.

40. Benjamin P. Laird, *Creating the Canon: Composition, Controversy, and the Authority of the New Testament* (Downers Grove: IVP Academic, 2023), 13.

number of written accounts that describe the origin and exploits of various deities or address one aspect or another of ancient worship. For the most part, however, written texts appear to have played a less foundational role in Greco-Roman religion than in Jewish and Christian circles. According to Larry Hurtado: "Reading, writing, copying, and dissemination of texts had a major place—indeed, a prominence—in early Christianity, that except for ancient Jewish circles, was unusual for religious groups of the Roman era."[41]

It goes without saying that the biblical authors expected their contents to be read, which history proves is precisely what happened. At multiple pivots in the Bible's storyline there is clear expectation to read its contents. The significance extends to today's evangelical. "The ideal reader of the Christian canon is one who devotes himself to diligent reading and re-reading of these biblical 'books.' In this sense, the ideal reader of the canon is one who consistently engages its contents."[42] Quite simply, the Judeo-Christian legacy is one of reading and writing. Evangelicals are, and should be, a biblically and theologically literate people.

The Evangelical Contribution to Education

Evangelicalism's contribution to education is often overlooked. But, as Brandon Crawford points out, "The Church has always been at the forefront of education as well."[43] It's hard to imagine today that the world's most historic and prestigious schools were founded by evangelicals in both the UK and the US, including Wycliffe Hall at Oxford and the schools of divinity at Cambridge, Edinburgh, and so on. In America, Harvard, Yale, and Dartmouth were established by Congregationalists, Princeton by Presbyterians, and Brown by Baptists (all evangelical traditions).

---

41. Larry W. Hurtado, *Destroyer of the Gods: Early Christian Distinctiveness in the Roman World* (Waco: Baylor University Press, 2016), 105–6.

42. Spellman, *Toward a Canon-Conscious Reading of the Bible*, 215.

43. Brandon James Crawford, *Let Men Be Free: A Christian Vision for Ordered Liberty* (Douglasville: G3 Press, 2024), 139.

"Between 1815 and 1848, the number of colleges and universities in America jumped from 33 to 113," reports historian Thomas Kidd.[44] To be sure, not all of these institutions were evangelical. But most were, as even independent divinity schools and seminaries began to pop up to further educate recent graduates from universities like Oberlin College (1833) and Baylor University (1845). America's first independent evangelical seminary, Andover Seminary, was established in 1807 to serve as a "counterweight" of traditional Protestant theology to the unitarian controversy embroiling Harvard College (now University). Formed by Presbyterians and founded by Archibald Alexander in 1812, Princeton Theological Seminary in New Jersey became an evangelical heavyweight and early bastion for conservative evangelical theology, before its liberal drift in the early twentieth century. In the mid to late nineteenth and early twentieth centuries, conservative evangelical Protestants (considered today as "fundamentalists") continued to establish Bible colleges and institutes, academies, and seminaries as alternatives to secular institutions becoming increasingly friendly to evolutionary theories and other ideas contrary to a consistent reading of Scripture. "Evangelicals had maintained a network of institutions of higher learning for decades," explains Kidd. These included, "Wheaton College (1860) in Chicago and Gordon College (1889) in Massachusetts. Fundamentalists had also created schools such as Bob Jones University (1927)."[45]

The high premium that historic evangelicalism placed on education shouldn't be too much of a surprise given what the Bible teaches about man's place in the world as he reflects his Creator. He is to engage in critical and reflective thinking, and to love God with all of his "heart, soul, and *mind*" (Matt. 22:37, emphasis added). It just so happens that evangelicals who uphold

---

44. Thomas S. Kidd, *America's Religious History: Faith, Politics, and the Shaping of a Nation* (Grand Rapids: Zondervan, Academic, 2019), 107.

45. Ibid., 265.

the Scriptures as their supreme authority also become educated in geography, history, science, art, and music as well. "It is no coincidence that the Scientific Revolution occurred in the lands dominated by Christianity," observed Crawford, "for the Christian faith offers the only worldview fully compatible with the scientific enterprise."[46] The value evangelicals historically place on education stems from the value they place on the Bible and its Judeo-Christian worldview. "Biblical Christianity teaches that the universe is knowable. It also teaches that God created the universe in an orderly way, so that truths learned in a laboratory can be generalized to the material world universally."[47]

Indeed, historians find it difficult to ignore the value that evangelicalism has historically placed on issues of education (both secular and theological). There were, of course, frontier preachers in early American evangelicalism who did not deem formal theological training necessary to their circuit ministries.[48] Still, as Thomas Kidd notes, "Besides the global cause of missions, evangelical Christians also fostered an enormous campaign for religious literacy, education and moral reform."[49]

Estimates of up to six hundred magazines and other literature were produced by evangelicals between 1790 and 1830. With a commitment that reflected being "people of the Book," The American Bible Society or ABS (a historically evangelical organization founded in 1816) seized upon technological printing advances and produced more than one million copies of the Scriptures between a two-year period alone in 1829–1831.[50] "In 1839," relays historian Elesha Coffman, "the ABS made it a priority to place Scripture not only in every American household

---

46. Brandon James Crawford, *Let Men Be Free*, 140.
47. Ibid.
48. See the example of "Methodist exhorter" Peter Cartwright in Elesha J. Coffman, *Turning Points in American Church History: How Pivotal Events Shaped a Nation and a Faith* (Grand Rapids: Baker Academic, 2004), 134–36.
49. Thomas S. Kidd, *America's Religious History*, 106.
50. Ibid.

but in every American classroom."[51] By 1860, they were printing more than a million King James Version Bibles a year (without note or comment).[52]

The flood of Bibles being printed and disseminated along with evangelical literature inevitably resulted in a home-grown education among Americans. Such can be observed in standard printed communication as even "Nineteenth century letters attest to a very high level of biblical literacy."[53] The connection between producing Bibles and theological literature—which resulted in Christians becoming educated—has always made the most sense within the evangelical tradition. The sequence is simple. Evangelicals place a high premium on reading Scripture, which yields a desire to know more about the world described in Scripture, naturally resulting in the desire to read, study, and learn as a way of life. As argued in this chapter, the vintage faith should not retreat from participating in formal theological training. Instead, in keeping with its historic legacy, authentic evangelicalism contributes to—and even reforms—education as it encourages continual growth in one's biblical-theological knowledge. As Michael Shepherd sums up:

> Churches must not put limits on the education of its members. Pastors must be equipped and supported as experts in the teaching of the Bible in its original languages, and church leaders must make available every kind of excellent and high-quality resource to the membership for the people to grow as much as they can. The result will be a new breed of Christian churches— churches shaped not by tradition alone or by the changing trends of culture but by the study of Scripture itself.[54]

---

51. Elesha J. Coffman, *Turning Points in American Church History*, 138.

52. See Paul C. Gutjahr, *An American Bible: A History of the Good Book in the United States, 1777–1880* (Stanford: Stanford University Press, 1999), 35.

53. Elesha J. Coffman, *Turning Points in American Church History*, 140.

54. Michael B. Shepherd, *An Introduction to the Making and Meaning of the Bible* (Grand Rapids: Eerdmans, 2024), 170.

Evangelical Protestants have had the most sizable impact on education in the West. A major result of the Reformation—from which the evangelical movement was birthed—was the import put on the act of learning. Colleges, universities, and seminaries drew upon the Reformation principle *semper reformanda* (always reforming), which became a driving influence for evangelicals *always to educate and re-educate* in accord with their developing knowledge of Scripture.[55] As such, participating in theological education is fundamental for the vintage faith.

EXCURSUS
Balancing Scholarship in the Church and the Academy

In April 2024, the seminary where I teach full time hosted the regional Far West Evangelical Theological Society meeting. Doing so was a great honor, as this was the first time in the history of the school that ETS was gathered on the campus of Southern California Seminary for the annual conference. Though a "regional" gathering (in this case, a massive territory spanning from Colorado to Hawaii), scholars as far as Scotland and Australia flew in to read papers and enjoy the day's academic fellowship.

Regional ETS meetings are excellent opportunities for seminary students, pastors, and scholars who are society members to present their research to a room of peers and non-peers. This includes opening themselves up afterward for critique and encouragement—during what feels like a ten hour police interrogation (which in reality is only ten minutes of Q&A). Submitting a paper proposal and presenting one's academic work requires a love for learning, scholarship, as well as serious humility. Not all papers are accepted, which comes with its own sense of self-deflation for its victims (and it happens to us all!).

---

55. Owen Strachan, *Awakening the Evangelical Mind: An Intellectual History of the Neo-Evangelical Movement* (Grand Rapids: Zondervan, 2015), 174–76, offers a helpful defense of the legacy of higher education in evangelicalism and its need to continue.

If a paper is accepted, it's virtually guaranteed to get critiqued by other academics in the room while the presenter stands there doing their best not to look mortified. It truly is a vulnerable experience. But it is also a wonderful accountability process that helps refine a budding scholar's ideas as well as provide a fellowship for evangelical academics who often feel alone with their gift-set not always appreciated by those outside of academia. For those who sense a divine call to bless Christ's church through academic writing, teaching, and scholarship, there is no better place to test their ideas and cultivate that calling then at ETS meetings. I highly recommend becoming a member, if you're not already.

Since I served as Vice President of the region at the time SCS hosted, it was up to me to choose the conference theme and keynote speaker, as well as invite publishers, sponsors, etc. The theme I chose for that year was the title of this excurses—*Balancing Scholarship in the Church and the Academy.* The idea reflected my own passion of bridging the gap between pastor and scholar. I even co-host a podcast with that name, The Pastor Scholar Podcast: Bridging the Gap.[56]

As I see it, local churches need more exegetically and theologically astute pastors who have the skills to interact and engage with scholarly material. This requires a respect for learning at the highest levels along with a commitment to stay up on the ebb and flow of scholarly trends. A pastor who does this encourages their congregations not to fear the academy, but to see it as a supplemental resource for the church. Moreover, it's usually (though not always) in the "ivory towers" of the academy where some of the more troubling ideas emerge, that in time trickle their way down to unsuspecting congregants. Thus, a pastor has a *duty* to be informed of scholarship, if anything, to nip concerning trends in the bud *before* they get published in a commentary or

---

56. The podcast is part of a network of conversative evangelical / biblical-fundamentalist content creators called Foundations Media, that can be accessed at https://foundationsmedia.org/.

in a more accessible popular-level book, or even as the topics of an influential podcast.

At the same time, I believe the academy needs more shepherd-hearted professors and scholars. Too often, the competition of tenure, the pressures of publishing, and the weariness of grading papers turns once-enlivened professors into overwhelmed curmudgeons who forgot their sense of calling. They need to be reminded that students are not enemies (well … most aren't). They are sheep from various cultures sent by the Chief-Shepherd himself that are in need of equipping in how to love and minister biblically based on the inerrant Word of God in their own contexts.[57] This means that even if I have a student for only a three-hour lecture once a week, I am committed to the idea that, for those three hours, I am to equip them not only intellectually, but also *pastorally* as far as I'm able. This includes praying with students, asking them (and actually caring) about their marriages, jobs, future plans, as well as making sure I'm accessible outside of office hours and classroom times.[58] I have found that this practice actually helps embolden my own sense of calling. It's from the *pastor* side of the pastor-scholar idea that reorients my confidence in the Lord's direction on my life, especially when that dreaded

---

57. I apologize. The mission statement of SCS is so drilled into my head and heart from faculty meetings, I usually can't go a day without repeating some part of it.

58. One habit I developed early in my teaching career was to publish my cell number on all of my course syllabi, and constantly point students to it. I know for some professors, that is a horrid practice that only invites more headaches on your personal time (my wife sometimes adopts this position!). But after nine years of doing so—with every class I teach—I have had very few students take advantage of such access in a negative way (in fact, I can't think of any as I write this, though one or two probably have), and yet multiple occasions where I was able to walk a student off a ledge (so to speak) who had a genuine problem. In such cases, I am incredibly thankful for having the opportunity to minister God's grace to a student outside the classroom, and grateful that the student trusts me enough to seek counsel on a sensitive matter—all of which began with making my cell public to them.

"imposter-syndrome" creeps up—the infamous nemesis of every teacher and scholar.

What follows below are the remarks I gave that opened the regional ETS meeting that year. I didn't originally intend to include this portion in the book. But as my wheels were spinning while writing chapter five on evangelicals participating in theological education, I found myself going back to what I said that day to a room of over a hundred fellow professors, scholars, pastors, and college administrators. They are presented below just as I read them live.

"What indeed has Athens to do with Jerusalem? What concord is there between the Academy and the Church?" So said Tertullian around the year 200 in chapter seven of his *Prescription against Heretics*. His question has since become a (in)famous dictum. If anyone knows any statement by heart from the third-century apologist, it is usually that one, which seems to place all academic thought on one pole, and the Christian faith on the opposite pole. It is not uncommon, therefore, for many Christians to pose in their minds an impassible gulf, a chasm where the two—that is, the Church and the Academy—should never meet. Unfortunately, even in circles within evangelicalism, there remains a divide to this day; an either *or* option. Either, you go to church and learn theology from your pastor and hold to a stripped-down version of *sola Scriptura*, which in reality becomes *solo Scriptura* (or nuda Scriptura). Or, you join the rest of the liberals and apostates and get a Master's degree or PhD from some accredited seminary or university and eventually compromise all of your Christian values.

But is this not guilty of a disjunctive fallacy? How legitimate is this either / or option? In his helpful book *The Outrageous Idea of Christian Scholarship*, historian George Marsden framed the question this way: "Are we not serving two masters if we attempt to be faithful to our faith community and try also to gain a hearing among a wider academic audience?" As he saw it, the answer *can* be yes if a Christian is attempting to be a scholar at the expense of their Christian principles. But the answer *should* be "no" as Marsden argued, "Broadly understood, faith *in something or other* informs *all* scholarship."

For too long, the divide between the Church and Academy has forced Christians into thinking that the two are mutually exclusive. Yet, doing so, ignores thousands of years of Church history that demonstrates the brilliance, precision, and diligence of academic thought by Christian thinkers—even pastors.

There once was a time when the pastor was the smartest man in the village. He was trusted by the people because they knew he committed himself to learning the languages of Scripture, to reading voices of the past, and to have developed rigorous research methods that tracked down primary sources. He drew out implications that were insightful, encouraging, and valuable in the culture in which that pastor lived and ministered. And, chances were, that pastor had some sort of formal theological training. He had a dedicated space of academic mentorship where he developed in skills of critical thinking and joined it to his growing biblical literacy—resulting in the confidence of preaching the gospel of Christ, in season and out of season, to engage his people to live and minister biblically, based on the inerrant Word of God.

In a series of lectures given at Caxton Hall in Westminster, London in 1932 (later published as the book *The Importance of Christian Scholarship*), J. Gresham Machen contended, "If knowledge is necessary to preaching, it does seem probable that the fuller the knowledge is, the better the preacher will be able to do his work. Underlying preaching, in other words, is Christian scholarship." Similarly, the great twentieth-century Greek Grammarian A. T. Robertson was convinced that seminary education and Christian scholarship made for better preachers of the gospel. Robertson delivered his inaugural address at Southern Seminary on October 3, 1890, calling it, "Preaching and Scholarship." In it, he argued to incoming students: "If theological education will increase your power for Christ, is it not your duty to gain that added power? . . . Never say you are losing time by going to school. You are saving time, buying it up for the future and storing it away. Time used in storing power is not lost."

However, we do have an expression in our tradition that speaks to the theologian in his or her "ivory tower." That is to say, there are, unfortunately, Christian academics who have lost all relevancy to the local church. These may be scholars who write *solely* for other scholars. Perhaps they're professors in a university or seminary trying to secure that next annual contract under the grueling mantra "publish or perish." The competition that such a mindset produces among colleagues in seminary inevitably forces them to isolate from one another as well as from the local church. It becomes too easy to do so with the excuse of "having to do research." They then retreat to their studies, neglecting their families and the very Christians they should be equipping with their work. Only academic monographs or peer-reviewed articles in the most prestigious journals become what matter. "Let the pastor produce material for the church member, while us scholars are about the more important task of gaining tenure by a long list of publications that no one will ever read." That is, unless forced to read by another academic professor who assigns the $250 monograph that no student can afford anyway! How much scholarship has been hijacked by the so-called elite, prestigious venues with subscriptions that only top research university libraries can afford.

Going back to Tertullian, is this what he had in mind when he asked, What does Athens have do with Jerusalem? Turns out the answer is no. He based his statement on Colossians 2:8 where the apostle Paul says, "See to it that no one takes you captive by philosophy and empty deceit, according to human tradition, according to the elemental spirits of the world, and not according to Christ." The "Academy" that Tertullian condemned was the same Academy that Paul condemned—*empty and baseless human philosophy*; *the elemental spirits of this world*. In Tertullian's day, these were gnostic heresies that developed as off-shoots of Platonism. They included the heresies of Valentinus and Maricon, the philosophy of the Epicureans who denied the immortality of the soul. They included the heresies of Stoicism that based its ethics on a universal nature called Fate infallibly regulating the course of events.

It was not *Christian* education that Tertullian had a problem with. It was the fusing of worthless pagan ideas with Christian theology that he criticized. It is in that sense that Jerusalem and Athens *are* to remain separate and distinct. I will stop there with Tertullian since we indeed have a paper this afternoon literally entitled, "Has Jerusalem got Anything to do with Athens? In Defense of Tertullian's Famous Dictum."

As I thought about what the theme should be for our Far West meeting this year, I couldn't shake the idea of how important the role of "pastor-scholar" or "scholar-pastor" is—the advancement of knowledge at a premier level that serves *both* the Christian scholar as well as the average church member. But this raises questions:

Is it even possible to bridge that gap in a way that's meaningful? Or should a pastor be judged only by his ability to sermonize and a scholar for his or her ability to contribute something new to the field? Should a pastor write only devotional material aimed at a person in the pew, and the scholar more technical pieces? Or can one actually do both—preach to the glory of God as well advance knowledge in the world of academia? Is it reasonable to expect an academic who publishes technical commentaries, peer-reviewed articles, and magisterial theological textbooks and *also* have the bandwidth to be immersed in the adventures of messy church life—to preach expository sermons, counsel struggling church members, baptize new converts, officiate weddings and funerals, and so on? These are the questions that developed into the theme for this year's Far West meeting of the Evangelical Theological Society—*Balancing Scholarship in the Church and Academy*."

I can say that with the forty-eight papers presented that day—along with a wonderfully self-reflective keynote session by Dr. Thomas Schreiner on his years as a scholar-pastor and a stirring presidential address on Francis Schaeffer given by Dr. Justin McClendon—that day's events *did* fulfil the goal of balancing the church and academy.[59] May that gap continue to be bridged, as Christ continues to fill his church with both pastors and scholars.

---

59. As I write this chapter, I am the current president of ETS Far West and plan to present on the late scholar-pastor C. E. B. Cranfield for my address at the upcoming regional held in Spring 2025 at Talbot Theological Seminary at Biola University.

CHAPTER 6

Consistent Local Church Fellowship

The Crucial X-Factor

This book raised an important question in chapter one. If classic evangelicalism meant believing in the virgin birth, the reality of miracles, Christ's vicarious atonement, his second coming, and so forth, then why is there such confusion today over what makes up the vintage faith? Moreover, almost without fail, studies on evangelicalism are sure to insert discussions on three of the fundamentals covered so far (Scripture, Jesus, evangelism). Taken together, these historic positions should serve as the measure for identifying authentic evangelicalism. But if all agree that such ideas comprise the basics, why the contemporary crises over evangelical identity? Why the need for this book?

In earlier chapters I used the word "evan-jello-calism" as a way to describe the elasticity of modern evangelicalism. Everything under the sun today is being labeled "evangelical," without concern for the key, historic doctrines above. I also argued that, although these core beliefs are essential for evangelical identity, they don't go far enough. Something tangible has proven necessary to qualify someone as truly evangelical, which is this: *behavior*. In other words, authentic evangelicalism—what I've been calling a vintage faith—must be measured by *evangelical belief resulting in evangelical behavior.* If one really does believe in the absolute supremacy of Scripture, the exclusivity of Jesus for salvation, and the need to evangelize, then it follows that they will want to increase in their biblical-theological knowledge and do so among God's people. This last part is key. Maintaining consistent fellowship in local church settings is a clear fundamental for genuine evangelicalism. It is a direct application of believing the Scriptures are truly authoritative. Quite simply, without living out an evangelical belief in Scripture *among other evangelicals,* there is no true evangelicalism.

Some might consider my argument for the necessity of church fellowship (and theological education) peripheral to evangelicalism rather than fundamental. But I say that overlooking the significance of local church fellowship is a major cause for the erosion today. In other words, it is due to neglecting the importance of church life that has resulted in today's evan-jello-calism. Said positively, maintaining local church fellowship is *essential* for evangelical identity. It provides encouragement and accountability on a level that supersedes those offered by mega-conferences, politics, or Christian entertainment branded as "evangelical."

What about evangelism and missions work—do these not qualify as "behaviors" as well? As I laid out in chapter three, believing in the necessity of evangelism should not remain just a belief. It should result in action as well, such as evangelizing the lost. But it is particularly these last two chapters—participation in theological education and maintaining church fellowship— that distinguishes this book apart from others on the topic. And of those two, it is church fellowship that is most important for genuine evangelical identity. In fact, I maintain it's the X-factor in the discussion, the crucial variable in my metric, that ultimately has the most significant impact on genuine evangelicalism. As such, consistent local church fellowship serves as the fifth and final fundamental marker necessary for recovering a vintage faith.

The Power of Corporate Fellowship

Recent statistics concerning the drop in biblical literacy were quoted earlier in the book. It's interesting that these numbers coincide with the colossal drop of church membership, especially in the United States. The polls bear out that if a believer is not joined to a church, especially one that is devoted to training their people in the Scriptures, that person is going to have a weak biblical worldview. An authentic evangelical church fellowship that I have in mind consists of being committed to a local body of believers that is governed by a plurality of elders who are passionate about, and skilled in, the steady exposition of God's Word.

Additionally, an evangelical local church fellowship practices a set of ordinances commanded in the New Testament (e.g., baptism and communion), and every member is equipped, challenged, encouraged, discipled, and disciplined according to the truths of Scripture.[1] Accountability is embedded in such a fellowship, as each member ministers to one another as well as to those outside their congregation. Because of this some refer to the New Testament's structure for churches as "brilliantly conceived," even functioning as a "surrogate family."[2] The driving conviction of it all goes back to the first fundamental of this book, a high view of the authority of Scripture.

Mentioned in chapter two was the late evangelical scholar, Wilber Smith. In the mid-twentieth century, Smith was one of the original professors at Fuller Theological Seminary who became first faculty member to depart the school in the early 1960s over their doctrinal drift. The slide away from the institution's original conservative evangelical vision into progressive ideas began by newer faculty denying the inerrancy of Scripture.[3] Smith was

---

1. Though I believe official membership is a healthy practice for local churches, I do not believe it is required for a church to qualify as "evangelical." Any use of "member" throughout the chapter is for convenience.

2. Joseph H. Hellerman, *Embracing Shared Ministry: Power and Status in the Early Church and Why It Matters Today* (Grand Rapids: Kregel Ministry, 2013), 191.

3. George M. Marsden, *Reforming Fundamentalism: Fuller Seminary and the New Evangelicalism* (Grand Rapids: Eerdmans, 1987), 220–23.

convinced of the need for evangelical churches to hold to the highest view of the Bible and not be influenced by wavering academic institutions. Before his departure from Fuller over his conviction of biblical inerrancy, he pointed out the urgent need for the church to return to an unwavering stance on God's Word. He said:

> In this battle of increasing intensity, in an hour when the waves of unbelief are striking at, and have been broken through many of the doors of our churches, and have already overwhelmed too many of the doors of our churches, and have already overwhelmed too many of our more important educational institutions, the Church needs, for its own life, for the protection of its young, for power in meeting attacks upon her beliefs, for vigor and strength, for courage and hope, for power in winning souls, the Church needs to return to the Word of God.[4]

Smith connected every foible of the evangelicalism in his day to a weak view of the Bible. He also saw the life of the worldwide body of Christ being dependent on the firmest of bibliologies. Wavering in the slightest bit on the inspired, inerrant, authoritative Word of God, opens churches up to demonic and worldly attack. Christians need other Christians. Christ redeemed "a people for his own possession" (Titus 2:14), not any one individual. There is divine power in evangelical fellowships that are locked in arms submitting to Scripture in obedience to Christ. Indeed, the local church is one of the greatest blessings for believers, and one of the strongest weapons against those hostile toward believers.

Often overlooked is the fact that only five of the twenty-seven books of the New Testament are addressed to individuals.[5] All but four of Paul's thirteen letters were written to *local churches*. And

---

4. Wilbur M. Smith, *Therefore Stand: A Plea for a Vigorous Apologetic in this Critical Hour of the Christian Faith* (Boston: W. A. Wilde Co., 1950), 487.

5. The five individual letters are 1 and 2 Timothy, Titus, Philemon, and 3 John. I interpret "the elect lady and her children" in 2 John 1:1 as a metaphor for a particular local church.

the remaining New Testament writings either imply corporate readership or directly mention churches within its contents. For example, James addressed his letter to a corporate audience (James 1:1), and Revelation contains messages directed straight at seven local churches (Rev. 2–3). Despite the New Testament emphasis on the local church, a 2022 *The State of Theology* survey conducted by Ligonier Ministries found that 56 per cent of American adults and 26 per cent of American evangelicals *disagree* with the statement: "Every Christian has an obligation to join a local church." These numbers, while sad, are not shocking. "The entrenched cultural value of individualism makes it unsurprising that most Americans deem church membership as optional for Christians."[6]

Contrary to modern evangelical tendencies of prioritizing individual Christian experience, the preponderance of biblical emphasis is on corporate assembly, corporate belief, and corporate behavior. When Paul said he can "do all things through Christ," he said it to the *church* at Phillippi and wanted them to learn of the principle *together* (Phil. 4:13; 1:1). When he gave instructions for taking communion, it was to occur, "when you assemble *together as a church*" (1 Cor. 11:18, emphasis added). This is contrary to modern evangelicals who prefer to take the Lord's supper alone, online, or with only their immediate family.[7] Unfortunately, in today's world, "virtual" gatherings have become a norm.

But the New Testament knows nothing of the sort. Physical fellowship is the expected norm of biblical Christianity. If anything, it takes the focus off oneself and places it on others for whom Christ died. This breeds authentic humility (see Phil. 2:3). Bringing out the importance of Christian humility dependent on Christian fellowship, evangelical author Joel Muddamalle makes

---

6. See *The State of Theology* at, https://thestateoftheology.com/.

7. According to one recent study, approximately one-third of American practicing Christians worship exclusively online. See Jim Davis and Michael Graham with Ryan P. Burge, *The Great Dechurching: Who's Leaving, Why Are They Going, and What Will It Take to Bring Them Back?* (Grand Rapids: Zondervan, 2023), 171.

a more-than-practical point: "Humility is meant to be lived out in community. When we rejoice, laugh, grieve, and process the hard and holy parts of life with others, we remind our hearts that life is about so much more than me, myself, and I. A daily commitment to building others up and considering what is good for them is good for our souls."[8] As it turns out, our souls *need* other souls as well, which requires meeting together for mutual encouragement. Therefore, gathering *physically* is an essential element of what makes up a true evangelical church, and maintaining physical corporate fellowship is essential for true evangelicalism.

The Christian Church as a Mystery

The word "church" (*ekklēsia*) appears 114 times in the New Testament. Though its most basic sense simply means *assembly* or *gathering*, its overwhelming usage in the New Testament identifies a gathering of those who worship God through Jesus Christ.[9]

While the word is prominent throughout the New Testament, Matthew is the only Gospel writer to use *ekklēsia* and likely give it an immediate Christian connotation.[10] In its sole Gospel appearance, it is Jesus who uses the term when predicting a special kind of assembly. Just after Peter confessed Jesus as the

---

8. Joel Muddamalle, *The Hidden Peace: Finding True Security, Strength, and Confidence through Humility* (Nashville: Thomas Nelson, 2024), 210.

9. Tremper Longman III and Mark L. Straus, eds., *The Baker Expository Dictionary of Biblical Words* (Grand Rapids: Baker, 2023), 151–52.

10. Though I think it is most probable that Matthew had in mind what would later be identified as the *Christian church*, I say "likely" in recognition that "kingdom" language envelopes both chapters and the possibility that for Matthew, "church/assembly" and "kingdom" are interchangeable terms. But it must be remembered Matthew wrote his Gospel several decades after the birth of the church recorded in Acts and influenced by the developments of the term up to the time of his writing that identified *ekklēsia* as the *Christian church* (not kingdom). Matthew's original readers were undoubtedly familiar with the distinct connotation of *Christian church* for *ekklēsia*.

Messiah and Son of God, Jesus announced that he will build his *ekklēsia* or "church" (Matt. 16:18).[11] The future tense-form and personal pronoun—"*I will* build *my* church" (*oikodomēsō mou tēn ekklēsian*)—gives strong indication that this assembly is something distinct from previous gatherings. This *ekklēsia* will not be an ordinary gathering prescribed in the Mosaic law; it will be personal and powerful. When Jesus attached the pronoun "my" to "church," he made a declaration that this future assembly is *his assembly*—a church that even the powers of hell will never be able to overcome! Once the Holy Spirit fell on an assembly of Jewish believers on the Day of Pentecost in Acts 2, the church, which was still future in Matthew 16, became present.

Eventually, as the rest of Acts and the Epistles play out, the church included Gentile believers alongside Jewish believers. Paul declared that Jews and Gentiles *together* comprising the same body of worshippers was a "mystery" (Eph. 3:6, 9; Col. 1:26–27). The use of *mystērion* ("mystery") does not suggest the idea of ascendent knowledge that always remains hidden. A biblical mystery was something previously unknown, perhaps foreshadowed in the Old Testament, that human reasoning *alone* could not solve. Divine revelation was required to make the mystery known. As one dictionary puts it, a biblical mystery is "God's ultimate intention with Scripture."[12] In the Ephesian and Colossian letters, Paul identifies a mystery that was previously unknown but was now made known: a living body of Jewish and Gentile believers

---

11. I don't want to minimize the importance of Peter himself in the founding of the church. But I do think his proclamation that "Jesus is the Christ the Son of the Living God" is the "rock" upon which Jesus is building his church (not Peter). There are multiple historical and theological reasons why I believe this, but one is also grammatical. The immediate switch from the masculine nominative Πέτρος ("Peter") to the dative feminine ᾗ πέτρᾳ ("this rock") shows a clear textual distinction between Peter and his confession, the latter being the closest antecedent to "the church," that Christ said he will build.

12. Tremper Longman III and Mark L. Straus, eds., *The Baker Expository Dictionary of Biblical Words*, 537.

bonded together in worship of Jesus Christ—the Christian church. Thus, the church was a new entity in the history of God's people, needing divine revelation to disclose its reality.

An additional distinction is worth noting. The fact that because the church is a *mystērion* makes it not only different from Israel but also different from the kingdom of God. This is because, like Israel, the idea of kingdom is one of the most prevalent and explicit themes of the Old and New Testaments; neither were mysteries that couldn't be solved.[13] In fact, the kingdom was something Jesus explicitly taught his disciples to pray *would come* (Matt. 6:10) and later assured them it will come according to the Father's timing (Acts 1:6–7; cf. Luke 19:11; 21:31). Distinct from the coming kingdom, Jesus is currently building his *church*, his worldwide body of believers, over which he serves as its "head" (not "king") (see Col. 1:18). God's own Son purchased the church through his life, death, and resurrection—making it infinitely special—and continues to gather this global community through the work of the Spirit.[14]

The mystery of the Christian church also relates to the baptizing, gifting, and permanent indwelling of the Holy Spirit. Rather than the Spirit being *among* or *with* God's people, he *baptizes* and *resides in* God's people—both Christians individually and the Christan church corporately (see 1 Cor. 3:16; 6:19; 12:13; cf. John 14:16–17). This makes the church different from Israel, the latter of which enjoyed only temporary and corporate manifestations of the Holy Spirit.[15] This glorious truth could never be invented by human thought. The church is an incredible mystery that Scripture had to reveal.

---

13. See Tremper Longman III and Mark L. Straus, eds., *The Baker Expository Dictionary of Biblical*, 455–57.

14. John D. Hannah, *Our Legacy: The History of Christian Doctrine* (Colorado Springs: NavPress, 2001), 257.

15. See James Merrill Hamilton, Jr., "He Is with You and He Will Be in You: The Spirit, the Believer, and the Glorification of Jesus" (Ph.D. diss., The Southern Baptist Theological Seminary, 2003), ch 2.

One True Church, Multiple Assemblies

Though the Christian church comprises the universal body of believers in Jesus, it is important to note that the Christ's global body is expressed *tangibly through the local church.* As one reference work put it: "The concept of the church applies to local churches, where individuals support and encourage one another and worship together regularly, and also to groups of churches within a city or region, as well as all churches around the world."[16]

This means that every local church (little "c") that is biblical in its doctrine and practice is a manifestation of the Church (big "C"). The Bible never presents the Christian church as an abstract ethereal concept. Rather, it is a physical gathering of Jesus-followers in local assemblies, worshipping God together through various means like giving, baptizing, discipling, praying, signing, preaching, learning, sharing and so forth governed by a formal structure of elders and deacons (see 1 Tim. 3:1–13; Titus 1:5–9). Each of these means are subsumed under the concept of "fellowship" (*koinonia*)— the closest of partnerships and mutual interests, which revolves around Christ.[17] A church, therefore, functions not like a nation or kingdom. Instead, it is a more akin to a *family* that sacrifices for one another and encourages one another and shares with one another, and is led by elders who are "big brothers" in the faith— all out of love for one another.[18] The church is a family affair; a true fellowship.

Love and Accountability Before the Watching World

In John's Gospel Jesus gave the disciples—who formed the nucleus of what would be the Christian church—a command of love. But this love command came with unexpected accountability: the world.

---

16. Tremper Longman III and Mark L. Straus, eds., *The Baker Expository Dictionary of Biblical Words*, 152.

17. BDAG, 552–53.

18. See J. R. Miller, *Elders Lead a Healthy Family: Shared Leadership for a Vibrant Church* (Eugene: Wipf & Stock, 2017), 97–100.

Jesus said, "A new commandment I give to you, that you love one another: just as I have loved you, you also are to love one another. *By this all people will know that you are my disciples, if you have love for one another*" (John 13:34–35, emphasis added). It was discussed in chapter three how enemies of Christ can identify his disciples by their boldness (Acts 4:13). In John's Gospel, it is by their love—*for one another*. The third-class condition "if" (*ean*) in the final clause indicates the most probable reality given the requirement being met. The stated requirement is mutual Christian love. Jesus told his core group that all people—even outsiders—will know they belong to him *by their love for one another*. It is an astonishing reality that Jesus gave the unbelieving world the right to judge his own people. And the one measure he trusts that everyone will be able to properly gauge is how Christians *love other Christians*. Later in the same context, Jesus revisits this idea when he prayed to the Father that the world may know that he was sent by him as measured by the disciples' mutual love and unity (17:21).

The act of Christians loving one another does serve an evangelistic purpose. Non-believers should be enticed to believe in Jesus because of the observable love his children express toward each other, which reflects his love for them. Such brotherly love is ultimately to be an expression of the love they have toward God, as John later wrote: "If anyone says, 'I love God,' and hates his brother, he is a liar; for he who does not love his brother whom he has seen cannot love God whom he has not seen" (1 John 4:20). The idea is that the love expressed between believers who are visible serves as a microcosm of the love that they have (or don't have) for the God they say they believe in.

But the genuine love between Christians is not merely for the benefit of the watching world. Christians showing genuine love for one another, like in church and ministry settings, also gives them confidence of their own salvation. In other words, when a believer has real love for other believers for whom Christ died, that love has the powerful ability to crush the annoying dread of doubting one's standing before the Lord. To this, John also wrote, "We know that we have passed out of death into life, *because we love the brothers.* Whoever does not love abides in death" (1 John 3:14). Mutual Christian love has a real causal effect, the "because" in the verse. Loving one another *causes* Christians to *know* they have transferred from death to life, from condemnation to salvation. Fleshing out what he called "the principle of the practice of the purity of the visible church," the ever-relevant late evangelical thinker Francis Shaeffer said:

> One cannot explain the explosive dynamite…of the early church apart from the fact that they practiced two things simultaneously: orthodoxy of doctrine and orthodoxy of community in the midst of the visible church, a community which the world could see. By the grace of God, therefore, the church must be known simultaneously for its purity of doctrine and the reality of its community. Our churches have so often been only preaching points with very little emphasis on community, but exhibition of the love of God in practice is beautiful and must be there.[19]

As Schaeffer saw it, right doctrine and right behavior go together. This is a must for the vintage faith. The "orthodoxy of community" that Schaeffer spoke of is dependent on real love between believers in a church that is visible to those outside the church. It is also the emphasis of Paul and other writers of Scripture. A healthy evangelical church will be one marked by healthy evangelical doctrine *and* healthy evangelical behavior that is visible. The connection between genuine belief and its resultant behavior cannot be divorced.

Healthy Doctrine, Healthy Life

One of my favorite times of the year is May. The reason is because this is when the seminary where I teach holds its graduation ceremonies. Every professor gets excited about graduation.

The blasting of the traditional pomp and circumstance begins, and the faculty leads the march to the stage with our students

---

19. Francis A. Schaeffer, *The Church Before the Watching World: A Practical Ecclesiology* (Downers Grove: IVP, 1971), 62.

following. Every proud family member and friend is on their feet with huge smiles and balloons (some of whom no doubt amazed their graduate really is graduating!).

As professors we sit on the stage and enjoy the show from the most vulnerable seats in the house, staring at everybody who's staring back at us. The highlight is watching our favorite students (yes, we have favorites) walk across the stage and receive that coveted degree for which they worked so hard. But there is another reason I love that day. Each year, I get to join a group of international representatives from all over the world who begin the festivities by reading the same portion of the New Testament in their native languages. Being the New Testament professor, I am privileged to join them and read my part in Koine Greek—the very language through which God breathed out the holy text.[20] The passage we all read in various languages is Paul's admonition to Timothy: "Follow the pattern of the sound words that you have heard from me, in the faith and love that are in Christ Jesus. By the Holy Spirit who dwells within us, guard the good deposit entrusted to you" (2 Tim. 1:13–14).

In v. 13, Paul uses a phrase that often goes by unnoticed: "sound words" (*hygiainontōn logōn*). This word-picture is very important when considering the relationship between evangelical belief and behavior as members of the church. In fact, its main context is used within what have historically been called the "Pastoral Epistles," Paul's letters to Timothy and Titus that offer instructions on local church ministry. The apostle was fond of a few other phrases that meant the same thing as "sound words." He instructed Titus to teach "sound doctrine" (*hygiainousē didaskalia*) and to make sure his church was "sound in the faith" (*hygiainōsin en tē pistei*) (Titus 1:9, 13). This raises the question— what does it mean for doctrine or faith to be "sound"?

The idea of sound doctrine is common in conservative evangelicalism, but its meaning is largely assumed. The apostle

---

20. The annual experience is that much more special to me because it was my original language professor and mentor, the late Dr. Thomas Rohm, who did the reading for years before his passing in 2021.

Paul used the term in a very specific way. The word often translated "sound" (*y̆giainō*) is a term he borrowed from ancient Greek writers, which in the extant literature referred to a physical "health." It meant the opposite of spoil or going rotten—it was "healthy, wholesome, in good condition."[21] It's not surprising, therefore, that from this word eventually came the English phrase "good hygiene."[22]

The meaning of "physical well-being" for *y̆giainō* was kept not just in literature before the New Testament, but through the Gospels as well—particularly in Luke's account.[23] Luke, who was a trained physician with a proclivity for medical language, used this word for "health" on three separate occasions. In his Gospel, Luke records Jesus using the word when responding to the Pharisees and Scribes, that "Those who are *well* [*y̆giainō*] have no need of a physician, but those who are sick" (Luke 5:31). During another occasion, Jesus healed a centurion's servant from afar, and Luke records that when "they returned to the house, they found the servant *well* [*y̆giainō*]" (7:10). Later, in the parable of the Prodigal Son, Luke the physician again uses the word when referring to that son who returned to his father "in good health," or "safe and sound" [*y̆giainō*] (15:27). This was always the sense of the word, a physical health. Until Paul. The apostle was the first to use it in a specific church context.

In nine times throughout the Pastorals, Paul uses the phrase *y̆giainō* and its cognate *hygiēs*, but attaches something new to it. In doing so, he turned the idea of "health" into a technical word. It was now "healthy" *-teaching, -doctrine, -words, -faith*. Being a Hellenistic-Jewish scholar, Paul was fluent not only in Greek but also in Hebrew (and probably Latin), and he knew how to retain tangible word pictures that offer vivid metaphors. Sound

---

21. Franco Montanari, et al., *The Brill Dictionary of Ancient Greek* (Liden: Brill, 2018), 2176.

22. See Titus 2:8 that uses the derivative adjective *hygiēs* to describe speech that is "sound" or "healthy."

23. Outside of Luke and Paul, the word appears only one time in 3 John 2, with the same meaning of "good health" conveyed.

or healthy doctrine is teaching that is unspoiled, un-rotten, free from corruption. Sound words are teaching from the Holy Spirit entrusted to divinely appointed delegates—who the Bible calls prophets and apostles—and codified in the holy Scriptures. It is teaching *most* exemplified in "accordance with the gospel of the glory of the blessed God" (1 Tim 1:11).

What is most striking about Paul's use of this phrase "sound doctrine/faith" is that in each of its nine appearances, it is never defined but used in direct contrast to *false teaching* and *false teachers.* The contrast is what gives the definition. Sound faith is what contradicts the doctrine and character of heretics—those who spoiled the gospel of Jesus Christ and true biblical theology with their own twisted ideas. This shows a direct connection between the importance of healthy doctrine that leads to healthy living, for the opposite is also the case—unhealthy doctrine leads to unhealthy living. Notice the contrast:

- **1 Timothy 1:10:** "the sexually immoral, men who practice homosexuality, enslavers, liars, perjurers, and whatever else is contrary to *sound doctrine.*"

- **1 Timothy 6:3:** "If anyone teaches a different doctrine and does not agree with the *sound words* of our Lord Jesus Christ and the teaching that accords with godliness."

- **2 Timothy 1:13:** "Follow the pattern of the _sound words_ that you have heard from me, in the faith and love that are in Christ Jesus" (this is the one possible exception, but the overall context of the letter is pervasive with correcting false teaching).

- **2 Timothy 4:3:** "For the time is coming when people will not endure *sound teaching*, but having itching ears they will accumulate for themselves teachers to suit their own passions."

- **Titus 1:13:** "This testimony is true. Therefore, rebuke them sharply, that they may be *sound in the faith.*"

- **Titus 1:9:** "He must hold firm to the trustworthy word as taught, so that he may be able to give instruction in *sound doctrine* and also to rebuke those who contradict it."

- **Titus 1:16–2:1**: "They profess to know God, but they deny him by their works. They are detestable, disobedient, unfit for any good work. But as for you, teach what accords with *sound doctrine.*"

- **Titus 2:2**: "Older men are to be sober-minded, dignified, self-controlled, <u>sound in faith</u>, in love, and in steadfastness" (this in contrast to the the false teachers in 1:10–16).

- **Titus 2:8**: "and *sound speech* that cannot be condemned, so that an opponent may be put to shame, having nothing evil to say about us."

In contrast to false teaching or "unsound" doctrine, *sound doctrine* or healthy teaching is how Paul describes biblical orthodoxy—teaching enveloped by the grace and mercy of the gospel of Jesus Christ. That sort of doctrine which makes up core evangelical beliefs, leads to an evangelical lifestyle. The contrast is sharp. *Sound doctrine*—doctrine from the *true* Word—is fueled by love for Christ and Scripture. It is in direct contrast to false teaching that always has vanity, ignorance, and heresy at its core. A local church devoted to God's Word and faithfully committed to biblical literacy, will recognize that "sound knowledge" or "healthy doctrine" is always intertwined with good character. False teaching and false teachers will never have those two together—sound doctrine and good character—*and their crowds will reflect that lapse.*

Evangelical scholars analyzing Paul's letters to Timothy and Titus have pointed out that for Paul, the gospel of Christ is both right belief and right behavior, *together* acting as the antidote to heresy.[24] Sound or healthy doctrine that is taught and practiced by true men of God is needed in an ancient world of heresy and corruption just like it's needed in a modern world of heresy an corruption. As such, *sound doctrine* and *good character* should

---

24. Douglass J. Moo, *A Theology of Paul and His Letters*, Biblical Theology of the New Testament (Grand Rapids: Zondervan Academic, 2021), 320.

envelope the entire structure of a genuine evangelical church. If they don't, heresy and moral scandals are sure to occur within its ranks (Acts 20:29–30).

Revisiting the X-Factor

In a book several years ago, I introduced what I called the "X-Factor" for growing in one's biblical literacy. I argued that spiritual maturity and biblical literacy are connected by *fellowship*.[25] This element was necessary to include since the idea of fellowship is hardly ever considered in discussions on developing one's biblical literacy. But I am convinced that Christians develop both in their biblical literacy and spiritual maturity in *fellowship with other Christians*. The more I've thought it through, the more I've come to realize that fellowship is not just the X-factor for biblical literacy; it is also the X-factor of true evangelicalism. Fellowship is an essential component of sanctification that is never achieved alone.

What sets evangelical fellowship apart from other gatherings is that authentic fellowship incorporates Scripture, prayer, and the physical assembly of the saints—with meaningful participation in all three. Another word often used in contexts of fellowship is *discipleship*. The English word stems from both "disciple" and "discipline," but *discipleship* is a relatively modern term (sometimes used interchangeably with *fellowship*). Though the *word* discipleship does not appear in the New Testament, its concept certainly does. Paul refers to the process of discipleship in terms of believers in churches growing in unity, knowledge, and maturity (Eph. 4:13; Col. 1:28; cf. Heb. 5:14; 10:25).

It is in contexts of *discipleship* and *fellowship* where Christians most aptly learn the Bible's contours and are encouraged to persevere in the vintage faith. Assembling on the first day each week for worship and the faithful preaching of Scripture has been a premier way for learning the Bible and enjoying fellowship ever

---

25. Cory M. Marsh, *A Primer on Biblical Literacy* (El Cajon: SCS Press, 2022), 36–38.

since the birth of the church (Acts 2:42; cf. 20:7; 20:27).[26] As Paul stated, it is "through *the church* that the manifold wisdom of God is made known" (Eph. 3:10, emphasis added). There is something powerful when believers of different backgrounds and ethnicities assemble together and crack open their Bibles. In such instances, God's wisdom is on display, even to the angelic world—"the rulers and authorities in the heavenly places." Perhaps Jesus had this in mind when saying he is in the midst whenever two or three are gathered in his name (Matt. 18:20). God's wisdom displayed through church fellowship is unlike anything else on earth.

In fact, *daily* fellowship is the historic practice of the church as evidenced in the earliest Christian document outside of, and contemporary with, the New Testament. The *Didache* ["teaching"] *of the Apostles* is an ancient manual for worship, baptism, and Christian living. It also discloses that daily fellowship is expected among the saints: "And you will seek every day the presence of the saints in order that you may rest upon their words" (*Didache*, 4:2).[27] How much we need encouragement from the saints!

Unfortunately for much of modern evangelicalism, the twin concepts *discipleship* and *fellowship* have become catchalls for any type of program that has the name "ministry" attached to it. Whether there is active participation in biblical-learning, prayer, encouragement, admonishment, and so forth seems not to matter for churches that consider gatherings around football games or golf outings as equally valid fellowship or discipleship. But according to Andrew Burgraff, genuine discipleship is "the process of learning the teachings of Scripture, internalizing them to shape one's belief system, and then acting upon them in one's daily life."[28] This is a helpful definition, no doubt, but it lacks

26. Cory M. Marsh, *A Primer on Biblical Literacy*, 37.

27. This translation is adapted from Will Varner, *The Apostolic Fathers: An Introduction and Translation* (London: T&T Clark, 2023), 16.

28. Andrew T. Burgraff, *Discipleship Today: Applying Biblical Discipleship in Today's Context* (Cary: Shepherds Press, 2024), 19.

the crucial qualifier such as *fellowship, community, with other believers,* etc.[29]

Discipleship is never a lone enterprise. It requires other believers, teachers, pastors, mentors, and so forth engaged in a reciprocal relationship. Evangelical discipleship consists of teaching, encouraging, even disciplining one another in the vintage faith. However, there is a sobering caution that with the loss of evangelical discipleship comes the loss of evangelicalism's future. This is because genuine discipleship affects other areas of the vintage faith, such as biblical literacy, homiletics, theological education, and training the next generation. Evangelical writers Jim Davis and Michael Graham outline how important discipleship is for future generations of American evangelicals:

> Considering the world our children and grandchildren will likely grow up in, the need for discipleship is great. New Christians don't have the Biblical foundations our culture used to provide. We must make it our aim as church leaders to teach the Bible in our sermons. We must invest in Christian education. The main goal of our youth ministry, as fun as it may be, has to be discipleship. If we rely solely on entertaining worship or memorable experiences, we fall short of our goal, and our children will bear the cost of our shortsightedness. The more we enter exile the greater the need in the church for true discipleship.[30]

From this standpoint, it's clear that biblical discipleship can never be divorced from biblical fellowship. It also makes sense why the two, though distinct, are often conflated. Discipleship occurs naturally when fellowshipping with other believers. And fellowship is enjoyed when two or three believers are engaged in discipleship. All is governed by Scripture, prayer, and meaningful participation.

---

29. Though the definition lacks explicit indication of discipleship in community, Burgraff later makes clear that the roles of teachers, mentors, and church fellowship are "key factors in discipleship." Andrew T. Burgraff, *Discipleship Today*, 51–62.

30. Jim Davis and Michael Graham with Ryan P. Burge, *The Great Dechurching: Who's Leaving, Why Are They Going, and What Will It Take to Bring Them Back?* (Grand Rapids: Zondervan, 2023), 224.

It's not surprising that the crucial X-factor of church fellowship and discipleship is hardly discussed in critiques of evangelicalism. For instance, neither concept appears anywhere in Kristin Kobes Du Mez's scathing criticisms of "white evangelicals." In fact, the only "fellowship" Du Mez finds worthy of discussion is the secretive unit The Fellowship, a politically infused cabinet of behind-the-scenes powerbrokers associated with Billy Graham and former presidents.[31] The organizers of the National Prayer Breakfast since the 1950s, this group also called "The Family," interests Du Mez only as far as exposés of their supposed militant patriarchy and national power consolidation.[32] Her portrayal of such a network is anything but positive, and is as far removed from genuine evangelical fellowship as the shadowy Illuminati is. Similarly, Isaac Sharp's arguments for "other evangelicals"—liberals, feminists, homosexuals, and so on— entirely leaves out the need for church fellowship and discipleship in his critiques of "white" or "mainstream" evangelicalism. Instead, his construction of evangelical identity contends that any would-be adherent will always lack a sense of belonging if not "white."[33]

For these critics, race, gender, political lobbying, and social status serve as the metrics for evangelicalism. Works like theirs highlight the need for something beyond belief and something more spiritually meaningful than politics to be the metric of evangelical identity. Evangelicalism, according to its vintage expression, *must* include behavior. And, as this chapter has argued, evangelical behavior requires evangelical community—believers in fellowship and discipleship, encouraging one another to grow in truth and love, to call one another to repentance from sin, as they seek to glorify God in their bodies (Rom. 12:1–2). As such, fellowship also serves as a powerful evangelistic tool when confronted with

31. Kristin Kobes Du Mez, *Jesus and John Wayne: How White Evangelicals Corrupted a Faith and Fractured a Nation* (New York: Liveright, 2021), 35.

32. Ibid., 192.

33. Isaac B. Sharp, *The Other Evangelicals: A Story of Liberal, Black, Progressive, Feminist, and Gay Christians—and the Movement that Pushed Them Out* (Grand Rapids: Eerdmans, 2023), 118.

persecution, "so that the life of Jesus also may be manifested in our mortal flesh" (2 Cor. 4:10).

Accountability is baked into the idea of consistent local church fellowship. With the practice of loving and truthful accountability, believers engrossed in habitual sin are not left alone to dishonor God. They are also not left alone to fight their battles against their flesh. Christ, through his people, fights for that struggling or sinning believer with the intent of spiritually restoring them. Such accountability is what Paul called "bearing one another's burdens" and "fulfilling the law of Christ" (Gal. 6:1–2). This includes calling out the behavior that critics, like those throughout this book, contest are worthy of the label "evangelical." It is no wonder they portray aberrant lifestyles with sympathy rather than calling them what they are: sinful. One major reason why is that they simply don't value the need for biblical fellowship as stressed in this chapter. It is very difficult to maintain a sinful lifestyle when held accountable by a church.

Contrary to progressive or leftist evangelicalism, sin in the vintage faith is not celebrated or approved. It is seen as a cancer, killing the person and staining the purity of Christ's body. From Paul's admonition against homosexual lifestyles to James's and Peter's condemnation of pride, being discipled in true evangelical fellowship keeps in check those who claim evangelical beliefs while engrossed in anti-evangelical behavior. A lifestyle of consistent evangelical fellowship is a blessing! It acts as an incredible sanctifying tool in the life of any struggling believer and guards the purity of the church. Thus, the crucial X-Factor of evangelicalism—and final fundamental of the vintage faith—is consistent local church fellowship.[34]

---

34. I should point out that *consistent* fellowship doesn't demand *unending* or *unbroken* fellowship. Often, genuine evangelicals are between churches in their search for a permanent church home, or for various circumstances, are not able to attend church services. It is the *principle* of consistency that I argue for, which should be reflected in the evangelical's life of regular gathering together and serving fellow saints in a local assembly.

PART 3

A Few Rants and Things

CHAPTER 7

A Rant on Evangelical Politics

I imagine some readers saw this and the next chapter in the table of contents and flipped right to them, bypassing everything said up till now. I probably would do the same if I wasn't the one writing the book. This chapter heading was originally a placeholder in my outline. I hoped that by the time I got here, I would've thought of something a little more eloquent or academic sounding than a "rant" of things I think are crippling American evangelicalism. No such luck. A rant is what you get.

The elasticity of modern evangelicalism is due in part to the things covered here and in the following chapter. Political allegiances and voting blocs (the supposed "evangelical vote"), manufactured telegenic appearances, and the intoxication of social influencers and celebrity pastors are all to blame for their part in creating today's evan-jello-calism. Critics of evangelicalism, including those with whom this book has taken issue, are correct when taking to task mainline evangelicalism for its obsession with celebrity pastors and conflating politics with the biblical faith. I have argued throughout this book *against* such an evangelicalism, which I believe needs to be recovered according to its vintage expression (the five fundamentals in Part 2). This means categorizing evangelicalism according to political blocs, celebrity Christianity, race, and other such nomenclature is misguided at best and destructive at worst. But the fact that "evangelicalism" has been stretched to cover all these other ideas over the past three or four decades calls into question the usefulness of the label itself. Chapter nine will return to this thought, and even suggest the possibility of a name change.

For now, it bears recalling that the metric offered so far for a true "vintage faith," that is, a genuine and historic evangelicalism, includes the highest view of Scripture, the exclusivity of Christ, evangelism, education, and the necessity of consistent church fellowship. In none of these five fundamentals does race, politics, fame, and so forth play any role—despite what is often portrayed as American evangelicalism. Therefore, if any significance is drawn from my work, I hope it shows a contrast to the ubiquity of authors calling everything under the sun "evangelical" with what is *really* evangelicalism. Still, this does not mean we should ignore criticisms in so far as they really do reveal blind spots in need of correction. Those who are not favorable toward a theological tradition sometimes level the most accurate criticisms that insiders can't (or won't) see. Does contemporary American evangelicalism have a problem with confusing American politics with the vintage faith? Yes, it does. Does mainstream evangelicalism have an intoxication with celebrity culture? Undoubtedly so. That said, such criticisms do not in any way legitimatize progressive agendas that are welcoming of beliefs and lifestyles antithetical to evangelicalism's original identity, even if they call out the very things I call out here.

Protesting or Ranting?

What's the difference between a protest and a rant? I suppose the one is a formalized or organized complaint while the other is just complaining. I excel at the latter. But Protestantism was birthed as a "protest." Thus, *protesting* is in its blood. The original dissents in the sixteenth century centered on the Roman Catholic Church's monopolizing the ancient faith and packaging it as an industry. Catholic dogma taught that Christians were not justified through faith alone as Paul seemed to teach (Rom. 5:1; Gal. 2:16). Rather, they were *infused* with righteousness to the extent they obeyed whatever the pope and his delegates told them to do.

Out of the idea of a works-based righteousness, aberrant doctrines like a treasury of merit, purgatory, and costly indulgences were introduced with the "guarantee" that one can purchase reduced time for departed souls from the anguish of an indefinite limbo after their deaths. The clerical and financial abuses to maintain this lucrative industry—that would eventually finance the construction of St. Peter's Basilica and other portions of Vatican City off the capital gains from indulgences—were unreal.[1] As a reaction to centuries of horrific exploitation, Protestantism was inevitable. Gavin Ortlund notes, "Late medieval abuses— both financial and physical—help explain why renewal in the church could only come in the form of protest."[2] Evangelicalism, being a tradition within Protestantism, is fiercely independent. There is no pope or "mother church" to wield its oversight. There are denominations of course, and one might make the case that the state churches left in the Reformers' wake weren't too big a step away from the centralized governance of Rome.[3] Indeed, such an argument provided the seedbed for independent or non-denominational evangelical traditions like Brethrenism, chapel movements, and Bible churches to emerge.

However, there is an irony in Protestant traditions that stress the individual priesthood of all believers, precluding the warrant

---

1. Incidentally, with approximately 177 million acres of land ownership worldwide today, the Roman Catholic Church remains the second largest real estate holder on the planet. See "The World's Largest Landowners," https://www.madisontrust.com/information-center/visualizations/worlds-largest-landowners/.

2. Gavin Ortlund, *What It Means to Be Protestant: The Case for an Always-Reforming Church* (Grand Rapids: Zondervan Reflective, 2024), 56.

3. This is not meant to dismiss Protestant denominations as legitimate evangelical heirs (which they certainly are!). I am merely pointing out sentiments that have been expressed by independent movements.

for a centralized magisterium (here begins the rant!). Obvious differences in doctrine notwithstanding, modern mainstream evangelicalism shares a few embarrassing commonalities with medieval Catholicism. Politicizing the faith and turning it into a lucrative industry are relevant examples. Some conservative American evangelicals have a hard time distinguishing between secular politics and biblical Christianity. Republican "evangelicals" aren't alone, since those on the left are guilty of the exact same thing. Both sides exploit passages from Scripture for their own agendas. Though political conservatives are not any more guilty than political liberals in the crime of misusing Scripture, they do seem to get the most attention on a populist level.

One notable example is Bards Fest, an annual festival mixing Scripture, American patriotism, and right-wing politics founded by conservative podcaster Scott Kesterson. For its inaugural gathering in St. Louis in 2021, the festival's promoters hit the all-time height of hubris claiming it to be "The Greatest Spiritual Revival in Human History."[4] Apparently the Protestant Reformation or the birth of the church on the Day of Pentecost would fall short of this gathering in the American Midwest. The "greatest spiritual revival in human history" consisted of biblically-based messages alongside multiple speakers railing against vaccines and government conspiracies. It has since devolved into platforming anti-trinitarian heretics and female self-identified pastors and apostles as keynote speakers.[5] A charismatically confused, politically saturated Christian nationalist dream is the result, with attendees not able to distinguish biblical Christianity from zealous forms of national pride.

And when it comes to Christian celebrityism (more of a rant to be completed next chapter), evan-jello-calism is atrociously guilty. Celebrity pastors neglect old-fashioned (biblical!) pastoral care of their sheep in their competitive races to have the biggest churches, most social media likes, most best-seller books, most

---

4. See Bards Fest, https://bardsfest.com/2021-missouri/.
5. Ibid., https://bardsfest.com/2024-flemingsburg/#speakers.

interviews, biggest conferences, biggest stages, biggest staff, biggest syndicated radio shows, brightest lights, brightest sneakers, and tightest pants. (That may have gotten away from me at the end. I actually own a pair or two of skinny jeans. But this is supposed to be a rant). Scandals and moral failures are all too common within big name evangelicalism, where "pastors" (in title only) are not held accountable by their local churches. It's not surprising given an industry that fame-intoxicated pastors helped create and keep alive. Name branding and imaging are key components to their ministry philosophies, despite any Christian or pious-sounding language on their websites.

With the counsel of Proverbs 29:11 on my mind, I will do my best not to be "a fool [who] gives full vent to his spirit," in my ranting here and in the next chapter. Though I fully believe the problems discussed in these two chapters are real problems in need of change for first-world evangelicalism, this is not an official protest. These are merely my complaints, for what they are worth. I will present them as "wisely" as I'm able and "quietly hold back" enough to keep these chapters from never ending.

Evangelical Politics

It is impossible to keep the church out of politics entirely. The gospel comes with an ethic that will always overlap with conversations concerning secular politics.

The gospel message centers around themes of murder, law, corruption, innocence, judgment, righteousness, grace, mercy, forgiveness, and of course, love. If all these ideas simultaneously swirl around the death of Christ, how can the gospel *not* speak into political discourse? Clearly, they have implications for discussions on the value of life, justice, even race—all of which are perennial hotbed political issues. But as Jim Davis and Michael Graham point out, something is wrong when Christians on both the left and right are leaving the church in droves ("dechurching" is their word) because they are more passionate about national politics than the gospel of Jesus Christ.[6] The question is not if politics should ever enter a church; it is a question of *clear priority*. What takes the priority in one's church—Christ and his Word, or secular political trends? Davis and Graham delineate the differences and how they should play out in the local church:

> We must put primary issues in the primary spot and secondary issues and tertiary issues in their places. Certainly, the core historic Christian theological doctrines are primary. These include the divinity of Christ, his atonement for our sin, his resurrection, and our sure hope of eternity with God free from sin. There are primary implications of our doctrine that we should all agree on as well. If we are all made in the image of God, then we agree that racism is bad and the unborn should be protected. . . . Those who have dechurched because of politics should first ask themselves if they have the primary and secondary in the proper places. Did they possibly leave too hastily? Have the secondary issues become primary for them? Or did they rightly see that the church and clergy were guilty of the misalignment of the gospel ethic?[7]

In each church, there needs to be a clear distinction between primary issues and secondary and tertiary issues—with balance maintained consistently. Unfortunately, too many evangelical pastors are guilty of prioritizing secular political issues that interest them over the clear gospel message. Railing about cultural trends from the pulpit or endorsing political candidates and the various propositions while disguising them as "sermons" is a derelict of pastoral duty. The crime recalls Con Campbell's "political evangelical" grouping from chapter one. The pulpit should be reserved for Bible exposition, and nothing else. When a pastor preaches on biblical texts that do have significant bearing on a political issue, it is then—and only then—that modern-day relevance should be drawn, never neglecting that passage's

6. Jim Davis, Michael Graham and Ryan P. Burge, *The Great Dechurching: Who's Leaving, Why Are They Going, and What Will It Take to Bring Them Back?* (Grand Rapids: Zondervan, 2023), 167.

7. Ibid., 167–68.

historical and grammatical contexts. Any contemporary relevance or application of the text is *secondary* to the single-intention of the biblical author. Maintaining the proper balance between the *thing* (the text's meaning) and *implications of the thing* (the text's significance) guards the hermeneutical triad of every portion of Scripture, that is, its historical context, literary dimension, and finally its theological message and daily appropriation.[8]

It should be clear by now (for those who've read each chapter before this one), that all five fundamentals of what I term the "vintage faith" are governed by the very first one: the highest view of Scripture. The inspired and inerrant biblical canon gives the evangelical the authority by which to live out their Christian faith. With regularly increasing biblical literacy, evangelical thought is shaped by the regular intake of Scripture—which begins in the home and the local church as argued earlier. It is one thing to *claim* to hold to a divinely-inspired, inerrant, authoritative text and another thing to *practice* that belief. Pastors must demonstrate both consistently in their churches. If Scripture really is divine revelation from God, then it must be sufficient for framing one's political beliefs. Unfortunately, too many evangelical pastors don't maintain this dual necessity. Most trending evangelical sermons demonstrate the pastor's *lack* of belief in the power of Scripture by their constant need to "make it" applicable through forced interpretations, that are really not interpretations at all, but rather applications that suit the sermon more than the text itself. Nowhere is this more prevalent than in political sermons.

But what if evangelical pastors simply did just preach the text? Is it not a living and breathing word from God (Heb. 4:12)? Divine inspiration dictates the Bible really is miraculous. I submit that

---

8. See Andreas J. Köstenberger with Richard D. Patterson, *Invitation to Biblical Interpretation: Exploring the Hermeneutical Triad of History, Literature, and Theology* 2nd ed. (Grand Rapids: Kregel Academic, 2021), 49–69. I prefer "appropriation" to "application" since not every biblical text can be *applied* in the strictest sense of the word, but every passage can be *appropriated* somehow (e.g., what does it teach me about God and how should I respond?).

if pastors focused squarely on their primary task of preaching the Word faithfully each week, in season and out of season, it will inevitably inform their congregants' views of politics as they "mature to manhood" (Eph. 4:13). Thus, waiting till election season to preach about political issues or simply handing out pre-screened, pastorally-approved voting templates that ensure an "evangelical vote" is to show one's lack of commitment to faithful expository preaching with the *long-term* (hence "conservative") goal in view. Consistent biblical exposition equips and shapes evangelical minds to think evangelically according to Scripture. The pressure of the evangelical pastor should be to rightly communicate *the Bible* year-round, not to preach against trendy cultural fads, the problems of big government, the subtle evolutionary or transgender insertions from Disney, or which political candidate is going to save or destroy America. When evangelicals are shaped by a biblical worldview through regular exposure to the whole counsel of God, they naturally form biblical thoughts on these other matters—without the need of a zealous preacher ramming it down their throats at the moment of decision when it's too late.

In his compelling work, *Worshipping Politics*, history professor Luke Goble argues for a reframing of the relationship between faith and politics as "intentional formation" in place of reactionary decision-making that easily becomes divisive among Christians. In the case of the latter, pastors and their congregants can be guided more by emotion toward a specific political issue or candidate at the time a decision needs to be made, rather than shaped calmly by years of consistent Bible study that should prepare them for those voting decisions. In such cases, proof texting (a form of politicking the Bible!) becomes the "exposition" needed to justify a politically right or left measure. Proof texting—cherry picking / politicking the Bible—this way becomes another source of justification for decisions that are more emotive than contextual. Describing a person's emotional/affective process as their inner "elephant" that roams where it wants and the rational process as the "rider" left to explain that direction, Gobel argues, "Scripture can serve as a source to *train* the elephant in a way that is prior to any one moment of decision of justification."[9] He goes on to point out the biblical witness that underscores the ancient understanding of the relationship between obedience and *training* versus just obedience and command (e.g., Deut. 11:18; Prov. 3:3; 6:21; 7:3). Now, obviously *interpretations* of the sacred text (not merely quoting them) will play a foundational role in how they are communicated and received when preached. I have already pointed out the indelible link between an evangelical view of the Bible and a literal or grammatical-historical interpretation of it (see chapter two), which I believe is the biblical and proper hermeneutic. However, even though the method is sound, not every evangelical applies it with the same amount of consistency which results in the various interpretations of important, but secondary and tertiary matters.

The point here is that a truly evangelical presupposition is one that understands that the Bible shapes all of life including our beliefs, affections, and desires, and the preacher's job is to preach it as consistently as possible—and let the chips fall where they may when it comes to voting time or when confronted with the newest societal evil. This is *intentional formation* by Scripture instead of reactionary engagement of political culture. Though he does not necessarily argue for an evangelical case centered around the Bible as strongly as I do here, Goble is nevertheless correct in his assessment that having a transformative effect on society requires a source from which that transformation springs. "A different understanding of self-sacrificial love, of life in death to self, of spiritual identity," he says, noting also that, "The problem is that the degree of contact and influence in society can be in direct competition with the depth of formation in Christ and his body."[10] Clearly, the Bible is what offers that unique understanding of Goble's virtues, which shapes a person's political beliefs and is no match for the views of secular culture that attempt to compete with it.

---

9. Luke J. Goble, *Worshipping Politics: Problems and Practices for a Public Faith* (Eugene: Cascade, 2017), 47.

10. Ibid., 186.

Dangers of the "Conservative v. Liberal" Narrative

It is easy for modern evangelical leaders to use politically loaded words to their advantage and create unhealthy, judgmental political climates within their ministries. This is especially the case with influential evangelical pastors who intentionally position themselves within the broader cultural and political divide, and arbitrability demonize whatever *they* say is "liberal."

Unfortunately, many pastors have effectively used the "conservative v. liberal" narrative as a way to cover abuse, bully congregants from the pulpit, and as a weapon to control their people. A sad reality exists in some of the largest conservative evangelical churches where a congregant who may align themselves with what are considered liberal ideas is ostracized from genuine pastoral care. Moreover, a congregant's claim of experiencing trauma and abuse within the church is dismissed, perhaps justified by the same "conservative v. liberal" narrative. Not only do such mega-machines bring shame on the name of Christ with their politicizing the pulpit, but they contribute to the mountain of scandal and real pain left in their wake as their witness to the watching world (see chapter six). Genuine cases of abuse that are documented by progressive authors or journalists critiquing mainstream evangelicalism should not be casually dismissed as "liberal agendas." Instead, they should be taken with the upmost seriousness befitting of the justice, mercy, and humility expected by God (Micah 6:8).

Such dismissals of abuse or trauma (whether spiritual, physical, or sexual) occur more easily in churches that have built significant ideological barriers over the years by exploiting the "conservative v. liberal" narrative. Those claiming some form of abuse from their pastor—who may employ hundreds of people holding tightly to their jobs—are too often viewed as politically motivated and dismissed as such, rather than received as legitimate grievances by legitimately hurt people. This polarization not only clouds the truth but also isolates victims, making it harder for them to find justice or support outside of conservative circles. This, of course, is *not* the norm of every large evangelical church (or smaller church). But where they do occur, a line can often be drawn showing that guilty conservative churches have essentially insulated themselves from broader scrutiny by their framing of instances of abuse around political narratives rather than ethical or legal terms—adding to the hurdles for abused Christians trying to find healing among God's people.

The Supposed Evangelical Vote

If you've made it this far in my rant on evangelical politics, let me add another: my absolute hatred of evangelicalism being defined or portrayed as a political bloc or voting constituency.

Why have we allowed secularists to invent a false category under our noses?

Political polls are academic and theoretical, and, as touched on in an earlier chapter, are hardly ever trustworthy. Questions are framed in a certain way and people of certain ethnicities and economic statuses targeted. An "evangelical vote" determined by skin tone, affluency, or FICO score is entirely superficial and manufactured. *Let's put an end to ethnic polling being the determinative factor in what makes someone a Christian, Protestant, or evangelical!* This means at the very least there is no such thing as the "evangelical vote." None whatsoever. It is completely fabricated by those who have made up the senseless term. It ends up feeding a secular media that craves viewers by exploiting Christianity and especially evangelicalism.

Current media trends, influenced by critical race theorists, can yield the impression that there is a set norm with voting constituencies that *must* be followed. The rule is "blacks" support democratic candidates while "whites" support republican interests. But researchers know this is simply not accurate. For example, the past decade saw a rise of American black evangelical leaders who express numerous concerns over leftist policies that violate biblical principles. A notable case involves African American evangelical leaders uniting against Hillary Clinton when she ran against Donald Trump in 2016.

An "Open Letter" was addressed to the female presidential nominee and signed by multiple representatives of historically black denominations that included Harvard lecturer and director of the Seymore Institute for Black Church and Policy Studies Jaqueline Rivers, as well as Charles Blake, the presiding bishop of the Church of God in Christ. The document condemned liberal policies advocating for abortion and the "well financed war" waged by the gay and lesbian community on the "faith of our ancestors."[11] Contrary to the attention Sharp, Kobes Du Mez, and other progressive authors quoted earlier, afford to oppressive "white" evangelicalism in their respective works, instances of black evangelical protest against progressive, leftist constituencies hardly get the attention they deserve (usually none at all). I suspect the reason is because such cases don't feed the appetites of journalists with leftist agendas or fit neatly within misleading polls that pretend categories such as "white = conservative" or "black = liberal" evangelicals are legitimate taxonomies. Though at times a pattern can be detected to support these fabricated categories, thankfully, as Kidd expresses, "Some conservative Protestants have shown a willingness to break with those ethnic voting patterns."[12] Yet, these numbers don't play into the criticisms of evangelicalism being "white," whether by Sharp, Du Mez, or any other critic of "white evangelicalism."

But is there truth to Kobes Du Mez's statement: "Evangelicals may self-identity as 'Bible-believing Christians,' but evangelicalism itself entails a broader set of deeply held values communicated through symbol, ritual, and political allegiances."?[13] In one sense, yes. Evangelicalism is often communicated by the cross as a symbol of Christ's atonement as well as by the "rituals" of baptism and communion. And despite my protest (or rant), American evangelicalism is too easily conflated with republican

---

11. See Thomas S. Kidd, *Who Is an Evangelical? The History of a Movement in Crises* (New Haven: Yale University Press, 2019), 146.

12. Ibid.

13. Kristin Kobes Du Mez, *Jesus and John Wayne*, 297.

political allegiances. So descriptively, according to some popular perceptions, Kobes Du Mez has a valid point. But prescriptively, she is far from accurate. Evangelicalism *should not* be defined or thought of this way. It gives the false impression that mainstream evangelicalism is nothing but Trumpism filled with white republicans.

Admittedly, there are pockets of American evangelicals who are just as comfortable wearing red MAGA hats at church events as they are wearing cross necklaces. And, as my comments about the Bards Fest earlier pointed out, too many evangelical leaders are guilty of creating confusion between right-wing politics and evangelicalism. Still, it's not like Trump supporters are the only ones politicking for evangelical identity. I am writing this book during a (very) heated presidential race, and the newest evangelical lobbyists vying for attention are "Evangelicals for [Kamala] Harris." The group is comprised of multiple self-identified evangelical pastors, professors, and scholars who are registered democrats and far left-of-center politically. Despite their public self-identification as "evangelicals," polls, books, and blogs aren't published equating such a constituency with the "evangelical" voting bloc. It remains more convenient for critical authors and publishers to equate evangelicals almost exclusively with right-wing / white conservatives, despite the very public evidence to the contrary (e.g., the various progressive evangelical groups listed in chapter one).

What could be the reason? Simply this: race peddling sells. Criticisms of republican evangelicals inevitably morph into epithets of race, guns, cowboy hats, Islamophobia, homophobia, xenophobia, and so on, which fuel the appetite of the American industry that progressives casually label "evangelicalism." In other words, ridiculing the "majority," however perceived, is big business and always ends in sales commensurate with cultural trends. This version of evangelicalism, most expressive in the US, has become a two- or three- or four-headed monster with meaningless identity to the exclusion of the very *evangel* itself (contra chapter three). Virtually all of it is justified by a supposed white male chauvinist voting constituency created by pollsters fixing the adjective "evangelical" to it.

Biblical Patriotism v. Confused Nationalism

Since I write as an American, naturally my perspective is one coming from a citizen of the US. I am also what pollsters would consider to be "conservative" in my political beliefs (as if that was a surprise by now).

But I also recognize the need to have a politically "liberal" constituency in order for my nation to operate on some form of balance. A plane cannot fly without both the right *and* left wing operating in unison. Though one may prefer one side over the other or pretend the plane can operate just fine with one wing, the truth is, take away either wing and the plane will crash (or in cartoons, fly in circles). As much as I prefer my "right wing," I genuinely am thankful for another side that is clearly needed for my country to thrive. This must be the case, otherwise the US—which has never been governed by just one party—wouldn't be the most powerful and influential nation on earth. My attitude is the same even when I adamantly disagree with propositions advocated by the opposite constituency (in California where I live, there are more than I can count!). That said, let me be clear: I do not support progressive ideas that threaten the safety and commerce of the United States. But I say all this because I'm convinced that one can be an American patriot without falling into an overly emotional or dangerously fanatical version of nationalism.

For example, I am a proud veteran of the US Army. After almost thirty years, I still maintain friendships with some of the men with whom I served. I grew up under that old school patriotic mindset that believed every able American should serve their country at some point, so I enlisted when I was eighteen and fresh out of high school. I really did view it as my patriotic duty so as not to lazily reap the benefits of the freedoms that so many of my countrymen died or were injured to maintain. I believe that still. As such, I joined up out of principle, not for any educational or financial benefits. But this stems from my American patriotism, not any form of Christian or other type of nationalism.

What are some differences between what I call patriotism and nationalism? Maybe this will help (remember this is a rant). Patriots serve their country. Nationalists attend rallies. Patriots risk their lives for their fellow citizens. Nationalists amass arsenals to protect their own houses. Patriots are willingly inconvenienced by their government and go wherever their government commands them to go (e.g., military). Nationalists fight to maintain every convenience afforded them, believing every inconvenience is a government conspiracy. Patriotic *Christians* trust that God has determined that they are citizens of the country where they live. Nationalistic *Christians* are paranoid about every secular agenda and *functionally* distrust God who's determined their citizenry of the country they refuse to serve. Are my comparisons fixed rules? Of course not. Sometimes patriots adopt the ethos of nationalism, and other times nationalists adopt the more stable ideals of patriotism. But again, this is supposed to be a rant. As these differences suggest, I am a strong advocate for patriotism and hold much contempt for nationalism.[14]

Patriotism is not something genuine evangelicals should dismiss. In fact, it's biblical. Paul told the Athenian crowds, "God made from one man every nation of mankind to live on all the face of the earth, having determined allotted periods and the boundaries of their dwelling place" (Acts 17:26). A person lives where they live and for how long they live there because God "determined" [*horisas*] it so. I am an American because God determined me to be born (and currently live) in America. You live in the country where you live because God determined it so. If you or I move to someplace else, guess what? God determined

---

14. The nationalism I critique in this section is the cultural conflation of right-wing zealots with biblical Christianity, not the amillennial or postmillennial theological visions of Christian nationalism. I take exception with the later groups as well, but on different exegetical and theological grounds than what I rant about here. The former form makes a brief appearance below.

[*horisas*] that also. But the text makes clear that our "allotted periods" and "boundaries" are for a specific purpose: "to seek God, and perhaps feel their way toward him and find him. Yet he is actually not far from each one of us" (v. 27).

For a nation to survive in a fallen world, war is unfortunately necessary at times. The history of Israel is filled with necessary bloodshed. Citizens *should* serve their country and be thankful for it. They should also pray for its welfare and for its leaders to act justly and wisely (see Jer. 29:4–9; 1 Tim. 2: 1–3). Serving one's country—whether militarily, politically, or civically—demonstrates a thankfulness for God's determinative will for them having a country. But it also comes with a purpose as Paul laid out: to "seek" (*zēteō*) and "feel" (*psēlaphaō*) their way toward God who is not far from any one citizen. In other words, the Lord determined *where* people live in order to praise and worship the only true and sovereign Creator *who is there all along.*

The warrior-king David expressed something relevant in poetic contrast: "Some trust in chariots and some in horses, but we trust in the name of Yahweh our God. They collapse and fall, but we rise and stand upright" (Ps. 20:7–8). David wrote as a king seasoned from battle for his nation. Even though he led Israel into multiple wars, he kept his trust in God above all his and other nations' military might. Like David, patriotism says I love the nation where God determined I should live, and I will do my part to ensure its health—even risk my life in service for it. Nationalism says everything about the government is dripping with lies and conspiracies and the only battles worth fighting are those against anybody I don't trust.

In his published dissertation arguing for an evangelical patriotic alternative over nationalism, Adam Wyatt draws clear distinctions between patriotism, cosmopolitanism, and nationalism. According to Wyatt, "Nationalism at its core is the belief in the superiority of a nation and can lead—not always—to a desire to dominate others, particularly in minority groups. Cosmopolitanism is a liberal philosophy that seeks to ignore national ties by stressing the importance of seeing all people as fellow citizens regardless of national citizenships."[15] With these two political philosophies as bookends, Wyatt rightly argues for a *via media* he calls "patriotism," which is biblically sustainable. "Patriotism," he explains, "is loyalty toward one's own home country—and one's own home country alone—and personal identification with one's own home country, culture, and people."[16] The differences can appear subtle at first, but they are stark. Embedded in the idea of nationalism is an attitude of national superiority, while embedded in the idea of cosmopolitanism is a complete erasure of nation for world-citizenry. In between these poles is a genuine patriotism that has loyalty and thankfulness as its core virtues, bringing it back to Paul's admonition in Acts 17 above.

While there's biblical precedent for patriotism, there's also a biblical precedent for nationalism, though the latter is *not* commended in Scripture. In his study, Wyatt makes a compelling case that when Jesus overturned the tables of the money-changers and merchants in Mark 11, he did so not merely in defiance of the commercialization of the Jewish sacrificial system. He did it also out of defiance of a corrupt Jewish nationalism. Jerusalem Jews at this time were zealous nationalists who had forcefully taken over the court of the Gentiles, the largest of the four major divisions of Herod's Temple complex. They set up their shops in the one area set apart for Gentiles, which kept all foreigners away from the closest place they could worship Yahweh. Apparently, these leaders and merchants didn't believe the court of the Gentiles carried any real significance for Israel, so they decided to turn it into a bustling Walmart.

Into the scene, steps Jesus. As Wyatt argues, "Jesus was upset at the total disregard for the court's sanctity that was designated for the Gentiles who had not yet become full members of the Jewish faith. All of the court's commercial activity was effectively

---

15. Adam Wyatt, *Biblical Patriotism: An Evangelical Alternative to Nationalism* (Denver: GCRR Press, 2021), 97.

16. Ibid., 95.

denying the Gentiles, and the nations of the world, access to the temple."[17] By caring only for their nationalistic interests, these Jews effectively rejected any prescriptive for the temple that included Gentile accessibility. In a rare act of violence, Jesus made his righteous anger over the situation known. He flipped over tables and drove out the nationalists with a whip while appealing to Isaiah the prophet: "Is it not written, 'My house shall be called a house of prayer for *all the nations*'? But you have made it a den of robbers!" (Mark 11:17; cf. Isa. 56:7).

Christian Nationalism, Flags, and Worship

From its founding, the United Stated was primed for Christian nationalism. The founding fathers who held to a theological eschatology were primarily postmillennial in their outlook.

According to Adam Wyatt, they viewed "the new American republic as the primary agent of redemptive history because it was seen as the principal seat of the kingdom. Through the [revolutionary] war's connection to millennialism, Christianity was infused with nationalism."[18] The idea went back to Puritan ideals of national faith that understood theocratic utopias to be a real possibility before the return of Christ. Justified by a hermeneutic that conflated the church with Israel meant that divine covenants designated for the Jewish nation were transferred to other nations who make Christian covenants with God. Thus, America was forged as the new "city on a hill," as coined in John Winthrop's 1630 sermon, with parallels drawn between American settlers and the ancient Israelites in search of the promised land. The promised land was now America. A colonial flag as its national symbol soon emerged.

By the time of America's Civil War in the nineteenth century, national flags began to play a pivotal role in churches. Up until then,

---

17. Adam Wyatt, *Biblical Patriotism*, 159. Wyatt also refers to Ronald Kernaghan, *Mark*, IVPNTC (Downers Grove: InterVarsity, 2007), 218.

18. Adam Wyatt, *Biblical Patriotism*, 35.

flags were mainly reserved for naval and merchant ships, but a shift in national loyalties between the North and South resulted in flags becoming symbols of patriotism.[19] Both northern and southern sensibilities began morphing into displaying their respective flags in their respective churches, along with hymns and liturgy that infused patriotic themes. The displaying of American flags in churches continues to this day in large corners of evangelicalism. What message does this portray? A careful balance must be met. As Wyatt argues, "If the symbol of national faith is the American flag, it can also be the central object of its worship. This is not to say that flags, in and of themselves, are always idolized, but great care must be taken to distinguish between the flag and the country it represents and the proper object of worship, which is God."[20] Because a national flag is a powerful visual symbol, it can communicate a message that associates loyalty to America (or any country) with loyalty to Christ. This is not necessarily so, as a flag can just as well communicate gratefulness for the nation to whom God determined that Christian should be a citizen. It's also not just an American evangelical phenomenon. In a 2021 article, *Christianity Today* posed the question about national flags during church services to evangelical pastors from eleven different countries around the world.[21] While some did see it as their political or nationalistic duty to display their country's flag in their place of worship, others did so with a spiritual orientation of hoping to direct worship to the God who is sovereign over that nation. Some pastors choose not only to display their own nation's flag but flags of other nations as well to show a love for

---

19. See John Wilsey, *American Exceptionalism and Civil Religion: Reassessing the History of an Idea* (Downers Grove: IVP Academic, 2015), 23. Also Harry S. Stout, *Upon the Altar of the Nation: A Moral History of the American Civil War* (New York: Penguin, 2007), 28–29.

20. Adam Wyatt, *Biblical Patriotism*, 185.

21. Morgan Lee, "Do Flags Belong in Churches? Pastors Around the World Weigh In," *Christianity Today*, July 2, 2021, https://www.christianitytoday.com/ct/2021/july-web-only/flags-church-sanctuary-patriotism-nationalism.html.

neighboring countries. And still others refuse to fly a national flag at all during worship so as not to conflate Christ with national politics. As the survey revealed, evangelicals from all around the world hold to a variety of opinions about displaying national flags in churches, precluding any agreed upon consensus. But it also revealed this is a delicate issue that deserves careful thought.

There is a risk involved for American evangelical churches that display the national or patriotic flags during worship services. Though not guaranteed, doing so *can* serve as a visual hermeneutic that at best confuses the relationship between God and country, or at worse equates that relationship. One of the first things Hitler did as leader of the Third Reich was to demand German churches display the Nazi flag to prove their loyalty to him and socialist Germany. A lesson for American evangelicals becomes all too real. If loyalty to the nation is conflated or confused with the worship of Christ *because* that flag accompanies the pulpit— then how is that church not guilty of similar idolatry?[22] Christ must reign supreme in evangelical churches, not any nation or national leader. Therefore, e*vangelical leaders must be cognizant of the risk when considering displaying a flag in their places of worship.* Personally, as patriotic as I am (even sporting a few patriotic tattoos!), I am also very uncomfortable with the idea of an American flag waving while and where corporate worship takes place because I don't think the risk is worth it.

Conclusion

I really did do my best to keep this chapter manageable. Originally, my "rant" was going to be a single chapter covering all the points above on politics as well as my disdain for evangelical celebrityism. But I realized halfway through (like most rants) that would turn this chapter into an inordinately long scroll of gripes. Instead of cramming it all into one place that would probably come off more obnoxious than insightful, I've decided to break my rant in two, with chapter eight focused on the evangelical intoxication with

---

22. See Adam Wyatt, *Biblical Patriotism*, 185.

celebrity culture. But both rants are related. The more I thought about them, the more the overlap became obvious. Evangelical politics and evangelical celebrities sometimes converge into one big contribution to a version of evan-jello-calism saturated with things apart from its vintage fundamentals.

CHAPTER 8

A Rant on Evangelical Christian Celebrityism

Over the years I've repeated more times than I can remember this single thought: *we must kill Christian "celebrityism."* I don't think I've ever said the same about evangelical politics (though I clearly made my thoughts known in chapter seven). I don't use the word "kill" lightly here. I view the obsession that American Christianity—particularly American evangelicalism— has with modern day "influencers" as a cancer. Among other things, it breeds a spirit of competition among evangelical leaders that is crippling Christ's body in the US. Jesus decreases while celebrities increase in their race for the most influential ministry. Pastors and influencers work *against* each other, not together in love as Christ commanded his disciples.

Why We Must Kill Christian Celebrityism

The word "celebrity" pulls double duty as both a noun and adjective. The idea relates to someone who is influential enough to be publicly *celebrated.* My word "celebrityism" goes beyond any one individual who is praised. It calls attention to a modern movement of evangelicals obsessed with high profile business, political, and celebrity culture that's become ubiquitous within American evangelicalism. In Christian celebrityism, Christ is not celebrated; influential people and their platforms are.

Evangelicalism in the United States has an uneasy intoxication with celebrity pastors.[1] The rampant celebrityism among American evangelicals today can probably be traced to the revival movements birthed in late seventeenth and early eighteenth centuries with emotionally charged preaching and dramatic antics. Eventually, truth became eclipsed by show; discipleship by the number of hands raised. There became a new expectation for ministers of the gospel. Pastors need not be well-educated expositors of Scripture. Rather, they should be dynamic, experience-mediating orators.[2]

Critics are well aware of the obsession American evangelicals have with fame. Indeed, scholars have also noticed an interesting overlap between celebrity and politics. One easily crosses over to the other (in either direction). Richard Lints writes about the modern church's inability to makes sense of and appreciate the differences among Christians due to a superficial homogeneity forced upon it by secular culture. "Mass culture in the West has transformed us into a global consumer culture," he says. "It created the illusion of heightened individuality while implicitly demanding conformity."[3] Lints is correct in his assessment of evangelical "global" consumerism. Secular political culture now views everything through a lens of superficial diversity, equity, and inclusion (DEI), influencing the American church to the extent that all *genuine* diversity and individuality among evangelicals is shunned and a superficial conformity takes its place. But what is the link between evangelical politics and celebrityism?

Lints draws the connection with the *influence of mass culture*: "It should also be noted that evangelicals have been especially prone to

---

1. The terms "celebrity pastor" and "Christian celebrity" are examples of two nouns joined to express an adjectival phrase. I figured grammar nerds would appreciate that detail.

2. See Nick Needham, *2000 Years of Christ's Power* (Ross-shire, UK: Christian Focus, 2023), 5:88.

3. Richard Lints, *Uncommon Unity: Wisdom for the Church in an Age of Division* (Bellingham: Lexham, 2022), 22.

the temptations of mass culture. Evangelical celebrities transcend all local realities, and as many of them became overtly political (and partisan), they damaged the ability to speak across cultural differences."[4] The relationship between evangelical politics and evangelical celebrityism is built upon the influence that popular culture has on the evangelical church. Evangelical pastors who relentlessly engage a culture war and prioritize *that* over faithful week in and week out biblical exposition ironically show their dependence on the very thing they spend their time denouncing. They devote more attention in sermons to attacking cultural-political issues than to proclaiming the gospel through consistent Bible exposition. The result is that they lead theologically infantile churches paranoid about secular culture rather than biblically literate congregants growing to theological maturity.

But as the previous chapter argued, an evangelical's regular exposure to Scripture will, over time, shape their discernment, awareness, and beliefs about everything. To understand Scripture correctly *is* to understand culture and politics correctly—and chasing down every secular fad for sermon content serves the pastor's interests, not the church's overall health. Building on Lints's point, such pastors cripple their witness for Christ and Scripture since the gospel transcends all cultural barriers and smashes through any perceived culture war.

Katelyn Beaty also offers recent criticism of the explosive influence of the evangelical celebrity. Defining celebrity as *social power without proximity*, she calls attention to the fakeness of it all:

> We think we know our favorite ministry heads, worship leaders, authors, activists, and evangelists, because we follow them on social media or hear them preach from a stage or read their words on a page. But we are presented with a presented, mediated self. And the absence of true knowledge, and true accountability, leaves abundant opportunity for their social power to be misused and abused.[5]

---

4. Ibid., 22, n.42.
5. Katelyn Beaty, *Celebrities for Jesus: How Personas, Platforms, and Profits are Hurting the Church* (Grand Rapids: Brazos, 2022), 18–19.

The need for accountability is key in Beaty's assessment of evangelical celebrity culture. A pastor or any evangelical leader whose ministry is placed in the public spotlight needs to be held accountable with regular contact, prayer, encouragement, admonishment, and so forth from the other men who help lead the church. Such accountability acts as a guard against the attacks and temptations of the world, the flesh, and the devil. From famous apologists to itinerate preachers, modern evangelicalism is plagued by celebrity ministers detached from any real accountability and whose legacies include all sorts of misconduct discovered after the fact. Celebrity evangelicals are almost never grounded in a healthy Bible-centered church with a plurality of pastors who love them enough to speak into their lives regularly and directly.

A dangerous irony that exists for Christian celebrities is public isolation. They become a public persona, but nobody really knows them. They aren't accountable and humble enough to bring other people into their process. Moral failures and scandals happen through a string of isolations when celebrity pastors don't have accountability with other men who love them enough to speak into their lives. Too often, a senior-pastor model of ministry, with one man at the top calling the shots, creates a church culture that is too afraid to speak up if that leader needs to be confronted or called to repentance. A healthy ministry is one operating as a "social context" of community and leadership, not as the isolated endeavor of one ambitious leader.[6] When moral failures and abuse are exposed in evangelical celebrityism, a line can almost always be drawn between the celebrity caught in egregious sin and absentee local church accountability. This is what Beaty meant with her caution of having social power without proximity. "We have too many institutions built around personalities—people with immense social power but little or no proximity. We are

---

6. See Joseph H. Hellerman, *Embracing Shared Ministry: Power and Status in the Early Church and Why it Matters Today* (Grand Rapids: Kregel Ministry, 2013), 178–80.

well passed thinking of celebrity as a neutral tool."[7] Celebrity is anything but neutral. As stewards of Christ, our aim should be to reveal the full beauty of *Jesus*, never ourselves. I am doggedly convinced that for Christ to increase in mainstream evangelicalism *we must kill Christian celebrityism*.

Mega-pastors, Mega-jobs, Mega-ghostwriting

Especially prone to the problem of celebrity Christianity are megachurches with "mega-pastors" driven by relentless "vision casting" that effectively keeps everyone in the church under their control.[8]

Problems of pastoral pride and bullying are inevitable in most megachurches, "because of a structure that elevates one man over the rest to the point of his becoming virtually unassailable."[9] Rising to a pharaoh status on top of a pyramid, so to speak, the name-brand celebrity doesn't need to submit to anybody.[10] Congregants become too imitated or awe-struck by the celebrity pastor to speak up when it's needed.[11] This is especially the case for paid staff members whose jobs are dependent on the one man on top. Evangelical megachurches and celebrity ministries are built on an economic principle that is the perennial justification for everything American—*jobs*. Providing jobs is the impenetrable vindication for evangelical mega-pastors who have morphed themselves into a name brand that keeps people employed. And

---

7. Katelyn Beaty, *Celebrities for Jesus*, 19.

8. Ibid., 43–62.

9. Constantine R. Campbell, *Jesus v. Evangelicals: A Biblical Critique of a Wayward Movement* (Grand Rapids: Zondervan Reflective, 2023), 152.

10. I borrow the pharaoh / pyramid metaphor from Joel Tetreau, *The Pyramid and the Box: The Decision-Making Process in a Local New Testament Church* (Eugene: Resource, 2013), 8.

11. As an aside, this conversation underscores the importance of church leadership structure and polity. I am convinced there is no such thing as celebrity in a genuinely functioning model ruled by a plurality of elders. The accountability demanded by the model makes it impossible for any one man to become *his own* accountability, which is often the case with senior pastor and megachurch models.

because people's livelihoods are at stake, Christian employees keep their mouths shut if the Christian celebrity violates biblical ethics for the sake of the "ministry."

Related to problems of mega-pastors and celebrity culture concerns the best-kept secret in evangelicalism—*the egregious yet accepted industry of ghostwriting.* A sad reality is that celebrity pastors hardly ever write their own books but reap a mountain of fame and money from them anyway. Ghostwriting is the practice of hiring a skilled writer to author a book in place of someone under the agreement that the true author's identity remains hidden from public knowledge. Again, justified by providing jobs, the field of ghostwriting keeps armies of highly competent no-name writers employed for their skill, despite its unethical practice. It amounts to plagiarism since the real author gets no credit on the book and remains unseen (hence "ghost"), while the celebrity who didn't write it receives every accolade. The technical word for such a practice used in biblical studies is pseudepigraphy, or "false writing," referring to an ancient document pretending to be from a prophet or apostle to reap some personal benefit. Ancient examples include non-canonical works like Enoch, Testament of Job, the Gospel of Thomas, the Gospel of Barnabas, and others that are falsely attributed to a prophet or apostle hundreds of years removed from the actual time of writing. The practice was almost always considered deceitful and, once detected, a pseudepigraphal writing lost all authority since it was a fake.[12]

I should be clear that Christian authors aren't the only ones guilty of ghostwriting. Some bestselling secular books are also peppered with the practice. But somehow the act has become an industry standard within evangelical publishing, despite the clear biblical ethics violated. "Such deception is grounds for firing a lawsuit in other arenas," Beaty points out. "Yet the practice is

---

12. See the various essays in David B. Capes, ed., *Does It Matter Who Wrote the Bible? The Pastoral Implications of Pseudonymity and Anonymity in the New Testament* (Eugene: Pickwick, 2025).

common in publishing, including Christian publishing."[13] What a sad witness *to* the world when evangelicals become frauds *alongside* the world! Ghostwriting is, like ancient pseudepigraphy, a form of lying. It is condemned by Paul (2 Thess. 2:2), and clashes with John's clear ethics of truth-telling: "*I write to you*, not because you do not know the *truth*, but because you know it, and because *no lie is of the truth*" (1 John 2:21, emphasis added). Ghostwriting communicates to the unsuspecting reader that the celebrity pastor whose name appears on the cover wrote the work when they simply hired someone else to write it for them. Profits from sales skyrocket and the celebrity's ego inflates—and all of it's based on fraud. The celebrity is not alone in his scam, everyone involved in the practice contributes to the lie. It is a shared sin for the celebrity pseudo-author *and* the ghostwriter *and* the publisher (if they're aware). They act as a team willingly engaged in deceit for financial or other personal gain.

Unfortunately, ghostwriting has become an indispensable tool for Christian celebrityism—with pride stirring the pot. The pseudo-author with celebrity status refuses to acknowledge the ghostwriter's efforts with a simple "and," "with," or even a footnote crediting them to something (which hardly any reader would notice anyway!). Instead, the celebrity Christian wants to be celebrated for his or her supposed genius *and no one else*. This violates the Pauline ethic of bringing in "many witnesses" who confirm one's teaching, whether oral or written (2 Tim 2:2). The truth is that no one is a genius on their own. Everyone is dependent on others for previous knowledge. The practice of footnoting and giving credit to where credit is due should be a non-negotiable for any Christian author. Doing so demonstrates humility and shows that the writer is aware that he or she is entering into an ongoing conversation that's older than him or her. As such, others need to be credited for their ideas when helping advance that conversation.

As any genuine pastor will freely admit, shepherding a local church is extremely hard work. An eclectic group of human souls

---

13. Katelyn Beaty, *Celebrities for Jesus*, 107.

are under the pastor's care for which he's accountable. A legitimate author will also tell you that researching and writing *well* is hard work, and writing for publication is tremendously difficult. One man doing *both* with excellence—pastoring and publishing—is remarkably challenging and rare (practically impossible). Chances are excellent that when a celebrity Christian leading several large ministries seemingly pumps out multiple bestsellers a year, there is fraud taking place—the book is written by someone else, the publisher turned a blind eye, and the Christian reader is clueless to the deception (or chooses to ignore it). Evangelical pastors who fall into the dark trappings of celebrity culture in their races to be *New York Times* bestselling authors stain their pulpits and shame the name of Christ.[14] Tragically, Christian celebrityism has turned American evangelicals from being people *of* the book to being people *deceiving others* with their books.

The (Mis)Use of Technology in the Church

From radio and television to podcasts and Instagram reels, there would be no celebrity pastors without modern technology. This raises a question. If evangelical celebrityism is an aberration of the vintage faith (which I argue it is), and is dependent on modern technology (which also I argue is true), does that make technology itself evil?

The question is not simple. An immediate response is that technology is inherently neutral. Much like a gun or a car, what matters is how it's used. A gun can protect the innocent *and* kill the innocent. A car can transport kids to school *and* be used as a deadly weapon.[15] Any evil committed using these

---

14. Warren Throckmorton, "How the Religious Right Scams Its Way onto the *New York Times* Bestseller List," *Daily Beast*, November 16, 2014, https://www.thedailybeast.com/how-the-religious-right-scams-its-way-onto-the-new-york-times-bestseller-list/.

15. As I write this in January 2025, two domestic terrorist attacks were just carried out in the US using cars as weapons in both New Orleans and Las Vegas. While only the terrorist died in the latter, sadly, fourteen were killed and thirty-five were injured in the former (as of

things lies squarely with the evil *person* behind them. Guns and cars are neutral, but their users are not. Evangelicals, therefore, would do well not to adopt a gnostic perspective that equates the material world with evil, while supposing only what is spiritual or intellectual is what matters. But what about instances where technology is *not* so neutral? This is a reality as well. The late cultural critic Neil Postman cleverly coined the word "technopoly" in his assessment that warned of a society shaped by technology rather than supported by it. Technology can become sovereign over national life, even redefine historically held beliefs on politics, religion, education, family, and so forth to fit its purveyors' agendas.[16] More recently, former professor of mass media and strategic communication at the University of Tennessee at Martin, Arthur Hunt, made similar arguments. Hunt tied the American Christian fixation with technology to a post-modern obsession with images, even tracing it historically to ancient pagan cultures and idolatry.[17] Technology is *not* inherently innocent or neutral according to these scholars.

Today, algorithms in social media are intentionally engineered to elicit views and responses to whatever their curators want to be seen. A person's social media outlets are controlled by private owners who purposely expose their users to their products, politics, and social ideals. Evangelicals are not immune to this technological phenomenon; if anything, they're prime targets and even become facilitators of it. With the ubiquitous onslaught of Artificial Intelligence (AI) platforms, pastors can now preach sermons and write lessons without ever having to craft them on their own thanks to technology *designed* for this very function.[18]

---

today's reports).

16. Neil Postman, *Technopoly: The Surrender of Culture to Technology* (New York: Vintage, 1993).

17. Arthur W. Hunt III, *The Vanishing Word: The Veneration of Visual Imagery in the Postmodern World* (Eugene: Wipf & Stock, 2013).

18. On the Pastor Scholar Podcast, we dedicated an entire episode to the use of AI in churches and specific platforms targeting pastors, which can be found at foundationsmedia.org.

Justified by the American ideal of "expediency," pastors no longer must spend their time in the deep trenches of exegesis to understand the biblical text on their own with guidance from the Holy Spirit (2 Tim. 2:15; 1 John 2:27). Instead, they can let an artificial bot do the work for them so they can spend time needed to build their individual ministry platforms. Turns out, technology isn't so neutral after all.

The use and misuse of technology is nothing new for evangelicals. In the early 1990s, emeritus professor of communication at Calvin University, Quentin Schultze, published a monograph entitled *Televangelism and American Culture* analyzing what he called "the business of popular religion."[19] The book was written before the rise of internet-driven technologies, and by today's standards, may be a bit dated. But the insights Schultze offers in his study critiquing American "televangelism" (evangelical television preachers during the mid to late twentieth century) can be applied to today's evangelical celebrity culture.[20] According to Schultze, "Television is not a neutral medium; it invariably communicates some messages better than others." Nevertheless, he cautions that "nearly all criticisms…levele[d] against the medium are the result of how it's used, not its inherent nature."[21] He added this last part after interacting with several writers who were critical of converging modern technology and the gospel, believing technology was anything but "neutral."

For example, British writer Malcom Muggeridge gave several provocative lectures in the mid-1970s that strongly decried the non-neutrality of technology and argued that television threatens the reality of Christ into a make-believe world of fantasy.[22] Such

---

19. Quentin J. Schultze, *Televangelism and American Culture: The Business of Popular Religion* (Eugene: Wipf & Stock, 1991).

20. Given my comments earlier about mega-pastors and mega-churches I find this thought from Schultze worthy of pause: "The closest thing to televangelism incarnate in the local church is the so-called megachurch." *Televangelism and American Culture*, 220.

21. Ibid., 49.

22. One thinks of the wildly popular Christian film industry and

technology apparently "exploits the weakness and wretchedness of men" by appealing to human fallenness that promotes *eros* over *agape* [lust over love], celebrity status over a broken and contrite heart.[23] Though Muggeridge's take is going on fifty years old and may be overstated, it's hard not to see some similarity with what he noticed then and today's celebrity-intoxicated, technologically-competitive evangelical culture. Too many current pastors have borrowed the tactics of their televangelist forebearers and have advanced, not the gospel or biblical theology, but their own evangelical cults of personalities that compete with one another for the most likes and followers on social media. These pastors tend to have the same spiritual "gift" of exaggeration that inflates attendance and membership numbers, baptisms, financial giving, saved souls, along with the size of their social media imprint. Evangelical celebrity influencers now use technology to purchase fake social media accounts, fake followers, and fake likes run by others to help "boost" their platform and name branding.[24] Technology-fraud is the industry standard for Christian celebrityism, running hand in hand with the ghostwriting covered earlier.

Let me offer a sobering reason for the pervasive number of evangelical cults of celebrity we see today—*American capitalism infused with popular media technology influencing evangelicalism to create a facade of ministry success.* The difficulty that American pastors face is separating ministry faithfulness to the local body of believers that Christ has given them from what is perceived to be "successful" by the American dream. "It was inevitable that American views of success would influence religion," argues Schultze. "Increasingly, the successful preacher was the one most

---

meteoric shows today, like The Chosen, that always insert bits of non-biblical fantasy genre into their portrayals of Christ or other stories from Scriptures.

23. Quentin J. Schultze, *Televangelism and American Culture*, 48.
24. Katelyn Beaty, *Celebrities for Jesus*, 110–11.

able not only to evangelize unsaved souls or revive waning ones, but also to create visible symbols of success."[25]

The modern industry of evangelicalism demands that the successful preacher be persuasive and well liked, regardless of his (or her) character. A compound of "television" and "photogenic," the word "telegenic" is now an industry term used of a person's attractive appearance on a screen (TV, computer, mobile device, etc.) that positively impacts viewers. Just like the danger of mingling mass politics with electronic media resulting in entertainment-driven news,[26] an unguarded mingling of technology with evangelicalism can confuse entertainment with the gospel. This may result in more likes, more followers, more opportunities, and more money for the telegenic evangelical. But something is missed that a true vintage faith offers. Biblically saturated pastors are committed to shepherding the sheep *among them* (which is by necessity smaller churches), *not* building platforms in a race to influence the world (see 1 Pet. 5:2). At the least, conservative evangelical pastors should think twice about appearing on the same channel or participating in the same events with questionable people, despite the reach it affords.

If creating jobs isn't the pretext, the most well-worn excuse by doctrinally sound celebrity evangelical pastors for appearing on programs that are known to host theologically aberrant celebrities, or for starting their own television or YouTube ministries, is that it expands the gospel's reach. This is superficial evangelism. It assumes that God *needs* them alongside heretics or *needs* them to become famous worldwide for non-believers to hear the truth. But the fact is most audiences are already part of the celebrity's constituency. One study showed that less than 4 per cent of all religious broadcasting viewers are non-believers. In some cases, 85 per cent or higher of viewers are already converted. A study done by Institute of American Church Growth of 40,000 Christians showed only 0.01 per cent of them said they attend church as a

---

25. Quentin J. Schultze, *Televangelism and American Culture*, 73.
26. See Neil Postman's classic, *Amusing Ourselves to Death: Public Discourse in the Age of Show Business* (New York: Penguin, 2005).

result of mass evangelism.[27] The numbers suggest that television in particular has never been an effective evangelistic medium. It is largely *confirmatory*, not conversion driven.

The televangelism phenomenon became the progenitor of twenty-first century American evangelical celebrityism. For many celebrity preachers, their studio audience or conference stage is their "church," funded by relentless pleas for donations disguised as "offerings." Viewers are passive, not active. No one is serving one another with their gifts and talents. Once Christians become a mere "audience," they are nothing more than consumers who can be manipulated to the ends of the celebrity who changes rapidly with the shifting tides of the marketplace without concern for the people they supposedly serve.[28] Additionally, with the rise of public preachers skyrocketing into stardom through a medium that can be accessed by millions, the gospel message of Christ's sacrifice for unworthy sinners tends to become one of prosperity or mere positive thinking.

Viewers are pressured to "sow seeds of faith" by giving to their celebrity preacher who needs the funds for airtime. Wildly popular television preachers like Oral Roberts championed what became known as the "prosperity gospel," where "Belief could now be expected to produce not just healing from illness, but health, wealth, and happiness."[29] The most influential among them counseled US presidents or founded universities they named after themselves.[30] There is an important commonality between television preachers and online pastors. Virtually none of them are (or were) held accountable by a local church governed by a plurality of qualified elders. Instead, they have studios, producers, literary agents, and public relations personnel. With private jets

---

27. These percentages are taken from Quentin J. Schultze, *Televangelism and American Culture*, 187–88.

28. See Gary Gilley, *This Little Church Went to Market: The Church in the Age of Entertainment* (Minneapolis: Evangelical Press, 2005).

29. Jonathan Root, *Oral Roberts and the Rise of the Prosperity Gospel* (Grand Rapids: Eerdmans, 2023), 70.

30. See Nancy Gibbs and Michael Duffy, *The Preacher and the Presidents: Billy Graham in the White House* (New York: Center Street, 2007).

and a collection of mansions that follow, the love of money, fame, greed, abuse, follow as well.

Public platforms and powerful influence, mixed with a malevolent use of technology, eventually results in abuse and scandal enveloping Christian celebrityism. Inevitably exposed is the hard truth that many "evangelical" celebrity pastors are in fact false teachers who peddle forms of the gospel for sordid gain. The New Testament is not silent in its warnings of such charlatans (1 Tim. 6:5; Titus 1:7; 1 Pet. 5:2; Jude 16).

Apostolic Perspectives on Christian Celebrityism

Admittedly, it is easy to point the finger at Big Eva celebrity culture in modern America. Furthermore, the telegenic, high profile prosperity preachers make especially easy targets for those who, like me, are within the stream of conservative traditions committed to inductive hermeneutics and expository preaching. But the seeds of Christian celebrityism were not first laid in the soil of charismatic prosperity preachers. Rather, celebrity culture sprang up in the local church around the most orthodox Bible expositors in history.

Apollos was a close associate of the apostle Paul and his intimate circle.[31] An Alexandrian Jewish convert to Christ, he was a powerful preacher, introduced in the New Testament as, "an eloquent man, competent in the Scriptures. He had been instructed in the way of the Lord. And being fervent in spirit, he spoke and taught accurately the things concerning Jesus though he knew only the baptism of John" (Acts 18:24–25). After some mentoring by Priscilla and Aquilla, Apollos would go on to play a role in the establishment of the church in Corinth and "greatly helped those who through grace had believed, for he vehemently refuted the Jews in public, showing by the Scriptures that the

---

31. Andrew J. Wilson, "Apostle Apollos?" *Journal of the Evangelical Theological Society* 56.2 (June 2013): 325–35, makes an interesting case that though Apollos does not fit neatly into the customary evangelical categories of the apostolate, Paul considered Apollos to be a fellow apostle.

Christ was Jesus" (vv. 27–28). Each of the ten times his name appears in the Bible is in a venerated context, highlighted by Paul's commendation of Apollos as an effective teacher for the benefit of the church (1 Cor. 4:6; 16:12).

Apollos may also be the first "celebrity" preacher in church history. In fact, Paul uses the word for "famous" when commending an unidentified "brother" for his preaching, which is a fitting characteristic of Apollos: "With [Titus] we are sending the brother who is *famous* [*epainos*] among all the churches for his preaching of the gospel" (2 Cor. 8:18).[32] Commentators have suggested multiple candidates for the identity of this anonymous "brother." Luke and Barnabas have been popular candidates as early as the fourth century while some contemporary scholars prefer to view the "brother" as a newly-elected representative of a church council.[33]

Though it's unwise to be dogmatic, I think a solid case can be made for the unnamed brother being Apollos as he was quickly gaining *epainos*—"fame, praise, celebration"—in his preaching abilities and the Corinthians knew him well.[34] This also fits the distinction Paul seems to draw between Titus's pastoral heart in vv. 16–17 and the "famous preacher" in v. 18—who, in the apostle's previous letter to the church, explicitly identified Apollos as a "brother" who decided not to visit the church at that time *despite* Paul urging him to (1 Cor. 16:12).[35]

---

32. The Greek in v. 18 can also be translated "… whose praise is in the gospel throughout all the churches." Variations of this translation are reflected in the KJV, NASB, and LSB, while the ESV, NET, and CSB reflect the translation given above.

33. Gerald Lewis Bray, ed., *1–2 Corinthians*, Ancient Christian Commentary on Scripture (Downers Grove: InterVarsity Press, 1999), 276; V. G. Shillington, *2 Corinthians*, Believers Church Bible Commentary (Scottdale: Herald Press, 1998), 182.

34. See William O. Walker, Jr., "Apollos and Timothy as the Unnamed 'Brothers' in 2 Corinthians 8:18-24," *The Catholic Biblical Quarterly* 73.2 (April 2011), 318–38.

35. I can't resist saying that, to me, this distinction has celebrity preacher written all over it! I can imagine Apollos in the modern-

What I want to point out here is the fact that Christian celebrityism is not restricted to the standard prosperity gospel and word of faith culprits nor did it start with them.[36] Tribalism over famous preachers runs in the bloodline of doctrinally conservative Christian circles, beginning with Apollos, Peter, and Paul—all three of whom held to the highest view of Scripture. And Paul didn't hold back in calling out factitious parties in the Corinthian church who celebritized each one of them (including himself):

> I appeal to you, brothers, by the name of our Lord Jesus Christ, that all of you agree, and that there be no divisions [*schismata*] among you, but that you be united in the same mind and the same judgment. For it has been reported to me by Chloe's people that there is quarreling among you, my brothers. What I mean is that each one of you says, "I follow Paul," or "I follow Apollos," or "I follow Cephas," or "I follow Christ" (1 Cor. 1:10–12).

> For while there is jealousy and strife among you, are you not of the flesh and behaving only in a human way? For when one says, "I follow Paul," and another, "I follow Apollos," are you not being merely human? (1 Cor. 3:3–4).

Multiple elements of these two passages are interesting, but what I want to emphasize is that the Corinthian believers did not latch on to charismatics or heretics. They were not forming cliques or *schismatas* ("divisions") around the sons of Sceva who were trying to cast out demons in the name of Jesus who Paul proclaimed (Acts 19:13). They were not building factions around the preeminent "super apostles" intoxicating this same church in Corinth, who in reality were false teachers (2 Cor. 11:5). Instead,

---

day context of preaching tours, conservative evangelical conferences, crusades, etc. where he's a frequent keynote speaker with little time for the local church. Still, you have to admire him and his love for truth.

36. Parts of what follows are adapted from my chapter, "Recovering Biblical Literacy," in *Fight the Good Fight: Reclaiming Biblical Fundamentalism*, ed. Richard Bargas (Grand Rapids: IFCA Press, 2024), 54–55. Used with permission.

they were forming tribes around the best, most faithful Bible teachers Christianity had to offer—*Apollos, Peter, and Paul!* The Corinthians' exclusive loyalties to their favorite preachers threatened the unity of the church. But Paul was clear to point out that he and the others merely planted and watered the soil, while *God* caused all visible growth (1 Cor. 3:6–7).

Today, there are silly wars among conservative evangelicals that reflect the celebrity factions in Corinth. Party lines are drawn between whose radio ministry or podcast is *truly* Reformed or what Study Bible is *more* orthodox or what translation is *most* literal. Unbridled dogmatism runs rampant in such conversations and is especially pervasive on social media. Disagreements over the finest theological detail or technical term become excuses to anathematize one's fellow believer with appeals made to a favorite author, pastor, or theologian (living or dead) to justify the unruly condemnation. Those who claim an evangelical identity should learn from Paul about the dangers of attaching one's spirituality or theological bona fides to a famous name.

Before a finger of blame is pointed at trending celebrities with outrageous ministries, it is healthy to examine one's own tendency. If those sitting under the instruction of *divinely chosen apostles who exposited Scripture better than anyone* can fall into celebrityism, then we can too. But the lesson cuts both ways. Doctrinally sound evangelical *pastors* and *preachers* whose ministries are widening (or have widened) into the public space, need also to learn from Paul. They need to be the *first* to remind their followers that *God in Christ* is the ultimate "Senior Pastor" (*archipoimeno*, see 1 Pet. 5:3) who deserves all the glory for visible growth due to their efforts while *they* are mere gardeners.

Public Minister v. Christian Celebrity

As this "rant" draws to a close, I want to be clear that this chapter is not a condemnation of public ministry as a whole. Christ has used—and continues to use—very public ministers of the gospel who are faithful to the text and to their local churches.

"There have always been men . . . like Chrysostom or Knox or Whitefield or Spurgeon or Lloyd-Jones or ten thousand others who have been 'famous among all the churches for [their] preaching of the gospel,'" observes Kevin DeYoung, "it is not a capitulation to culture to admit this fact. And it's not bad to acknowledge these men and commend them to others. Could actually be quite biblical."[37] Indeed, we should pray for and expect certain ministries to widen publicly and influence the larger society with the gospel of Jesus (even through books written on the vintage faith!).

Rather, my rants throughout this chapter were aimed specifically at *celebrity* Christianity, not *public* Christianity. If it were the latter, I'd be condemning myself since this book is *published*, distributed *publicly*, and hoped to be read by the *public* (all related words). Consequently, being a public minister or public theologian does not necessitate the trappings of celebrity status. Neither should *fame* or *popularity* be confused with *celebrity*. Though similarity exists, this chapter, borrowing from Beaty's work, defined celebrity as an intentional social power *without* proximity. There is a difference between this definition of "celebrity" and simply being "well-known" or "famous" (as in the case of Apollos earlier).

If celebrity is intentional *social power without proximity*, then I suggest being well-known or famous *without* celebrity is having *social influence within proximity*. The Christian leader must kill any desire for personal "power" and find joy in "influencing" others for the glory of God *within* proximity (see Mark 10:42–45). To maintain social influence *within proximity* suggests that the well-known, public, or "famous" evangelical pastor knows the people they are called to shepherd, and they actually know something of the pastor's life—not some polished persona that a celebrity would portray. In other words, the difference between being famous and being a celebrity is in being

---

37. Kevin DeYoung, "When Paul Sent the Celebrity Pastor," The Gospel Coalition, May 8, 2012, https://www.thegospelcoalition.org/blogs/kevin-deyoung/when-paul-sent-the-celebrity-pastor/.

held accountable. Accountability is the great separator of the two, and for the public minister, is cherished as a grace and implemented into his ministry model. Accountability keeps individual ambition and power (to which we're all susceptible) in check while allowing for the most public influence of the gospel.

Conclusion

Evangelicalism is not the only Christian tradition with celebrities. But its addiction to celebrityism is most obvious, especially in the United States. I've already made the case for what makes up a true and authentic evangelical faith, and having the biggest church, most followers, or reposted tweets appear nowhere in the argument.

I concede that more may be added to my five fundamentals in part two of this book, but I am certain that not one of them can be eliminated if we are to recover the vintage faith. A genuine, historic evangelicalism is established on a set pattern of beliefs that results in behavior reflecting those beliefs and nothing else. Any definition for evangelicalism that includes celebrity culture or politics has absolutely no bearing on what this book has argued as a true vintage faith. In the final chapter that follows, I will return to an idea I brought up earlier in the book about the usefulness of the label "evangelicalism." Is it worth retaining or should we finally retire it for something else? Can something that is *vintage* be recovered as an effective model of theological identity in a *modern* world? These are not identical questions, but they both highlight the need for our answers to be based on fundamental truths from a fundamental source.

CHAPTER 9

A Case for Biblical Fundamentalism

Now that we've essentially reached the end of the book, I want to return to an idea first brought up in chapter one and echoed at various points throughout this volume: the usefulness of the label evangelicalism. I am not the first academic to struggle with the name, as D. G. Hart was shown to renounce it entirely, though not its theology. For Hart, evangelicalism has become such a wide category of "unstable constellation of personalities and organizations" that it ceases to be of any value.[1] Unfortunately, Hart has a point.

Nor am I the first to consider what Richard Mouw described as a "perverse theological fantasy" he had in mind about announcing to the world a name change.[2] For Mouw, his excitement was curbed with the reality that his suggestion of "neo-fundamentalism" as a new label for conservative evangelicalism would never be accepted—despite any kernel of seriousness in his idea. Though I like the term that Mouw suggested, the "neo-" prefix can

---

1. D. G. Hart, *Deconstructing Evangelicalism: Conservative Protestantism in the Age of Billy Graham* (Grand Rapids: Baker Academic, 2004), 31.

2. Richard J. Mouw, *The Smell of Sawdust: What Evangelicals Can Learn from Their Fundamentalist Heritage* (Grand Rapids: Zondervan, 2000), 57.

unwittingly recall aberrant—even polar opposite—movements from *Neo*-Orthodoxy to *Neo*-Nazism. It's not that "neo" is a bad word in itself, it just tends to suggest an abnormal or irregular iteration of something. Additionally, if the word "neo" has such baggage, then I doubt qualifying it with "fundamentalism" is going to help!

Besides, the "neo" prefix has already been used within the context of modern conservative Protestantism to identity what emerged in the mid twentieth century as *neo* or *new evangelicalism*. Birthed in the wake of the modernist–fundamentalist wars, neo-evangelicalism was an academic distancing by conservative scholars from what they perceived to be an anti-intellectual form of fundamentalism.[3] But this particular label has become less and less used of an existing constituency as its movers pass into eternity and their movement consigned to the pages of history. In any case, what I have been arguing for to this point is anything but "new." In fact, the opposite is my case. This book calls for recovering something *vintage* and *historic*—a tradition with positions that are stable and verifiable in Scripture, not reactionary to the evolving fads of culture.

Time for a Name Change?

"For everything there is a season," said *Qōhelet*, "and a time for every matter under heaven" (Eccles. 3:1). I'm unsure if King Solomon had in mind the value of changing names of things when he wrote that verse. But he does go on to include that, among all the various seasons of life, there is "a time to keep, and a time to cast away" (v. 6). I can't help but see some relevance for this discussion that asks if we should keep "evangelicalism" as a label or cast it behind us.

The previous two chapters on politics and celebrity pastors pulled back the curtain a bit to expose a few areas of the American

---

3. Owen Strachan, *Awakening the Evangelical Mind: An Intellectual History of the Neo-Evangelical Movement* (Grand Rapids: Zondervan, 2015), 109–26.

industry I have termed, "evan-jello-calism." To exorcise the "jello" out of the movement is to set free a vintage faith from modern-day entrepreneurs and captors of the fundamental beauty, power, and theology of biblical Christianity. Earlier in Part 1 of this book, I also called attention to theological liberals and progressives who disavow practically everything genuinely evangelical (basically the ideas in Part 2), but for whatever reason refuse to relent and drop the label "evangelical" for themselves. These types have served as adversaries to my thesis in the sense of offering a contrasting conversation with their ubiquitous fixation of "white," "oppressive," "republican," and other useless descriptors they attach to "evangelicalism." The fact that so many "others," to use Isaac Sharp's term, choose to classify themselves as "evangelicals," despite their beliefs and lifestyles being antithetical to the history of the evangelicalism, elevates the need for a possible name change.

Recall the point raised by Mouw in chapter one: "If a term we use to describe ourselves ceases to live up to the standards of truth-in-advertising than we should drop it."[4] Mouw made this observation twenty-five years ago when considering dropping the label evangelical[-ism] because its usefulness had by then become increasingly suspect. It is that context which gave rise to his fantasy of re-branding the tradition as "neo-fundamentalism" above. My sentiments are certainly with Mouw on this point. As this book contends, the vintage faith has been hijacked by those who have no right to the name *evangelicalism* but still apply it to themselves or apply it to others who go outside the metrics this book offers. But maybe a different label without the "neo" prefix would be helpful. As such, I suggest that the term *biblical fundamentalism* is the best alternative to identify what is traditionally understood as conservative evangelicalism.

The Fundamental Principle of Biblical Fundamentalism

For "biblical fundamentalism" to make inroads as a useful label that identifies genuine or conservative evangelicals requires defining

---

4. Richard J. Mouw, *The Smell of Sawdust*, 20.

the terms. Like "evangelicalism," the term "fundamentalism" has become an elusive phrase. Also like "evangelicalism," the word "fundamentalism" comes with its own baggage.

Derision has been the legacy of Christian "fundamentalism" ever since Curtis Lee Laws, a Baptist minister and editor of the *Watchman-Examiner,* offered the neologism in 1920. He coined the term in defense of conservatives who fought for "the great fundamentals" and did "battle royale" against modernists who attacked the veracity of Scripture and other classic evangelical doctrines.[5] Despite how the word is used in today's culture, which is almost always in some contemptuous context (e.g., *militant*-fundamentalism), the word *fundamentalism* itself is not bad or good; it's neutral. Its meaning simply builds on what is *essential, basic, or necessary*—all three of which Microsoft Word considers synonyms for *fundamental* (go ahead and check). According to the *Oxford English Dictionary* (the magisterial last word on English lexemes if there ever was one), the English term "fundamental" is defined as both an adjective and a noun. As an adjective, "fundamental" means "a foundation or core; of central importance," and as a noun, "a central or primary rule or principle."[6]

If we take these neutral ideas as our launching pad, a fundamentalist would be someone who simply *holds to a core foundation of beliefs by a central rule or principle.* The question then becomes, *what* core beliefs and by *what* central principle? It is precisely here that the adjective "biblical" adds the necessary qualifier for the type of fundamentalism argued in this chapter. The "central rule" or "principle" from which identifies a "biblical fundamentalist" is *Scripture*—and *Scripture alone*—for core beliefs and authority over daily Christian living (aka, *sola Scriptura*).

---

5. Owen Strachan, *Awakening the Evangelical Mind*, 39–40.

6. Okay, this technically comes from the "concise" OED which I had pre-loaded in my Bible software program! See Catherine Soanes and Angus Stevenson, eds., *Concise Oxford English Dictionary* (Oxford: Oxford University Press, 2004), s.v. "fundamental." Logos Bible Software.

This immediately distinguishes *biblical fundamentalism* from any other type of fundamentalism that sources its identity apart from the Bible. It also extends past the five "fundamentals" this book identifies as the irreducible minimum or the *sine qua non* of evangelicalism. Biblical fundamentalism includes them but extends to other beliefs and convictions that are *sourced in Scripture* and are fundamental to knowing the biblical God, the world he created, and our place as his image bearers. I suppose "biblical worldview-ism" would capture the same idea. But "biblical worldview-ist," sounds weird to me. Besides, biblical/biblicist and fundamental/fundamentalist are historic terms that have a legacy worth resurrecting (and harmonious with my fixation of all things "vintage"!).

Who Wants to Be Labeled a "Biblicist"?

Like "fundamentalist/fundamentalism," the terms "biblicist/biblicism" are not wildly popular among the evangelical elite. Because a *biblical fundamentalist* can also be called a *biblicist* in the right context, the idea of biblicism for how I and others understand it should be explained.

For some scholars, biblicism conjures up images of selective proof texting to justify one's orthodoxy.[7] For others, it gives the impression of an "ahistorical mindset" that devalues all insights and formulations from Christian thinkers throughout history.[8] And still others view biblicism as an extreme form of literalistic interpretation, "with no respect for Scripture's poetic devices or Aristotelian rationalism."[9] One dictionary even conflates "biblicism" with "bibliolatry," the latter being a pejorative term

---

7. Michael S. Horton, "Why Historical Theology Matters: The Trinity and the Dangers of Biblicism," *Theo Global Journal* 1 (Nov 2024), 233.

8. Matthew Barrett, *The Reformation as Renewal: Retrieving the One, Holy, Catholic, and Apostolic Church* (Grand Rapids: Zondervan Academic, 2023), 21.

9. J. D. Douglas, ed., *New Twentieth-Century Encyclopedia of Religious Knowledge*, Second Edition (Grand Rapids: Baker, 1991), s.v., "Biblicism."

to castigate those who value Scripture to the extent of apparently *idolatrizing* the Bible.[10] If being a biblicist relates to any one of these views, it's not surprising that astute Christian thinkers would want to stay as far from it as an identity as possible!

Now, I must admit that there are people in this world who probably fit within one of those descriptions. That said, I believe it's unfair to tag a group of people with a label that is used entirely differently by those who intentionally self-identify as biblicists and contribute to the academic community. Unfortunately, scholars who push a *version* of the label onto others who define it differently tend to be the most published and influential within academic evangelicalism and therefore become the standard bearers of what they believe a word *should* mean, despite what it *did* mean before them. These are often voices within the current Reformed evangelical trend of returning to a form of catholicity that *can* (not always) resemble the medieval scholasticism justifying the "dark ages" when the Roman Catholic Church kept the light of God's Word from their people.[11] I say it's better to go directly to those who are informed from the inside and self-identify with a label, and consult *their* definition for how *they* use the term. Doing so reveals a more accurate portrayal of biblicism that looks markedly different from those given above.

---

10. See J. J. Scott Jr., "Biblicism, Bibliolatry," in *Evangelical Dictionary of Theology*, ed. Walter A. Elwell (Grand Rapids: Baker, 1984), 152. Interestingly, this entry does not appear in the subsequently revised editions.

11. Let me be clear, I do think there is much that can be learned from supposed retrievals of classic theology and the like. I even enjoy personal friendships and collegial associations with many who fit within, and publish as advocates of, this modern trend. It is the issue of *charity* and *respect* for other Christians that I value most. Unfortunately, some within this crowd have failed to demonstrate these ethics toward those who don't view themselves as accurately portrayed in their scholarly re-definitions of historic terms like "biblicist" or "fundamentalist." The re-branding of "biblicism" by some often amounts to elitist and unloving derogatory statements toward other believers within evangelicalism, thereby violating Jesus's clear ethics in Matthew 7:12 and John 13:35.

For example, according to *self-identifying* biblicists John MacArthur, Richard Mayhue, and the faculty that produced a respected textbook on biblical doctrine, "biblicism" is defined simply as, "a very strong and even unquestioning commitment to the authority of the Bible."[12] This simple definition is not reflected at all in the sample offered by those who deride the term above. In MacArthur and Mayhue's view of biblicism, there is no worship of the Bible (bibliolatry) nor a disrespect for Scripture's poetic devices as suggested in those derogatory statements.

They are not alone, as some writers choose to highlight the historical pedigree of the idea of biblicism. Previous scholars like Alfred Russell even document the term "evangelical biblicist" as in use centuries ago to differentiate the non-conformists or puritan separatists from the "sacramentarian ecclesiasts" who held onto vestiges of aberrant Roman Catholic dogma in the wake of the Reformation.[13] Adding the qualifier "biblicist" proved helpful to identify someone who held to the *fundamental doctrines of the Christian faith* more than what "evangelical" could simply express. The latter term was eventually redefined by historical-critical scholars, and in the course of time became the catch all phrase that it is today. As Russell pointed out, the higher criticism made popular in German theological circles eventually spread to the UK and to the US, and as it did, "'Evangelical' gradually ceased to be the designation of true Biblicists and became merely a blanket phrase covering practically all Non-Romanists."[14] Ironically, the term evangelical now not only blankets "non-Romanists" (i.e., non-Catholics) who desire the label, but even extends in some uses to cover non-Protestants (i.e., Catholics and others) as well.

As chapter one pointed out earlier, by *sola Scriptura*, we mean that *ultimate authority* lies with the written revelation from God

---

12. John MacArthur and Richard Mayhue, eds., *Biblical Doctrine: A Systematic Summary of Bible Truth* (Wheaton: Crossway, 2017), 925.

13. Alfred U. Russell, "In Defence [*sic*] of Fundamentalism" *Central Bible Quarterly* 02.1 (Spring 1959): 43.

14. Ibid.

expressed through his chosen prophets and apostles, called the Bible. The principle does *not* mean that other authorities don't exist or should never be consulted (e.g., history, tradition, scholarship, etc). Contrary to some definitions of biblicism, a Christian biblicist does not supplant *sola Scriptura* with *solo* [or *nuda*] *Scriptura* as if believing God hasn't gifted countless teachers throughout church history with spiritual and intellectual prowess that elevate their insights to levels higher than mere opinions. Rather, the biblicist (or *biblical fundamentalist*) understands that Scripture is the inerrant, infallible, and authoritative Word of God that can be understood by the Holy Spirit indwelt believer in Jesus Christ who's applying a consistent method of interpretation.

How I and others apply the term in no way identifies someone who *disparages* the study and insights of extra-biblical literature. They just recognize there is a pecking order where nothing on earth can usurp the *Bible's authority*—and that recognition is reflected in their conversations and scholarship. "While not a perfect term," admit MacArthur and Mayhue, "we have chosen [to identify as] *biblicist*s, because at the core of our conviction lies an unshakable trust in God's inerrant and infallible Bible, rightly interpreted."[15] Clearly, to believe the Bible carries God's authority is to read it in such a way that would result in that belief which shares with the Protestant principle of Scripture's clarity. Thus, as argued earlier in chapter two, biblical inerrancy, biblical authority, and biblical clarity are all indelibly linked with a consistent interpretive approach that justifies these staple evangelical ideas. If this is what being a biblicist *truly* means, then frankly, no genuine evangelical should ever disparage the term even if disagreements over hermeneutics arise.

A Modest Intellectual History of Biblical Fundamentalism

As argued so far, the biblical fundamentalism for which I advocate is not to be confused with what is normally thought of when one hears the word "fundamentalism." Quite simply, a *biblical*

---

15. John MacArthur and Richard Mayhue, eds., *Biblical Doctrine*, 26.

fundamentalist holds to the great fundamentals of the Christian faith for its theological identity, as far as those beliefs are rooted in Scripture.

What I and others envision for the term falls within the historic stream of "a theologically conservative standpoint taken by orthodox Christian Protestant believers," as defined by Phillip Johnson. "It denotes a reiteration of orthodox doctrine in reaction to secular and liberal theological views."[16] As such, biblical fundamentalism is a form of evangelicalism that seeks to *reform* to what it once was where the Bible and essential doctrines of the Chistian faith were treated with the highest respect possible. It has always served as a bold and unashamed contrast to those who borrow from Christian capital in order to *appear* intellectual and/or godly while living lives denying the power of God (2 Tim. 3:1–5).

Biblical fundamentalism places itself within the historical milieu of the founding of three influential evangelical seminaries: Dallas Theological Seminary (DTS), Westminster Theological Seminary (WTS), and Fuller Theological Seminary (FTS). The principal founder of DTS, Lewis Sperry Chafer, rejected the early cultural "fundamentalism" of Carl McIntire and his aggressively separatist American Council of Churches founded in 1941, and instead participated in the founding National Association of Evangelicals (NAE) in 1942. According to historian John Hannah, Chafer was also critical of William Bell Riley's emergent fundamentalism in the World Christian Fundamentals Association as it converged onto secondary and tertiary matters in the 1940s to 1950s. Instead, Chafer and DTS maintained a strong commitment to academic theological education based on the fundamentals of orthodox Christianity derived from viewing the Bible as fully inerrant and authoritative. As a *biblical fundamentalist* seminary dedicated to training pastors,

---

16. Philip Johnson, "Fundamentalism, Christian," in *The Evangelical Dictionary of World Religions*, ed. H. Wayne House (Grand Rapids: Baker, 2018), 196–97.

scholars, and missionaries, historians do not consider Chafer or DTS within a stream of fundamentalism characterized by anti-intellectualism, militant separatism, or combativeness—the usual traits of cultural fundamentalism.[17]

A contemporary to Chafer, and similar in his fundamentalist convictions, J. Gresham Machen began publishing a series of articles in the *Princeton Theological Review* in 1905 defending the virgin birth of Christ.[18] A professor teaching at the end of Princeton Seminary's "old" tenure, marked by previous luminaries Hodges and Warfield, Machen distinguished himself as a world class New Testament scholar and apologist for biblical Christianity. After Princeton Seminary "reorganized" itself around theologically liberal "modernist" interpretations of the Bible in 1929, Machen led an exit from the historic school alongside conservative evangelical thinkers Cornelius Van Til, Oswald Allis, John Murray, and others to establish WTS in Philadelphia. "In intense struggles between fundamentalists and modernists during the 1920s and 1930s Machen emerged as an international champion of biblical authority and evangelical theology."[19] Like Chafer, Machen was not a *cultural* fundamentalist in any way, and didn't like the term "fundamentalist."[20] Nonetheless,

---

17. John D. Hannah, *An Uncommon Union: Dallas Theological Seminary and American Evangelicalism* (Grand Rapids: Zondervan, 2009), 17, 23.

18. See the fascinating exchange between Chafer and Machen as the former lends his advice to the latter on founding a seminary, which in turn reveals both men's ecclesiological differences. Stephen J. Nichols, "A Brief Exchange between Lewis Sperry Chafer and J. Gresham Machen," *Westminster Theological Journal* 62.2 (Fall 2000), 281–91.

19. D. F. Kelley, "Machen, John Gresham," *Evangelical Dictionary of Theology*, 3rd ed., eds. Daniel J. Treier and Walter A. Elwell (Grand Rapids: Baker Academic, 2017), 681.

20. Machen opposed prohibition, defended various civil liberties, and did not hold to a young earthy creationist view. See the insightful biography by D. G. Hart, *Defending the Faith: J. Gresham Machen and the Crisis of Conservative Protestantism in Modern America* (Phillipsburg: P&R, 2000).

every scholar places him as a key figurehead in conservative, fundamentalist evangelicalism as he published multiple works defending the fundamentals of the vintage faith—*The Origin of Paul's Religion* in 1921 and *Christianity and Liberalism* in 1923 being the most enduring, the latter as a defense of biblical authority and response to Harry Emerson Fosdick's infamous sermon "Shall the Fundamentalists Win?"

Though Fuller Seminary would become the scholarly bastion of "new [or neo] evangelicalism," at the time the school was established in 1947, evangelicalism and fundamentalism were not considered separate entities. As argued earlier, the terms were then interchangeable to describe the same large group battling a common foe. In his history on FTS, George Marsden writes, "Fundamentalism was thus a coalition of cobelligerents fighting against their common enemies, modernism and secularism."[21] This helps shed light on why Richard Mouw, quoted earlier, is sympathetic to evangelicalism's heritage of fundamentalism as he would come to serve as president of FTS for twenty years (1993–2013). Fuller's historic fundamentalist roots shouldn't be forgotten though the school suffered a massive missional drift that today looks nothing like its founding vision. The original faculty, with men like Harold Ockenga, Wilber Smith, Carl F. H. Henry, Everette Ferguson, Harold Lindsell, and others, were "loyal to a version of classical Protestant Christianity, they were loyal to the American evangelical heritage, and they were loyal to fundamentalism."[22] Fuller was formed on the notion that the Bible was inerrant and therefore its supernatural accounts were historically accurate.

Wilbur Smith, who appeared in earlier chapters, is an excellent example of Fuller's earliest faculty who were doggedly committed to the divine authority of Scripture. The school was thoroughly *evangelical*, argues Marsden, in its zeal for the biblically revealed

---

21. George Marsden, *Reforming Fundamentalism: Fuller Seminary and the New Evangelicalism* (Grand Rapids: Eerdmans, 1995), 5.
22. Ibid., 3.

gospel of salvation from sin through the atoning work of Christ. At the same time, it was thoroughly *fundamentalist* in its academic defenses of biblical inerrancy, not merely in the Bible's religious matters, but also in its science and history. "The early Fuller was in striking ways a fundamentalist institution with a thoroughly fundamentalist constituency," notes Marsden. "Though *evangelical* may have been the more respectable term to use, few would have questioned the fundamentalist identification."[23] At the founding of FTS, "to be a fundamentalist meant only to be theologically traditional, a believer in the fundamentals of evangelical Christianity, and willing to take a militant stand against modernism. *Conservative* was sometimes a synonym"[24] Marsden's description looks very similar to what this chapter calls *biblical fundamentalism*, that is, a conservative evangelicalism that rejects secular agendas influencing the church and/or attacking the veracity of Scripture.

According to this modest intellectual history, biblical fundamentalism enjoys a rich legacy of the highest academic caliber that represents the best of evangelical thought. As originally fundamentalist institutions, the charter faculties of Dallas, Westminster, and Fuller Seminaries comprised the brightest minds to teach and produce scholarly works reflecting their biblical worldview which they believed was verifiable and academically defensible. Consequently, any thought of cultural retreat or anti-intellectual sentiments fits nowhere within the history of genuine biblical fundamentalism.

Biblical Fundamentalism v. Cultural Fundamentalism

A realist view of history dictates that offering a new term to replace an old one can either back-fire or advance positively. Rather than entirely replace *fundamentalist* [*-ism*], this chapter offers a term that retains the core or classical understanding of

---

23. Ibid., 3.
24. Ibid., 10.

Christian fundamentalism while marking a clear demarcation from unhelpful ideas often attached to the word.

Too often, Christian fundamentalism is explained as a movement relating to cultural, socioeconomic, or psychological developments. Anti-intellectualism, anti-higher education, white supremacy, King James Only-ism, restrictive attire, restrictive music in worship, even restricting the color of the church carpet are, whether rightly or wrongly, among popular associations with fundamentalism. In any event, these ideas are not at all what I have in mind for the label "biblical fundamentalism." Instead, those arbitrary positions would more accurately be subsumed under the idea of "cultural fundamentalism," since they comprise man-made laws and ideas *outside of Scripture* which some groups unfortunately force upon their people.

In a recent multi-contributor volume seeking to reclaim *biblical fundamentalism*, Gary Gilley offered six major differences between cultural fundamentalism and biblical fundamentalism.[25] According to Gilley, differences in *authority*, *sanctification*, *leadership*, *attitude toward others*, *separation*, and *fear* are what distinguish a genuine biblical fundamentalism from a fundamentalism that is governed by trends outside of Scripture. It's not surprising that first difference is one of *authority*, as this is where all roads meet (see chapter two of this book). Whereas biblical fundamentalism believes God's inscripturated Word is the "final authority on everything it touches (2 Tim. 3:16–4:5)," says Gilley, *cultural fundamentalism* "tends to add personal preferences and convictions to the inspired revelation, and, in reality, these additions hold more weight than Scripture in matters of practice."[26] The other five also contain sharp differences between the biblical fundamentalism argued in this chapter—which sources its identity in Scripture alone—and the

---

25. Gary E. Gilley, "Biblical or Cultural Fundamentalism?" in *Fight the Good Fight: Reclaiming Biblical Fundamentalism*, ed. Richard P. Bargas (Grand Rapids: IFCA Press, 2024), 24–26.

26. Ibid., 25.

cultural counterfeit that most people imagine when the word "fundamentalism" is brought up.

This is a major reason why I believe even the phrase "Christian fundamentalism" is not as helpful as it once was. One can be a genuine Christian and yet be held captive by a version of fundamentalism that reflects a *type of Christian culture* more so than it does Scripture alone.[27] The important adjective *biblical* is what modifies *fundamentalism*. Any legalistic notion to control or persuade believers that is sourced outside of clear biblical norms is also outside of biblical fundamentalism. Self-identifying biblical-fundamentalist Joel Tetreau describes a "highjacking" of the term *fundamentalist* over the years due to extremists who isolate themselves from any engagement with culture or who demand agreement with them on non-essential matters. Though they rail against culture, these types ironically represent a *cultural* fundamentalism that is found in pockets of American evangelicalism in their combative opposition to any who disagree with them on non-essential matters.

Describing this as an "Issue-Driven Fundamentalism," Tetreau explains how pervasive this cultural type of fundamentalism is to what he also describes as "slaves to group-think":

> There are those that would suggest a true fundamentalist must be a Calvinist. Then there are those that believe a true fundamentalist could never be a Calvinist. Some would say that a fundamentalist must approach church music a certain way, or that a true fundamentalist must make sure that the women in his church never attend church in anything but a dress. Theologically, an issues-driven fundamentalist might believe that a true fundamentalist must believe in pre-tribulation rapture or must be a Baptist and could never be a Presbyterian.[28]

---

27. The spectrum is wide as forms of Christian fundamentalism can be found from independent fundamental Baptist churches to the uber-Reformed "Moscow Mood" of Doug Wilson in Moscow, ID.

28. Joel Tetreau, "The Highjacking of Fundamentalism," *Voice* (Jan–Feb 2020), 37–38.

Historically speaking, Christian or biblical fundamentalism was never envisioned as one denomination over another. Nor was it a retreat from all things cultural or academic. Rather, historic fundamentalism was rooted in a genuine concern for theological purity (as best attained through inductive hermeneutics). It aimed to guard timeless truths and doctrine, originating with the biblical prophets and apostles, and boldly defended by the Protestant Reformers.

It is also important to point out how dishonest the narrative is that historic fundamentalism was a whites-only movement that stifled the voices of black Christians, as often argued by progressive authors. Scholars are now challenging the idea that fundamentalism was ever an exclusively white phenomenon. The truth is that those who define evangelicalism or fundamentalism in terms of "whiteness" are the ones guilty of muting the historic constituency of black fundamentalists that helped shaped fundamentalism. In his historical-theological study on "Black Fundamentalists," Daniel Bare argues that conservative black Christians have been marginalized or excluded from the histories of early Protestant fundamentalism *despite* their self-identification as "fundamentalists" and others identifying them as "fundamentalists."[29] In fact it was due to their unwavering stance on the fundamentals of Christianity that informed many black fundamentalists' views on politics and the nation, and upon which later civil right leaders would build. "Rhetorically connecting their fundamentalist faith with such American ideals as emancipation, liberty, and democracy," reports Bare, "these conservative religionists [black fundamentalists] offered visions of a religiously inflected Americanism, and at times a reciprocal patriotically inflected Christianity, which promised hope for both the propagation of true religion and the advancement of their

---

29. Daniel R. Bare, *Black Fundamentalists: Conservative Christianity and Racial Identity in the Segregation Era* (New York: New York University Press, 2021), 187.

race."[30] Bare's study gives a much needed corrective to Kristin Kobes Du Mez's and Isaac Sharp's arguments that American evangelicalism is a white male problem. It's unfortunate that such a large marginalized group of African Americans who valiantly defended Christian fundamentalism over against liberal theology remain absent from the works of critical scholars who view evangelicalism in terms of race. Biblical fundamentalism, however, embraces its ethnic diversity since the only thing that matters is Scripture and the great fundamental doctrines of historic Christianity sourced in Scripture.

As Bruce Shelley explains, "Fundamentalism should be understood primarily as an attempt to protect the essential doctrines or elements (fundamentals) of the Christian faith from the eroding effects of modern thought."[31] In other words, historic Christian fundamentalism sought to guard and defend the "fundamentals" of the historic and divinely revealed Christian faith (Jude 3). But unfortunately, there exist "Christian fundamentalists" in corners of the world who are known more for what they're *against* than what *they're* for. These types are reminiscent of what scholars often call the "Colossian heresy" or "Colossian philosophy" warned against by Paul when chiding impressionable believers in the church: "Why, as if you were still alive in the world, do you submit to regulations—'Do not handle, Do not taste, Do not touch'" (Col 2:20-21). As the apostle goes on to point out using a word that appears nowhere else, such invented dogmas only promote "self-made worship" or "work-for-yourself religion" (*ethelothrēskia*) that only *seem* wise but are actually *useless* in making one holy (v. 23). All of this leads to why I believe *biblical fundamentalism* is a helpful moniker that retains the core convictions of traditional Christian fundamentalism by upholding the values of conservative evangelicalism while

---

30. Ibid., 160.
31. Bruce L. Shelley, "Fundamentalism," in *Dictionary of the Christian Church*, Rev. Ed., ed. J. D. Douglas (Grand Rapids: Zondervan, 1978), 396.

rejecting legalism, anti-cultural retreatism, and anti-intellectual mischaracterizations.[32]

Practically speaking, the term *biblical fundamentalism* is narrow enough to keep at bay theological liberals and progressive evangelicals who either attack the historical veracity and divine power of Scripture and/or adopt secular cultural virtues influenced by trendy social wokist agendas. But it's also wide enough to include genuine evangelicals across the denominational spectrum who uphold orthodox theology and the centrality of the gospel of Jesus Christ. "True, biblical fundamentalism," argues Richard Bargas, "includes Christians from different denominations, those who reject denominations, [and those] who would differ on secondary and tertiary issues of doctrine."[33] This means it's not as restrictive as some forms of Christian fundamentalism have been. If we had to broaden the scope, *biblical fundamentalism* is synonymous with *biblical Christianity* and a *biblical fundamentalist* is someone who identifies with the *fundamentals* of the Christian faith as long as those fundamentals are *biblical*—not cultural, political, ethnic, celebrity-driven, or anything else commonly used as a gauge for evangelicalism.

The Bugaboo of (Biblical) Separation

Today's evan-jello-calism has forgotten that the church is in a real spiritual battle and that a real enemy exists. The problem is ancient as Paul warned Timothy to halt the spreading of false doctrine which he attributed to demonic influence (see 1 Tim. 1:3–7; 4:1–5). If Christians guard the deposit entrusted to them and follow the pattern of sound words (2 Tim. 1:13–14), and if pastors hold firm

---

32. See Madison Trammel, *Fundamentalists in the Public Square: Evolution, Alcohol, and Culture Wars After the Scopes Trial* SHST (Bellingham: Lexham Academic, 2023), 21–22; 128–29 for how Carl F. H. Henry's popular narrative condemning fundamentalism's anti-intellectualism or cultural retreatism did not accurately portray the Christian fundamentalism of the early to mid twentieth century.

33. Richard P. Bargas, "The Surprising Legacy of Biblical Fundamentalism," in *Fight the Good Fight*, 114–15.

to biblical doctrine and rebuke those who contradict it (Titus 1:9), then by necessity the church will look different than the world. It will be *distinct, separate,* and *set apart,* or in theological terms, "sanctified." Unfortunately, much in today's evangelicalism mirrors the world rather than offering something different; something *separate* from all the counterfeits.

In their annual State of the Church Report for 2023, American Pastors Network reported that on a global scale, American evangelicalism is continuing to lose respect and substantial impact in the world *because* it fails to separate from worldly influence:

> And culturally, Christianity is not seen as being "different" than the rest of society. Where once being a Christian meant that you separated yourself from the vices of the day, that gap has just about disappeared. The problem is that if the Church has become like the world, it has nothing to offer the world! This is a far cry from what the first-century church was like and the revolutionary impact it had upon the world. It was that "cause-driven" attitude that attracted the lost and motivated the saved. Neither is happening today.[34]

The cause of Christ advanced by the church since its earliest days is gospel-saturated with its embedded ethics of holiness, righteousness, and conviction over sin. It views the whole counsel of God codified in the Scriptures as supreme in its authority. These biblical realties demand a separation from those who are duplicitous and feign or discard them. Thus, the *biblical* fundamentalist practices *biblical* separation.

Biblical separation is not a controversial doctrine. All Christians understand there are times to separate from others who deny the faith in either word or by deed. The precedent is ancient for God's people. Moses led an exodus of mass separation of the people of God away from pagan Egypt (Exod. 12:33–14:30). Drawing an analogy from when Israel was called to separate

---

34. Jamie Mitchell, "2023 State of the Church Report: A Time for Courage," American Pastors Network, 6. Available at https://americanpastorsnetwork.net/.

from her idolatrous and influential neighbors in the OT, Paul commanded the Corinthian church they likewise are not to be "unevenly yoked," "mismated," or "be badly coupled" (*heterozygeō*) to unbelievers because no genuine fellowship exists between light and darkness (2 Cor. 6:14–18).[35] The apostles taught a doctrine of separation in various places referring to people who appear to be believers but whose doctrine and/or lifestyles prove otherwise (e.g., Rom. 16:7; 2 Thess. 3:14; 2 John 10).

Discussions on biblical separation invariably overlap with those on ecumenism, the latter being a historical identity marker for theological liberalism. "Doctrine, truth, and group distinctives are ignored or greatly minimized for the sake of a united front," explains Rolland McCune, and "Ecumenism refers to the efforts expended to implement such unity."[36] The "unity" referred to here happens when evangelicals lock arms with people who deny the deity of Christ or the need for repentance or minimize the infallibility of God's Word for a shared cause at the moment deemed more important than unalterable biblical truths. It occurs when evangelicals unite with pro-choice advocates or with LGBTQ+ leaders who demand exceptional rights, despite the biblical witness to their sin. Unfortunately, the evangelical church at large can be guilty of unifying over things valued in secular society at the expense of biblical doctrines which are trans-cultural. But ecumenism at the expense of biblical truth is dangerous. "If truth is not the basis of unity," rightly cautions Richard Bargas, "then any unity established will be a false harmony that leads to confusion and even opposition to the revealed truth of the Word of God."[37]

But most times, ecumenism occurs in the name of God, Christ, or of Christianity. This type of ecumenism is partnering or extending a hand of fellowship with those who teach doctrines

---

35. For these glosses, see BDAG, 399; MSG, 833.

36. Rolland McCune, *Promise Unfulfilled: The Failed Strategy of Modern Evangelicalism* (Greenville: Ambassador, 2004), 65.

37. Richard Bargas, "Four Fatal Errors of Ecumenism," *Voice* (Sep–Oct 2024), 6.

and/or live lives contrary to Scripture *even though they claim to believe in the biblical God.* An interesting example of this occurred in the days of Zerubbabel when he oversaw the rebuilding of the temple in Jerusalem. Enemies of God identified as "adversaries" approached Israel's leaders and asked if they can partner with them in rebuilding the temple, even claiming to worship the same God as Israel. "But Zerubbabel, Jeshua, and the rest of the heads of fathers' houses in Israel said to them, 'You have nothing to do with us in building a house to our God; but we alone will build to the LORD, the God of Israel, as King Cyrus the king of Persia has commanded us.'" (Ezra 4:3). These potential ministry partners were fakes. Their true colors were revealed as they turned to intimidation tactics against the true people of God and did whatever they could to frustrate their progress of building (vv. 4–16). God's people must always be on alert for those who may claim to be one of them, but whose lives and doctrine signal otherwise. In such cases, ecumenism or partnering in ministry with those who deny core tenets of the faith or act unbecoming of the gospel is condemned by Scripture.

This would include fellowshipping with the "other evangelicals" from Isaac Sharp's study of "liberals, progressives, feminists, and gay Christians" which is also shared by Kristin Kobes Du Mez's and other trending volumes. What these and other voices fail to recognize is the gravity of sin and warnings of false doctrine that is so pervasive in the Bible. True Christians *must* separate from those who have no conviction over these vices. As Paul said, "bad company ruins good morals" (1 Cor. 15:33): For the biblical fundamentalist, just like for the historic evangelicals, there is no communion with anyone who denies the fundamentals of the Christian faith or lives life approving what is clearly evil (Rom. 1:32).

This does not mean that biblical separation requires separating from people over tertiary matters or personal preferences. Moreover, biblical separation should *never* be done with spite toward others and certainly *never* with violence. There is a unity the NT calls for which believers should always strive to maintain; though, it's a unity based on truth. As Kevin Bauder writes,

> Unity is a function of what unites. Fellowship is something held in common. What Christians hold in common is not merely the gospel, but the whole counsel of God. . . . We should conduct ourselves so that even in our separation we are earnestly endeavoring to maintain the unity of the Spirit in the bond of peace (Eph 4:3).[38]

This type of separation is different than cultural fundamentalists who practice second- and third-degree separation to the point of becoming "us four and no more!" Christians who separate from others *who don't* separate from others is a sequence outside the tents of biblical separation. Biblical fundamentalism practices *biblical* separation (of the first degree) which includes one party separating from another party, *not* separating from fellow believers who don't share the same level of conviction on when to separate.

This means that contrary to cultural fundamentalism, biblical fundamentalism does not make separation *the thing* over everything else. Instead, genuine Christian unity is the aim until it is absolutely necessary to separate. According to biblical fundamentalist Dave Deets, "Many cultural fundamentalists prioritize separation over the biblical necessity of unity. So they separate at all costs and hope for unity at the end of the day. . . . The proper relationship between separation and unity is that unity is the priority, and we can no longer be unified when we *have to* separate."[39] When does it become obvious that we *must* separate? According to Deets, "Instead of looking at how quickly and over what trivial matters we can separate and hope for unity later, we seek to be unified as long as possible on doctrine, and when we can't, we are grieved to have to separate."[40]

---

38. Kevin T. Bauder, "Fundamentalism," in *Four Views on the Spectrum of Evangelicalism*, eds. Andrew Naselli and Collin Hansen (Grand Rapids: Zondervan, 2011), 36, 38.

39. Dave Deets, "Defending Orthodox Doctrine: A Call to Arms?" in *Fight the Good Fight*, 67, emphasis in original.

40. Ibid.

A Vintage Fundamental Faith

Every term used to identify a theological tradition has weaknesses. Ask three different Christians to define "reformed," and you'll get four different answers ("Calvinist," "confessional," "covenantal," "reformational," et al.). Nuances and exceptions always accompany group labels, as this book has demonstrated with the label, "evangelicalism." With that in mind, I fully acknowledge that my suggestion of a new term probably has blind spots, has the potential to be misunderstood, or even to be rejected outright. Nevertheless, I do think it is a good label for conservative Christians to consider as an alternative to evangelicalism.

What I and others call *biblical fundamentalism* is simply the historic evangelical faith that I've argued for throughout this book. In the sense of holding to biblical fundamentals, a vintage faith that is evangelical *is* fundamentalist, which is precisely how the terms were used in the early to mid twentieth century. John Hannah helpfully distinguishes between *fundamentalist* and *fundamentalist controversy*, the latter designating political confrontation, while the former carries a sense of consternation toward the contemporary religious scene. The fundamentalism of the McCarthy era in the 1950s or rise of the Moral Majority in the 1980s represent the latter, even as the term *fundamentalism* changed its original meaning of identifying those who were simply conservative evangelicals. "As the term was used before the fundamentalist controversy, and to lesser degrees shortly thereafter, it was a synonym for *evangelical, conservative, orthodox*."[41] A vintage faith reclaims its heritage when the terms *evangelical* and *fundamentalist* were used interchangeably.[42]

This chapter is not the only or final word on the matter. In other words, it's not *the* case for what some would call *biblical fundamentalism*; it's merely *a* case for it. The idea for the word never received an official welcome nor is there a strict consensus of its meaning. I don't even know where the term originated, but

41. John D. Hannah, *An Uncommon Union*, 39.
42. See Ibid., 23.

it is one I've continually returned to over the years to describe what this book also calls a *vintage faith*. Synonymous labels used in previous chapters are *authentic evangelicalism, genuine evangelicalism*, even *historic evangelicalism*. The term *conservative evangelicalism* has also appeared several times interchangeably with what I've called a *vintage faith* and now here *biblical fundamentalism*.

I suppose one could also add *fundamentalist-evangelical* or *evangelical-fundamentalist* to the constellation of labels to describe the same idea of a Christians who holds to the *fundamentals* of historic evangelicalism and therefore the *fundamentals* of the Christian faith.[43] Such a name could be helpful in immediately distinguishing itself from the mushy "evan-jello-cals" who will presumably take serious exception to large portions of this book, as I and others do theirs. Either way, when pollsters can somehow identify "Jews, Muslims, Hindus, and Buddhists" as "evangelical," the label has become utterly useless.[44] The word "evangelical[ism]" has become limitless and expandable to include everything under the sun—that by biblical norms or by the historical understanding of the movement—would contradict them in the most obvious ways. Because of this, I think the term *biblical fundamentalism* is a worthy alternative for conservative evangelicals if we're ever to drop the label evangelicalism for good.

---

43. In fact, see John D. Hannah, *An Uncommon Union* (chapter three) for similar uses of these terms.

44. Ryan Burge, "The Rise of the Non-Christian Evangelical: Some Jews, Muslims, Hindus, and Buddhists are Identifying as Evangelicals - Why?" *Graphs About Religion*, Feb 26, 2024, https://www. graphsaboutreligion.com/p/the-rise-of-the-non-christian-evangelical?

CONCLUSION

Hope for Identity Recovery

We've *officially* reached the end. As this book sought to show in the beginning and ending chapters, there are clear identity crises in contemporary evangelicalism. Especially within American evangelicalism, race, politics, celebrity, different religions, even sexual preference are now customary culprits for identifying something as "evangelical." If "evangelicalism" can mean anything, it means nothing.

As earlier chapters pointed out, something other than culture or self-identification needs to serve as the gauge for identifying true evangelicals. Allowing pollsters, progressive authors, or self-perception to function as benchmarks for what makes up evangelicalism has caused some scholars (me included) to question the value of the term "evangelicalism." It's become an eroded category with the elasticity of an infinite umbrella stretched to cover anybody who feels entitled to the label. Because of this identity crisis, the previous chapter (chapter nine) offered *biblical-fundamentalism* as a worthy possibility for a name change— if used to identify conservative and historic evangelicalism that sources its identity in the Christ of Scripture and fundamentals of the Christian faith. It may not be a perfect term, but I think it's more helpful than the label "evangelicalism" as defined by an evolving constellation of ideas outside of the Bible.

In between the opening and closing chapters lay the DNA of what this book offered as the fundamentals for evangelical identity. Chapters two through six centered on identifying *what* makes up a genuine *evangelicalism* rather than *who* is an *evangelical*. In what was presented as a model for recovering a "vintage faith," genuine evangelicalism should be defined by a five-fold pattern of *beliefs* that lead to genuine evangelical *behavior*. Though I acknowledge more can be added to the list, I am convinced none can be taken away for a true—*vintage*—expression of evangelical Protestantism to exist. As I argued in those chapters, authentic evangelicalism can be identified by five fundamental positions: a high view of Scripture; the exclusivity of Jesus for salvation; a zeal for evangelism; participation in theological education; and the necessity of consistent local church fellowship. All five of these basic identity markers are governed by position one—the supremacy of Scripture's authority.

Though I am not the only one who has reasoned for a set pattern of *beliefs* to identify evangelicalism (rather than by who self-identifies as an evangelical in polls), the significance of this book is that it includes *behaviors* as part of the metric which serve as concrete demonstrations of professed evangelical beliefs. Quite simply, if one *believes* the Bible to be divinely inspired, inerrant, infallible, and authoritative, then that person will *live* accordingly. This extends my "fundamentals" of evangelical identity past conversion and what is customarily considered essential to believe in order to be saved (the latter covered in chapter three). As I argued, a focus on soteriology to the neglect of other important doctrines is too narrow to comprise a vintage evangelical identity. As such, obedience to the Great Commission (chapter four), growing in one's theological education (chapter five), and committing to regular fellowship with the saints (chapter six) results in spiritual maturity demonstrating evangelical behavior that *reflects* evangelical belief. As these chapters contended, the *sine qua non* of evangelicalism is belief, behavior, identity.

The behavior aspect of my model has accountability among the saints embedded in it, thereby baring any "other evangelical" from identifying with the tradition of evangelicalism. This leads to an additional significance of the book. It also serves as a contrast to the current conversation dominated by critical scholars and progressive evangelicals publishing works that identify modern evangelicalism in unhelpful terms. Labels such as "white," "republican," "oppressive," "militant," "fascist," "Trumper," and other descriptors are common among critics and intended more as derision than they are as accurate descriptors. Guilty of *ad hominem* rhetoric and straw man fallacies, their uses are influenced by a leftist culture advocating for a *version* of evangelicalism inclusive of beliefs and lifestyles that are actually antithetical to evangelicalism's true identity.

Still, are critics of evangelicalism ever correct in their appraisals of the conflation of politics or evangelicalism's intoxication with personality cults? Indeed, they are. As the "rants" in chapters seven and eight pointed out, evangelicalism mixed with secular politics and celebrity Christianity are real dangers. They both tend to conflate biblical Christianity with ideas or stage presence that mimics godless culture rather than separating from it. Constantine Campbell posed a question worth considering: "Will [evangelicals] double down and continue along this perilous path of compromise with political parties, or will they stop, reflect and change course?"[1] As chapter four pointed out, the church's commission has nothing to do with making disciples of political parties; the church's task is to make disciples of Christ.

Christians serving in politics is a wonderful thing, and I believe their influence in government is certainly needed. But doing so should not be confused with the mission of the *church*, which is to make *spiritual disciples*, not political allegiances. A genuine evangelical's politics are the *result* of their theological commitments informed by Scripture, not their equal and certainly not their cause. Therefore, the concept of an "evangelical vote" is imaginary, and evangelical churches should consider if waving

---

1. Constantine R. Campbell, *Jesus v. Evangelicals* (Grand Rapids: Zondervan Reflective, 2023), 2.

national flags in their spaces of worship visually communicates a form of nationalism conflated with the biblical God. A vintage faith looks forward to the geo-political utopia that everyone longs for which will occur when the King of kings returns to this earth (Acts 1:11; cf. Matt. 19:28).

"What, then, makes an evangelical an evangelical?" asks historian Thomas Kidd. "Evangelicals' political behavior is important," he answers, "and it has a troubling history. But at root, *being an evangelical entails certain beliefs, practices, and spiritual experiences.*"[2] Kidd is correct, and along with the metrics offered in this book, secular political agendas appear nowhere in his definition as a measure for authentic evangelicalism. "Partisan commitments have come and gone. Sometimes evangelicals have made terrible political mistakes," he continues. "But conversion, devotion to an infallible Bible, and God's discernible presence are what make an evangelical an evangelical."[3]

As for the celebrity culture of mainline evangelicalism, it is crippling the body of Christ, particularly in America where consumerism is elevated to biblical status. The message of hell-bound sinners in desperate need of repentance and salvation in Christ followed by a sanctified life in community is supplanted by studio audiences, fake social media accounts, dishonest book sales, and the trendy conferences of Big Eva. As chapter seven contended, we must kill Christian celebrityism. Such a call goes beyond the problem of merely "celebrity *pastors,*" as most of them are "pastors" in name only. Celebrity culture in American evangelicalism affects all who do business in the name of Christ. Dissatisfied with shepherding the flock the Chief Shepherd has given them, these types focus on building the biggest "ministries" without any real accountability. Borrowing from a current definition of celebrity as "social power without proximity," I believe the biblical precedent for any Christian minister is

2. Thomas S. Kidd, *Who Is an Evangelical? The History of a Movement in Crisis* (New Haven: Yale University Press, 2019), 155, emphasis added.
3. Ibid., 156.

social influence for Christ within proximity. All "power" belongs to Christ alone and the genuine pastor will not lord it over his people (see Matt. 20:25–28). Instead, he will work to *influence* them by modeling Christ to them within a structure of *accountability*, as Paul did the Corinthians (1 Cor. 11:1).

These conversations on politics, celebrity, self-identity, consumerism, etc. place a spotlight back on the need for this book. Evangelicalism has an identity crisis. John Hannah's diagnosis is somber:

> Modern Evangelicalism is in a state of crisis. The very community that historically has been deeply interested in transcendent, timeless truth seems more focused on the merely private, personal, and temporal than ever before. If I could be so blunt, the church has lost its soul, at least some think so. The Evangelical Church, I believe, is on the brink of becoming another of the many social, do-good agencies whose mission-purpose is to help people more fully enjoy this life, but neglect the implications of eternity.[4]

Has evangelicalism really lost its soul, at least in the Western world? If this book and others like it sounding the alarm are a real indication, then the answer has to be yes or very close to it. But as I've also argued, not all is lost. In answering the question *What is a true evangelical identity?* I contend that by recovering the fundamentals of its vintage expression, as argued throughout, there is hope in restoring evangelicalism's powerful influence for Jesus's sake in the US and abroad.

The elasticity of the term "evangelical[-ism]" over the past thirty or so years demands that its vintage form be recovered according to *core fundamental evangelical beliefs that flesh out in genuine evangelical behavior.* More might be added to my "five fundamentals," but none can be taken away. In any event, political allegiances, race, sexual-identity, celebrity, nationality, even mere

---

4. John D. Hannah, *Our Legacy: The History of Christian Doctrine* (Colorado Springs: NavPress, 2001), 340.

self-identification as an "evangelical" cannot—*must not*—ever be considered a factor in evangelicalism.

Rather, as this book has maintained, a more stable and objective evangelical identity is rooted in several realities: the highest love for Christ and Scripture, loving the lost with the gospel, loving to grow in the knowledge of God and of the world, and loving to do life together with fellow saints as the body of Christ. Love envelopes all five of these fundamentals of a true vintage faith. "So now faith, hope, and love abide, these three; but the greatest of these is love" (1 Cor. 13:13).

Bibliography

Akenson, Donald Harman. *The Americanization of the Apocalypse: Creating America's Own Bible*. New York: Oxford University Press, 2023.

Anderson, Leith, and Ed Stetzer. "A New Way to Define Evangelicals." *Christianity Today*, April 2016, https://www.christianitytoday.com/2016/03/defining-evangelicals-in-election-year/.

Ascol, Tom. "Theoretical Inerrantists." Founders Ministries, n.d., https://founders.org/articles/theoretical-inerrantists/.

Bare, Daniel R. *Black Fundamentalists: Conservative Christianity and Racial Identity in the Segregation Era*. New York: New York University Press, 2021.

Bargas, Richard P. "The Surprising Legacy of Biblical Fundamentalism." In *Fight the Good Fight: Reclaiming Biblical Fundamentalism*. Edited by Richard P. Bargas, 114–120. Grand Rapids: IFCA Press, 2024.

Bauder, Kevin T. "Fundamentalism." In *Four Views on the Spectrum of Evangelicalism*. Edited by Andrew David Naselli and Colin Hansen, 19–49. Grand Rapids: Zondervan, 2011.

Bauer, Walter, William F. Arndt, F. Wilbur Gingrich, and Frederick W. Danker. *A Greek-English Lexicon of the New Testament and*

Other Early Christian Literature. 3rd ed. Chicago: University of Chicago Press, 2000.

Beaty, Katelyn. *Celebrities for Jesus: How Personas, Platforms, and Profits are Hurting the Church.* Grand Rapids: Brazos, 2023.

Bebbington, David W. *Evangelicalism in Modern Britian: A History from the 1730s to the 1980s.* London: Routledge, 2005.

———. *The Evangelical Quadrilateral: Characterizing the British Gospel Movement.* Waco: Baylor University Press, 2021.

Belcher Jr., Richard P. *The Fulfillment of the Promises of God: An Explanation of Covenant Theology.* Fearn, Ross-shire: Mentor, 2020.

Benzinger, Brandon C., and Adam W. Day, eds. *What Can You Do with Your Bible Training? Traditional and Nontraditional Vocational Paths.* Eugene: Resource, 2023.

Bowman Jr. Robert M., and J. Ed Komoszewski. *The Incarnate Christ and His Critics: A Biblical Defense.* Grand Rapids: Kregel Academic, 2024.

Bray, Gerald Lewis, ed. *1–2 Corinthians*, Ancient Christian Commentary on Scripture. Downers Grove: InterVarsity Press, 1999.

Burge, Ryan. "The Rise of the Non-Christian Evangelical: Some Jews, Muslims, Hindus, and Buddhists are Identifying as Evangelicals - Why?" *Graphs About Religion*, Feb 26, 2024, https://www.graphsaboutreligion.com/p/the-rise-of-the-non-christian-evangelical?fbclid=IwAR3LLvzldpB09LFr8vboN8JU qrJVYFwCDRJ10Pqzj3KbN5LNzgxhFHXv27M.

Burgraff, Andrew T. *Discipleship Today: Applying Biblical Discipleship in Today's Context.* Cary: Shepherds Press, 2024.

Burk, Denny, James M. Hamilton Jr., Brian Vickers, eds. *God's Glory Revealed in Christ: Essays on Biblical Theology in Honor of Thomas R. Schreiner.* Nashville: B&H Academic, 2019.

Burnett, Christopher Ryan. "Defining Biblical Missions through 'Missiological Propositional Assertion.'" PhD diss., The Master's Seminary, 2022.

Campbell, Constantine R. *Jesus v. Evangelicals: A Biblical Critique of a Wayward Movement.* Zondervan Reflective, 2023.

Capes, David B. *Matthew Through Old Testament Eyes: A Background and Application Commentary.* Grand Rapids: Kregel Academic, 2024.

———, ed. *Does It Matter Who Wrote the Bible? The Pastoral Implications of Pseudonymity and Anonymity in the New Testament.* Eugene: Pickwick, 2025.

Carson, D. A. "The Purpose of the Fourth Gospel: John 20:31 Reconsidered." *Journal of Biblical Literature* 106 (1987): 639–51.

———. *Exegetical Fallacies.* Grand Rapids: Baker, 1993.

Carter, Joe. "The State of Theology: What Evangelicals Believe in 2022." The Gospel Coalition, September 22, 2022, https://www.thegospelcoalition.org/article/state-theology-2022/.

Casillas, Ken. *Beyond Chapter and Verse: The Theology and Practice of Biblical Application.* Eugene: Wipf & Stock, 2018.

Chafer, Lewis Sperry. *Systematic Theology.* Vol 3. Dallas: Dallas Seminary Press.

Charles, J. Daryl. *The Unformed Conscience of Evangelicalism: Recovering the Church's Moral Vision.* Dallas: Fontes Press, 2020.

Childers, Alisa, and Tim Barnett. *The Deconstruction of Christianity: What It Is, Why It's Destructive, and How to Respond.* Carol Streams: Tyndale Elevate, 2024.

Chou, Abner. *The Hermeneutics of the Biblical Writers: Learning to Interpret Scripture from the Prophets and Apostles.* Grand Rapids: Kregel Academic, 2018.

Coffman, Elesha J. *Turning Points in American Church History: How Pivotal Events Shaped a Nation and a Faith.* Grand Rapids: Baker Academic, 2004.

Crawford, Brandon James. *Let Men Be Free: A Christian Vision for Ordered Liberty*. Douglasville: G3 Press, 2024.

Cunliffe-Jones, Hubert, ed. *A History of Christian Doctrine*. Philadelphia: Fortress, 1980.

Daniel G. Reid, ed. *Dictionary of Christianity in America*. Downers Grove: InterVarsity, 1990.

Davis, Jim, and Michael Graham with Ryan P. Burge. *The Great Dechurching: Who's Leaving, Why Are They Going, and What Will It Take to Bring Them Back?* Grand Rapids: Zondervan, 2023.

Davison Hunter. *American Evangelicalism: Conservative Religion and the Quandary of Modernity*. New Brunswick: Rutgers University Press, 1983.

Deets, Dave. "Defending Orthodox Doctrine: A Call to Arms?" In *Fight the Good Fight: Reclaiming Biblical Fundamentalism*. Edited by Richard P. Bargas, 64–87. Grand Rapids: IFCA Press, 2024.

DeRouchie, Jason S., Oren R. Martin, and Andrew David Naselli. *40 Questions about Biblical Theology*. Grand Rapids: Kregel Academic, 2020.

DeYoung, Kevin. "When Paul Sent the Celebrity Pastor," The Gospel Coalition, May 8, 2012, https://www.thegospelcoalition.org/blogs/kevin-deyoung/when-paul-sent-the-celebrity-pastor/.

Dockery, David S., and Christopher W. Morgan, eds. *Christian Higher Education: Faith, Teaching, and Learning in the Evangelical Tradition*. Wheaton: Crossway, 2018.

Douglas, J. D., ed. *Dictionary of the Christian Church*, Rev. ed. Grand Rapids: Zondervan, 1978.

———, ed. *New Twentieth Century Encyclopedia of Religious Knowledge*. 2nd ed. Grand Rapids: Baker, 1991.

Du Mez, Kristin Kobes. *Jesus and John Wayne: How White Evangelicals Corrupted a Faith and Fractured a Nation*. New York: Liveright, 2021.

Elwell, Walter A., ed. *Evangelical Dictionary of Theology*. Grand Rapids: Baker, 1984.

Enns, Paul. *The Moody Handbook of Theology*. Chicago: Moody, 2014.

Estes, Douglas, and Daniel O. Alshire. "Facing the Future of Theological Education: Amid the Challenges, Daniel O. Alshire Sees Opportunities for Renewal." *Didaktikos: Journal of Theological Education* 5, no. 1 (Sep 2021): 17–23.

Farnell, F. David, ed. *Vital Issues in the Inerrancy Debate*. Eugene: Wipf & Stock, 2015.

Fazio, James I. *Two Commissions: Two Missionary Mandates in Matthew's Gospel*. El Cajon: SCS Press, 2015.

Fee Gordon D. *Gospel and Spirit*. Peabody: Hendrickson, 1991.

Fruchtenbaum, Arnold G. *The Book of Romans*, Ariel's Bible Commentary. San Antonio: Ariel Ministries, 2022.

Geisler, Norman L., ed. *Inerrancy*. Grand Rapids: Zondervan, 1980.

Gibbs Nancy, and Michael Duffy, *The Preacher and the Presidents: Billy Graham in the White House*. New York: Center Street, 2007.

Gilley, Gary E. "Biblical or Cultural Fundamentalism?" In *Fight the Good Fight: Reclaiming Biblical Fundamentalism*. Edited by Richard P. Bargas. 10–26. Grand Rapids: IFCA Press, 2024.

Gilley, Gary E. *This Little Church Went to Market: The Church in the Age of Entertainment*. Minneapolis: Evangelical Press, 2005.

Goble, Luke J. *Worshipping Politics: Problems and Practices for a Public Faith*. Eugene: Cascade, 2017.

Greenslade, S. L., ed. *The West from the Reformation to the Present Day*. Vol. 3 of *The Cambridge History of the Bible*. Cambridge: Cambridge University Press, 1963.

Grudem, Wayne, C. John Collins, and Thomas R. Schreiner, eds. *Understanding Scripture: An Overview of the Bible's Origin, Reliability, and Meaning*. Wheaton: Crossway, 2012.

Guinness, Os. *Fit Bodies, Fat Minds: Why Evangelicals Don't Think and What to Do About It*. Grand Rapids: Baker, 1994.

Gutjahr, Paul C. *An American Bible: A History of the Good Book in the United States, 1777–1880*. Stanford: Stanford University Press, 1999.

Hannah, John D. *An Uncommon Union: Dallas Theological Seminary and American Evangelicalism*. Grand Rapids: Zondervan, 2009.

———. *Our Legacy: The History of Christian Doctrine*. Colorado Springs: NavPress, 2001.

Hansen, Colin. "Introduction." In *Four Views on the Spectrum of Evangelicalism*. Edited by Andrew David Naselli, and Colin Hansen. 9–18. Grand Rapids: Zondervan, 2011.

Hart, D. G. *Deconstructing Evangelicalism: Conservative Protestantism in the Age of Billy Graham*. Grand Rapids: Baker Academic, 2004.

———. Defending the Faith: J. Gresham Machen and the Crisis of Conservative Protestantism in Modern America. Phillipsburg: P&R, 2000.

Hellerman, Joseph H. *Embracing Shared Ministry: Power and Status in the Early Church and Why It Matters Today*. Grand Rapids: Kregel Ministry, 2013.

Holland, Rick. "The Perspicuity of Scripture and Expository Clarity." In *To Seek, To Do, and To Teach: Essays in Honor of Larry D. Pettegrew*. Edited by Douglas D. Bookman, Tim M. Sigler, and Michael J. Vlach. 219–244. Cary: Shepherds Press, 2022.

Horton, Michael S. "Why Historical Theology Matters: The Trinity and the Dangers of Biblicism." *Theo Global Journal* 1 (Nov 2024): 233.

House, H. Wayne, ed. *The Evangelical Dictionary of World Religions*. Grand Rapids: Baker, 2018.

Hunt III, Arthur W. *The Vanishing Word: The Veneration of Visual Imagery in the Postmodern World*. Eugene: Wipf & Stock, 2013.

Hunter, James Davison. *American Evangelicalism: Conservative Religion and the Quandary of Modernity*. New Brunswick: Rutgers University Press, 1983.

Hurtado, Larry W. *Destroyer of the Gods: Early Christian Distinctiveness in the Roman World*. Waco: Baylor University Press, 2016.

———. *The Earliest Christian Artifacts: Manuscripts and Christian Origins*. Grand Rapids: Eerdmans, 2006.

Hyde, Daniel R. *This is the Word of the Lord: Becoming Confident in the Scriptures*. Fearn, Ross-shire: Christian Focus, 2022.

James M. Hamilton, Jr., "He Is with Your and Will Be in You." Ph.D. diss., The Southern Baptist Theological Seminary, 2003.

Johnson, Todd M. "Evangelicals Worldwide." *The Inquiry*. Gordon-Conwell Theological Seminary, March 25, 2020, https://www.gordonconwell.edu/blog/evangelicals-worldwide/.

Kelley, William, ed. *Collected Writings of J. N. Darby*. Vol. 7. London: Morrish, 1862.

Kidd, Thomas S. *America's Religious History: Faith, Politics, and the Shaping of a Nation*. Grand Rapids: Zondervan Academic, 2019.

———. *Who Is an Evangelical? The History of a Movement in Crises*. New Haven: Yale University Press, 2019.

Kimmel, Jospeh L. "Demons Seeking Identity? The Psychic Life of New Testament Exorcisms." *Journal of Biblical Literature* 143.1 (2024): 85–104.

Koehler, Ludwig, and Walter Baumgartner, eds. *The Hebrew and Aramaic Lexicon of the Old Testament*. Translated by Mervyn E. J. Richardson. 2 vols. Leiden: Brill, 2001.

Köstenberger, Andreas J. *A Theology of John's Gospel and Letters*, Biblical Theology of the New Testament. Grand Rapids: Zondervan Academic, 2009.

———. *Signs of the Messiah: An Introduction to John's Gospel.* Bellingham: Lexham, 2021.

Köstenberger, Andreas J., Benjamin L. Merkle, and Robert L. Plummer. *Going Deeper with New Testament Greek: An Intermediate Study of the Grammar and Syntax of the New.* Rev. ed. Nashville: B&H Academic, 2020.

Köstenberger, Andreas J., with Richard D. Patterson. *Invitation to Biblical Interpretation: Exploring the Hermeneutical Triad of History, Literature, and Theology.* 2nd ed. Grand Rapids: Kregel Academic, 2021.

Köstenberger, Andreas J., with T. Desmond Alexander. *Salvation to the Ends of the Earth: A Biblical Theology of Mission*, New Studies in Biblical Theology 53, 2nd ed. London: Apollos; Downers Grove: IVP Academic, 2020.

Kruger, Michael J. *Canon Revisited: Establishing the Origins and Authority of the New Testament Books.* Wheaton: Crossway, 2012.

Laird, Benjamin P. *Creating the Canon: Composition, Controversy, and the Authority of the New Testament.* Downers Grove: IVP Academic, 2023.

Lee, Morgan. "Do Flags Belong in Churches? Pastors Around the World Weigh In," *Christianity Today*, July 2, 2021, https://www.christianitytoday.com/ct/2021/july-web-only/flags-church-sanctuary-patriotism-nationalism.html.

Lindsell, Harold. *The Battle for the Bible: The Book that Rocked the Evangelical World.* Grand Rapids: Zondervan, 1976.

Lints, Richard. *Uncommon Unity: Wisdom for the Church in an Age of Division.* Bellingham: Lexham, 2022.

Longman III, Tremper, and Mark L. Straus, eds., *The Baker Expository Dictionary of Biblical Words.* Grand Rapids: Baker, 2023.

Luhrmann, T. M. "God Can You Hear Me?" The American Scholar, Jan 25, 2021, https://theamericanscholar.org/god-can-you-hear-me/.

Luther, Martin. "An Open Letter to the Christian Nobility of the German Nation Concerning the Reform of the Chistian Estate." In Martin Luther, *Three Treatise*, trans. Charles M. Jacobs, rev. James Atkison. 1–112. Philadelphia: Fortress, 1970.

MacArthur, John, and Richard Mayhue, eds. *Biblical Doctrine: A Systematic Summary of Bible Truth*. Wheaton: Crossway, 2017.

Madueme, Hans. *Defending Sin: A Response to the Challenge of Evolution and the Natural Sciences*. Grand Rapids: Baker Academic, 2024.

Marsden, George M. *Understanding Fundamentalism and Evangelicalism*. Grand Rapids: Eerdmans, 1991.

Marsh, Cory M. "Recovering Biblical Literacy." In *Fight the Good Fight: Reclaiming Biblical Fundamentalism*. Edited by Richard Bargas. 41–63. Grand Rapids: IFCA Press, 2024.

Marsh, Cory M. *A Primer on Biblical Literacy*. El Cajon: SCS Press, 2022.

Marsh, Cory M., and James I. Fazio. *Discovering Dispensationalism: Tracing the Development of Dispensational Thought from the First to the Twenty-First Century*. El Cajon: SCS Press, 2023.

Matthew Barrett, Matthew. *The Reformation as Renewal: Retrieving the One, Holy, Catholic, and Apostolic Church*. Grand Rapids: Zondervan Academic, 2023.

McClain, Alva J. *Romans: The Gospel of God's Grace*. Winona Lake: BMH, 1989.

McCune, Rolland. *Promise Unfulfilled: The Failed Strategy of Modern Evangelicalism*. Grenville: Ambassador, 2004.

McGrath, Allister. *Evangelicalism and the Future of Christianity*. Downers Grove: InterVarsity, 1995.

Miller, Chris. *Matthew*, New Testament Exposition Commentary. Elgin: Regular Baptist Press.

Miller, J. R. *Elders Lead a Healthy Family: Shared Leadership for a Vibrant Church*. Eugene: Wipf & Stock, 2017.

Miller, Timothy E., and Bryan Murawski. *1 Peter: A Commentary for Biblical Preaching and Teaching*, Kerux Commentaries. Grand Rapids: Kregel Ministry, 2022.

Mitchell, Jaime. "2023 State of the Church Report: A Time for Courage." *American Pastors Network*, 6. Available at https://americanpastorsnetwork.net/

Mohler Jr., R. Albert. "Confessional Evangelicalism." In *Four Views on the Spectrum of Evangelicalism*. Edited by Andrew David Naselli and Colin Hansen. 68–96. Grand Rapids: Zondervan, 2011.

Montanari, Franco, Madeleine Goh, and Chad Schroeder, eds. *The Brill Dictionary of Ancient Greek*. Liden: Brill, 2018.

Moo, Douglas J. *The Letter to the Romans*, The New International Commentary on the New Testament. 3nd ed. Grand Rapids: Eerdmans, 2018.

Moo, Douglas J., Eckhard J. Schnabel, Thomas R. Schreiner, and Frank Thielman, eds. *Paul's Letter to the Romans: Theological Essays*. Peabody: Hendrickson Academic, 2023.

Mouw, Richard J. *The Smell of Sawdust: What Evangelicals Can Learn from Their Fundamentalist Heritage*. Grand Rapids: Zondervan, 2000.

Muddamalle, Joel. *The Hidden Peace: Finding True Security, Strength, and Confidence through Humility*. Nashville: Thomas Nelson, 2024.

Needham, Nick. *The Age of Enlightenment and Awakening*. Vol. 5 of *2000 Years of Christ's Power*. Ross-shire, UK: Christian Focus, 2023.

Newport, Frank. "Fewer in U.S. Now See Bible as Literal Word of God." *Gallup*, July 6, 2022, https://news.gallup.com/poll/394262/fewer-bible-literal-word-god.aspx#:~:text=The percent20majority percent20of percent20Christians percent20(58,an percent20ancient percent20book percent20of percent20fables.

Nichols, Stephen J. "A Brief Exchange between Lewis Sperry Chafer and J. Gresham Machen." *Westminster Theological Journal* 62.2 (Fall 2000): 281– 291.

Noll, Mark A., David W. Bebbington, and George A. Rawlk, eds. *Evangelicalism: Comparative Studies in Popular Protestantism in North America, the British Isles, and Beyond, 1700–1990.* New York: Oxford University Press, 1994.

Noll, Mark A., David W. Bebbington, and George M. Marsden, eds. *Evangelicals: Who They Have Been, Are Now, and Could Be.* Grand Rapids: Eerdmans, 2019.

Olson, Roger E. "Postconservative Evangelicalism." In *Four Views on the Spectrum of Evangelicalism.* Edited by Andrew David Naselli. 161–187. Grand Rapids: Zondervan, 2011.

Ortlund, Gavin. *What It Means to Be Protestant: The Case for an Always-Reforming Church.* Grand Rapids, Zondervan Reflective, 2024.

Packer, J. I. *Evangelism and the Sovereignty of God.* Downers Grove: InterVarsity, 1973.

Pally, Marcia. *White Evangelicals and Right-Wing Politics: How Did We Get Here?* New York: Routledge, 2022.

Penner, Glenn M. *In The Shadows of the Cross: A Biblical Theology of Persecution and Discipleship.* Bartlesville: Living Sacrifice, 2004.

Peterson, Jacob W. "Math Myths: How Many Manuscripts We Have and Why More Isn't Always Better." In *Myths and Mistakes in New Testament Textual Criticism.* Edited Elijah Hixon and Peter J. Gurry. 48–69. Downers Grove: IVP Academic, 2019.

Peterson, Jacob W. "Math Myths: How Many Manuscripts We Have and Why More Isn't Always Better." In *Myths and Mistakes in New Testament Textual Criticism.* Edited Elijah

Hixon and Peter J. Gurry. 48–69. Downers Grove: IVP Academic, 2019.

Piper, John, and D. A. Carson. *The Pastor as Scholar and Scholar as Pastor: Reflections on Life and Ministry*. Edited by Owen Strachan and David Mathis. Wheaton: Crossway, 2011.

Piper, John. *"Love Your Enemies": Jesus' Love Command in the Synoptic Gospels and the Early Christian Parenesis*. Cambridge: Cambridge University Press, 1979.

Postman, Neil. *Amusing Ourselves to Death: Public Discourse in the Age of Show Business*. New York: Penguin, 2005.

Postman, Neil. *Technopoly: The Surrender of Culture to Technology*. New York: Vintage, 1993.

Quarles, Charles L., and L. Scott Kellum. *40 Questions About the Text and Canon of the New Testament*. Grand Rapids: Kregel Academic, 2023.

Bargas, Richard. "Four Fatal Errors of Ecumenism," *Voice* (Sep–Oct 2024): 6–9.

Root, Jonathan. *Oral Roberts and the Rise of the Prosperity Gospel*. Grand Rapids: Eerdmans, 2023.

Russell, Alfred U. "In Defence [*sic*] of Fundamentalism" *Central Bible Quarterly* 02.1 (Spring 1959): 43–44.

Ryle, J. C. *Knots Untied: Being Plain Statements on Disputed Points in Religion from the Standpoint of an Evangelical Churchman*. London: National Protestant Church Union, 1898.

Schaeffer, Francis A. *The Church Before the Watching World: A Practical Ecclesiology*. Downers Grove: IVP, 1971.

———. *The Great Evangelical Disaster*. Westchester: Crossway, 1984.

Schlatter, Adolf. *The History of the Christ: The Foundation of New Testament Theology*. Translated by Andreas J. Köstenberger. Grand Rapids: Baker, 1997.

Schultze, Quentin J. *Televangelism and American Culture: The Business of Popular Religion*. Eugene: Wipf & Stock, 1991.

Sharp, Isaac B. *The Other Evangelicals: A Story of Liberal, Black, Progressive, Feminist, and Gay Christians—and the Movement that Pushed Them Out.* Grand Rapids: Eerdmans, 2023.

Shepherd, Michael B. *An Introduction to the Making and Meaning of the Bible.* Grand Rapids: Eerdmans, 2024.

Shepherd, Michael B. *Textual World of the Bible* SBL, 156. New York: Peter Lang, 2013.

Shillington, V. G. *2 Corinthians*, Believers Church Bible Commentary. Scottdale: Herald Press, 1998.

Smith, Wilbur M. *Therefore Stand: A Plea for a Vigorous Apologetic in this Critical Hour of the Christian Faith.* Boston: W. A. Wilde Co., 1950.

Snell, Merwin-Marie. "Evangelical Hinduism." *The Journal of Religion* 6, no. 4 (Oct 1895): 270–277.

Spellman Ched, and Jason K. Lee, eds. *The Seminary as a Textual Community: Exploring John Sailhamer's Vision for Theological Education.* Dallas: Fontes Press, 2018.

Spellman, Ched. "The Canon After Google: Implications of a Digitized and Destabilized Codex," *Princeton Theological Review* 17, no. 2 (Fall 2010): 39–42.

Spellman, Ched. *Toward a Canon Conscious Reading of the Bible: Exploring the History and Hermeneutics of the Canon*, New Testament Monographs 34. Sheffield: Sheffield Phoenix Press, 2020.

Sproul, R. C., and Norman L. Geisler. *Explaining Inerrancy: The Chicago Statements on Biblical Inerrancy, Hermeneutics, and Application with Official ICBI Commentary.* Arlington: Bastion Books, 2013.

Spurgeon, Charles H. *The Greatest Fight in the World.* London: Paternoster, 1896.

Stout, Harry S. *Upon the Altar of the Nation: A Moral History of the American Civil War.* New York: Penguin, 2007.

Strachan, Owen. *Awakening the Evangelical Mind: An Intellectual History of the Neo-Evangelical Movement*. Grand Rapids: Zondervan, 2015.

Tatlock, Mark, and Chris Burnett eds., *Biblical Missions: Principles, Priorities, and Practices*. Nashville: Thomas Nelson, 2025.

Tetreau, Joel. "The Highjacking of Fundamentalism." *Voice* (Jan–Feb 2020): 37–38.

Tetreau, Joel. *The Pyramid and the Box: The Decision-Making Process in a Local New Testament Church*. Eugene: Resource, 2013.

The International Council on Biblical Inerrancy, "The Chicago Statement on Biblical Inerrancy." *The Journal of the Evangelical Theological Society* 21.4 (December 1978): 289–296.

Throckmorton, Warren. "How the Religious Right Scams its Way onto the *New York Times* Best Seller List," *Daily Beast*, November 16, 2014, https://www.thedailybeast.com/how-the-religious-right-scams-its-way-onto-the-new-york-times-bestseller-list/.

Trammel, Madison. *Fundamentalists in the Public Square: Evolution, Alcohol, and Culture Wars after the Scopes Trial*, Studies in Historical and Systematic Theology. Bellingham: Lexham Academic, 2023.

Treier, Daniel J., and Walter A. Elwell, eds. *Evangelical Dictionary of Theology*. Third Edition. Grand Rapids: Baker Academic, 2017.

Trueman, Carl. "Revoice, Evangelical Culture, and the Return of an Old Friend." Reformation 21, July 31, 2018, https://www.reformation2.org/mos/postcards-from-palookaville/revoice-evangelical-culture-and-the-return-of-an-old-friend.

Turner, David L. *Interpreting the Gospels and Acts: An Exegetical Handbook*. Grand Rapids: Kregel Academic, 2019.

Varner, Will. *The Apostolic Fathers: An Introduction and Translation*. London: T&T Clark, 2023.

Walker, Jr. William O. "Apollos and Timothy as the Unnamed 'Brothers' in 2 Corinthians 8:18-24." *The Catholic Biblical Quarterly* 73.2 (April 2011): 318–338.

Warfield, Benjamin B. The Inspiration and Authority of the Bible. Phillipsburg: P&R, 1948.

Weigel, George. *Evangelical Catholicism: Deep Reform in the Twenty-First Century Church.* New York City: Basic Books, 2014.

Wells, David. *No Place for Truth: Or, Whatever Happened to Evangelical Theology?* Grand Rapids: Eerdmans, 1993.

Wilsey, John. *American Exceptionalism and Civil Religion: Reassessing the History of an Idea.* Downers Grove: IVP Academic, 2015.

Wilson, Andrew J. "Apostle Apollos?" *Journal of the Evangelical Theological Society* 56.2 (June 2013): 325–335.

Witherington III, Ben. *Is there a Doctor in the House: An Insider's Story and Advice on Becoming a Bible Scholar.* Grand Rapids: Zondervan Academic, 2011.

Witherington III, Ben. *Sola Scriptura: Scripture's Final Authority in the Modern World.* Waco: Baylor University Press, 2023.

Wolfe, Adam. *The Transformation of American Religion: How We Actually Live our Faith.* Chicago: University of Chicago Press, 2003.

Woodbridge, John D., and Frank A. James III. *Church History: From Pre-Reformation to the Present Day: The Rise and Growth of the Church in Its Cultural, Intellectual, and Political Context.* Grand Rapids: Zondervan, 2013.

Wyatt, Adam. *Biblical Patriotism: An Evangelical Alternative to Nationalism.* Denver: GCRR Press, 2021.

Zaspel, Fred G. "Inerrancy, Adam & Eve, and B. B. Warfield (1851–1921)." *Detroit Baptist Seminary Journal* 29 (2024): 53–60.

Subject Index

D

E

Scripture Index

Christian Focus Publications

Our mission statement
Staying Faithful

In dependence upon God we seek to impact the world through literature faithful to His infallible Word, the Bible. Our aim is to ensure that the Lord Jesus Christ is presented as the only hope to obtain forgiveness of sin, live a useful life and look forward to heaven with Him.

Our Books are published in four imprints:

⟨○⟩ CHRISTIAN FOCUS

Popular works including biographies, commentaries, basic doctrine and Christian living.

⟨○⟩ MENTOR

Books written at a level suitable for Bible College and seminary students, pastors, and other serious readers. The imprint includes commentaries, doctrinal studies, examination of current issues and church history.

⟨○⟩ CHRISTIAN HERITAGE

Books representing some of the best material from the rich heritage of the church.

⟨○⟩ CF4KIDS

Children's books for quality Bible teaching and for all age groups: Sunday school curriculum, puzzle and activity books; personal and family devotional titles, biographies and inspirational stories – because you are never too young to know Jesus!

Christian Focus Publications Ltd,
Geanies House, Fearn, Ross-shire,
IV20 1TW, Scotland, United Kingdom.
www.christianfocus.com